Environmental Justice in Contemporary US Narratives

Environmental Justice in Contemporary US Narratives examines post-1929 US artistic interrogations of environmental disruption. Tracing themes of pollution, marine life, and agricultural production in the work of a number of historically significant writers including John Steinbeck, Ruth Ozeki, and Cherríe Moraga, this book outlines a series of incisive dialogues on transnational flows of capital and environmental justice. Texts ranging from *The Grapes of Wrath* (1939) to *Body Toxic* (2001) represent the body as vulnerable to a host of environmental risks. They identify "natural disasters" not just as environmental hazards and catastrophes, but also as events intertwined with socioeconomic issues.

With careful textual analysis, Athanassakis shows how twentieth- and twenty-first-century US writers have sought to rethink traditional understandings of how the human being relates to ecological phenomena. Their work, and this study, offer new modes of creative engagement with environmental degradation – engagement that is proactive, ambivalent, and even playful.

This book contributes to vital discussions about the importance of literature for social justice movements, food studies, ecocriticism, and the environmental humanities. The core argument of the book is that artistically imaginative narratives of environmental disturbance can help humans contend with ostensibly uncontrollable, drastic planetary changes.

Yanoula Athanassakis received her PhD in English (American literature), with a global studies emphasis, from the University of California at Santa Barbara, USA. She is Co-Founder of the Environmental Humanities Series at New York University (NYU) and Assistant Vice Provost for Academic Affairs, NYU, USA.

Routledge Environmental Humanities

Series editors: Iain McCalman and Libby Robin

The *Routledge Environmental Humanities* series is an original and inspiring venture recognising that today's world agricultural and water crises, ocean pollution and resource depletion, global warming from greenhouse gases, urban sprawl, overpopulation, food insecurity and environmental justice are all *crises of culture.*

The reality of understanding and finding adaptive solutions to our present and future environmental challenges has shifted the epicenter of environmental studies away from an exclusively scientific and technological framework to one that depends on the human-focused disciplines and ideas of the humanities and allied social sciences.

We thus welcome book proposals from all humanities and social sciences disciplines for an inclusive and interdisciplinary series. We favour manuscripts aimed at an international readership and written in a lively and accessible style. The readership comprises scholars and students from the humanities and social sciences and thoughtful readers concerned about the human dimensions of environmental change.

Environmental Justice in Contemporary US Narratives

Yanoula Athanassakis

Routledge
Taylor & Francis Group
LONDON AND NEW YORK

earthscan
from Routledge

First published 2017 by Routledge

2 Park Square, Milton Park, Abingdon, Oxfordshire OX14 4RN
711 Third Avenue, New York, NY 10017

Routledge is an imprint of the Taylor & Francis Group, an informa business

First issued in paperback 2018

British Library Cataloguing-in-Publication Data
A catalogue record for this book is available from the British Library

Library of Congress Cataloging-in-Publication Data
A catalog record for this book has been requested

ISBN: 978-1-138-89039-8 (hbk)
ISBN: 978-0-367-02700-1 (pbk)

Typeset in Bembo
by Apex CoVantage, LLC

For Anne and Apostolos

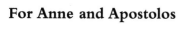

"Athanassakis expands our understanding of environmental justice through her brilliant engagements with the power of imaginative witnessing, social movements, and biological citizenship. Her book creates essential bridge-work between issues as wide-ranging as immigration, industrial agriculture, not-so-natural disasters, and cellular mutation. This ambitious, persuasive work will have a transformative impact across a range of fields, including the environmental humanities, transnational American studies, gender and ethnic studies, immigrant studies, food studies, trauma studies, biopolitics, and animal studies."

Rob Nixon, author of *Slow Violence and the Environmentalism of the Poor*

"*Environmental Justice in Contemporary US Narratives* dives into the lively, sometimes contentious debates surrounding ecocriticism, American studies, and media studies to make sense of their entangled intellectual roots. From John Steinbeck to Karen Tei Yamashita, Athanassakis brilliantly reads environmental justice fictions about food production, laboring bodies, citizenship, and globalization, for what they tell us about ecological destruction inherent in rampant – markedly American – global capitalism. The result is a richly satisfying, and much needed, recalibration of our understanding of the major contributions of transnational American studies to the fast rising field of the environmental humanities."

Joni Adamson, Professor, Environmental Humanities, and Director of the Environmental Humanities Initiative, Arizona State University, USA

Contents

Acknowledgments

This book is the culmination of years of support from various universities and foundations, and the patient support of family and friends. It is a moment to reflect on how the network of institutions, fellowships, and people grew from the Pacific Coast to the Atlantic and beyond.

My sincere gratitude goes to a number of foundations and institutions that afforded me the time and space to develop this project: first and foremost, the American Council of Learned Societies New Faculty Fellows Program; Rutgers University (particularly the departments of Human Ecology and Comparative Literature, and my students and colleagues in Women's and Gender Studies); Princeton University's Environmental Institute; the University of California President's Dissertation Fellowship program; the University of California's Humanities and Social Sciences Research Grant program; and the University of Illinois, Urbana-Champaign's English Department. At the University of California, Santa Barbara, I thank the English Department; the College of Creative Studies; the Interdisciplinary Humanities Center; the American Cultures and Global Contexts Center; and the Academic Senate. For their support with travel grants, I thank the American Studies Association of Turkey; the Modern Language Association; and the Santa Barbara Foundation.

In the course of this manuscript becoming a book, a number of people became de facto external reviewers, colleagues, and friends. For their inspiring work and great kindness at different stages of this project, I thank Bishnupriya Ghosh, Rob Nixon, Rita Raley, Joni Adamson, and George Lipsitz. For the fundamental role they played both as intellectuals and as friends, I thank Pavneet Aulakh, Karen Bishop, Allison Carruth, Heidi Hausermann, and Teresa Shewry.

A very sentimental thank you to the University of California, Santa Barbara at large and especially to the members of the English Department. I hesitate to single anybody out in the department because it was, as a whole, a magical place.

I thank New York University, where I was warmly welcomed and deeply supported from divergent angles. My deep gratitude to Katherine E. Fleming: a true friend and a steadfast source of motivation. I especially thank the Environmental Studies Department and the Animal Studies Initiative for providing a lively scholarly community. I also thank the departments of Comparative Literature, Environmental Studies, and English for housing my courses on environmental justice literature and veganism. My students at NYU were instrumental to the last stages of this project. I extend my gratitude to the Center for the Humanities, especially its director, Ulrich C. Baer, for supporting the Environmental Humanities Series, and for reading parts of this manuscript. I thank Zvi Ben-Dor Benite, for reminding me that the future holds great possibility for miracles. I must also thank Thomas Bender for bringing NYU into my life.

To my committee members at University of California, Santa Barbara, I thank you for your incisive feedback and the way that you stressed the importance of an earnest and creative approach to things: Giles Gunn, thank you for guiding me through not only literary history but also interdisciplinary theories of globalization; Carl Gutiérrez-Jones, you were a steadfast source of mentorship and an unparalleled example of collegiality; Shirley Geok-lin Lim, it was a gift to take your graduate courses and to work with you on the *Journal of Transnational American Studies*; Bishnupriya Ghosh, your comments at every stage continue to shape my thinking and I thank you for taking on yet another graduate student at a time when you could have easily said no – I thank you doubly so for reading the dissertation when it morphed into a book and giving me invaluable feedback.

The following list of dedicated souls includes people who read parts of this book years ago, and in many different forms (Bishnupriya Ghosh, Rita Raley, and Allison Carruth), and others who read it more recently. I am grateful to all of you: Ulrich C. Baer, Allison Carruth, Una Chaudhuri, Daniel Fleming, Katherine Fleming, Rita Raley, Teresa Shewry, and Stephen Hong Sohn.

My sincere thanks to Routledge and the editorial team that worked with me for the Environmental Humanities series. I especially thank the three anonymous reviewers of this book, whose comments were thorough and constructive. For their vision and its breadth, I thank the Series Editors, Professors Iain McCalman and Libby Ryan. I thank Kelly Watson for her professionalism and kindness throughout the process.

A number of artists were kind enough to let me use their art and reproduce it in this text. My warmest thanks to Marina Zurkow, a gifted artist whose generosity knows no boundaries. I thank you for allowing your whimsical art to grace the cover of this book and for lending it to our collective for New York University's Environmental Humanities Series; Suzanne Paola (pen name Susanne Antonetta), thank you for your insights on environmental justice and for the rights to reproduce an excerpt from *Body Toxic*; Alex Rivera, thank you for unlimited access to stills from *Sleep Dealer* and for your encouragement; David M. Allen, thank you for allowing me to reproduce your photograph from Cherríe Moraga's *Heroes and Saints*; to the staff members at the Library of Congress in Washington, DC, thank you for your help; to the staff members of the archives from North Dakota State University and also from the National Museum of Mexican Art, Chicago, thank you for your time.

This book would not have been the same without the friendship of many people, including Talin Dikranian, Alayna Fraser, Bethany Lepe, Raia Margo, Χρυσαυγή

Παπαδοσήφου, Alexa Schloh, and others that are listed here as readers, reviewers, and colleagues.

Finally, to my family, near and far, my deepest gratitude for your patience. I thank my mother, Anne, for never doubting that I would get done whatever I needed to get done. I'm not sure how this would have gone without your support. To my second father, Ken, for being positive and patient. To my brother, Nikolaos, for keeping things light and yet insisting everybody stay grounded. To my father, Apostolos, himself an academic and all too aware of the multiple pressures we face: thank you for never giving me unsolicited advice and even occasionally telling me in earnest, «πέταξέ τα» (cast it all aside). Thank you for modeling a deep love of teaching and scholarship in equal parts.

To all of the people and creatures who helped make this book a reality: I thank you.

1 Bodies interrupted

> To think we've gone and created immortality and the problem is how to mortalize it again. That we've not been able to make immortality for our bodies but have given them growths, splotches, sarcomas, melanomas, blastomas, calcifications, lesions – things to cut away and look for and then cut away again. We grow superbacteria, retroviruses, breastless women. But we've bombarded simple ores with atomic bits and filled them with radioactivity, something that lives as close to forever as we can imagine. We've made immortality for our waste, which grows larger and more important and more alive, and bulks itself out to inhabit the spaces we dwindle ourselves away from.
>
> Susanne Antonetta, *Body Toxic*

> Just like other rural areas around the country, the Pine Barrens have been victimized by immigration-driven population growth, yet the region is still beautiful. I have no doubt the author of this book has the medical ailments she claims, yet perhaps they have more to do with her lifetime of drug abuse than with living in New Jersey. My father grew up in the industrial badlands of Bayonne, New Jersey; he is 61 and has no major medical problems. In fact, my family is entirely from Jersey City and Bayonne, two cities that are far more industrialized than Ocean County, yet nobody in my family has ever had cancer. This book is another example of junk science giddily peddled by leftist Manhattanite editors who probably haven't been outside of Manhattan in years.
>
> Dan, Amazon.com

Environmental Justice in Contemporary US Narratives is about bodies that are interrupted and whose normal and natural trajectory is somehow short-circuited by unnatural and toxic forces. This book asks that we reevaluate and look anew at US-based narratives of the interrupted and derailed human body, a body that no longer seems to function like other bodies or whose path – when it does – we cannot help but register as an aberrance. Here, bodies are deeply material entities whose vital signs writers and artists channel in their environmentally conscious artworks. Here, the vital infrastructures of the body communicate with intensities that disturb habitual perceptions. *Environmental Justice in Contemporary US Narratives* focuses on "interrupted bodies" that exert their own agency, challenging the somatic containment intrinsic to the molar body.

Attentive to global capitalism and imperial states in projects of somatic containment, *Environmental Justice in Contemporary US Narratives* emphasizes the molecular and planetary scales of the distributed subject.

In all the chapters, we encounter interrupted bodies: one is a head without a body and a couple are disease-ridden and disfigured bodies. This is a time to recognize what we might consider to be rebellious bodies that disobey our standards of conduct. Just as the bodies have short-circuited, they cause a feedback loop in our ability to understand them, and they disrupt our perception of reality. As the characters in the stories ahead become unhinged and untidy, they shatter our world order and our ideas of somatic boundaries.

Bodies take up space and are, insofar as we conceptualize them, bound by that space. The further back we go, the more we see that humanity has always questioned the boundaries of bodies in space, and herein lies some of the most radical thinking of the twenty-first century.[1] In 1986 Mary Douglas noted "current gaps in research in risk perception" and stated that such research is by definition always reactive (3). The twentieth century witnessed concerted efforts to rectify such gaps: for example, Ulrich Beck's work (1992) has been taken up by scholars in the environmental humanities to investigate the idea of risk as experienced in everyday human life. What if our bodies are not in fact as hermetically sealed as we might think, and what if they are not obedient to the mind and subordinate to its wishes? The motivation to encourage humans to believe that our exposure to risk is spatially bound and can be mitigated by what we do with our bodies is growing exponentially and is monetarily incentivized. Messages to the public loudly proclaim that we can mitigate risk, but also increasing – and in direct relation to a unilateral push to ignore connections between communal risk and individual agency – is the static of such messages.

The tactics of resistance to official stories about necessary by-products of technological and industrial progress have become more sophisticated and they exhibit parasitic behavior: they feed off of denial and complacency. The fear of shaming and scaring the public becomes secondary to laying bare truths about our collective agency and the possibilities for meaningful change.[2] *Environmental Justice in Contemporary US Narratives* considers numerous texts that have become savvier, more urgent, and more complex than their predecessors in their responses to instances of corporate malfeasance and the orchestrated production of public skepticism of such malfeasance. These works speak frankly and creatively to their audiences about what, in one of my favorite quotes of all of the texts in this book, Susanne Antonetta blithely refers to as "separation and separation and separation" (2001, 11). A later discussion of this quote will illustrate its fuller context; for now, I offer it as both an epigraph and a coda. That is, it is the beginning and end – and even the middle – of *Environmental Justice in Contemporary US Narratives*.

The forced separation between ideas of biological and abiological matter (more than simply the separation between humans and their surroundings) shuts down emerging and productive discourse. "Separation and separation and separation" of mind from body, of inner from outer, and of toxic from clean are just a few of the examples that trouble the imaginations of the writers discussed in this book. What would it mean not only for mind and body to be less clearly demarcated but also for the body to have a material wisdom that the mind cannot compute? According to writers such as Susanne Antonetta (2001), John Steinbeck ([1939] 1976), coauthors John Steinbeck and Edward F. Ricketts ([1941] 2009), Bich Minh Nguyen (2007), and Cherríe Moraga (1994) (to name a handful), it would mean the eradication of much of humans' harmfully politicized behavior. It would mean, in fact, a profound reconsideration of the predatory environmental practices that are repackaged as necessary markers of progress. And finally, it would mean that an estrangement from our realities and usual practices of knowledge production would essentially force us to question how we go forward from here.

Body Toxic

Susanne Antonetta's *Body Toxic* (2001) narrativizes toxic harm from a material perspective. Antonetta spent part of her childhood in the Pine Barrens of southern New Jersey in the 1960s, and only later realized that the beauty of her surroundings was surpassed by its poisonous potential. Lurking not beneath but inside things like fresh-picked berries, fresh fish, and the water she both swam in and drank was a lethal combination of nuclear waste and pesticides that metastasized and surfaced in her body as spontaneous abortions and cancerous growths. Antonetta's "environmental memoir" is, by definition, also a corporeal one, demonstrating that the traditionally separate spheres of nature and human are in fact enmeshed. The mixing of these categories defies conventional binaries and points to the gap between industrial development and our ability to measure its cost.

In the Amazon.com comments about Antonetta's book, the divisive nature of the politics of the body is clear. Readers are incensed by what they see as Antonetta's *choice* to be ill by ingesting recreational drugs. Citing her illicit drug use as the cause of mental and physical illness becomes a manner not only of moral but also, strikingly, political balkanization. One reviewer, Dan (2004), points out that his own family does not have cancer but is from an area "far more industrialized than Ocean County" and suggests that it is Antonetta's "lifetime of drug abuse" that is at fault for her illness.[3] The reviewer's teleology depends on a direct relationship between visible industry and invisible illness. As Dan points out, Jersey City and Bayonne are "far more industrialized" than the geographic locations Antonetta identifies as places where she lived. What Dan is missing, however, is the manner in which visible industry in large urban centers often sends its means of production (and thus its pollution) elsewhere. Further refuting Antonetta's claims, Dan racializes pollution as the problem of "immigration-driven population growth" and declares that this memoir is yet "another example of junk science giddily peddled by leftist Manhattanite editors." Regardless of partisanship, the reviewer demonstrates the politicized nature of the body as matter in the twenty-first century.

Antonetta's story is one of extremes: her body is devastated, her mental faculties are foggy because of manic depression, and she uses recreational drugs to escape reality until her eighteenth birthday. Her tone does not elicit readers' empathy and although it is bleak and unsentimental, it manages to incite passionate responses from its audience. In her review of the book, Victoria Kamsler writes that Antonetta's "family is not admirable or even particularly likeable" and notes that, to her credit, Antonetta manages "to impart the sense that, nevertheless, they matter" (2002, 196). Not only does this family matter, but as Kamsler rightly states, this memoir also "expands our moral sensibility by showing us how to be concerned for people with whom we are *not* meant to identify" (2002, 196; emphasis in the original). Yet what Kamsler calls an "obsessively readable contribution to environmental ethics" (2002, 194) might make average ecocritics squeamish. We pay keen attention to readability and there is a distinct way in which this text is in fact not "obsessively readable" because it refuses to enable our wishes to engage with the people in it.

Body Toxic is one of three books that all examine areas where New York borders New Jersey and wherein greed trumps morality. Antonetta's text is uninviting and unsentimental; the narrative voice appears to march on and will do so whether or not the reader stays with the author. Certainly if we read this text with a focus on the ethics of corporate wrongdoing and companies' willed ignorance of the cost to human and nonhuman lives, we will read it with the same fervor with which we might read Dan Fagin's *Toms River* (2013). Fagin's sweeping and crushing study of villainous corporate practices is summed up by one of his shortest sentences, "Many waste handlers simply conclude that compliance doesn't pay" (2013, 176). Proving Ciba-Geigy's criminal intent produces the kind of cloak-and-dagger suspense that drives the reader to keep turning the pages of this spectacularly written piece of investigative journalism. While Robert Sullivan's *The Meadowlands* (1998) is written in a comparatively jocular tone, the purpose of that book is similar: to unearth tawdry histories of corporate and governmental negligence evidenced by buried chemical drums.[4]

An important distinction between the narratives of Fagin and Sullivan on the one hand and Antonetta on the other hand (besides the fact that she is author, narrator, subject, and object of her book) is that Antonetta does not include geographical coordinates and maps and she presents herself as unconcerned with details of time and place. Both Fagin and Sullivan illustrate what our collective dependence on a synthetic existence is doing to us and the spaces we inhabit. In *Contaminated Communities*, Michael Edelstein observes that such epiphanies are "lifescape changes" that require "cognitive adjustments" in five major areas ([1988] 2004, 65–71). When people begin to realize that they have been exposed to toxic substances and that the half-life of chemicals within them will be far longer than their own lifespans, what is needed is more radical than a mere cognitive adjustment. Fagin's and Sullivan's books begin with maps of the Meadowlands and Toms River areas, but Antonettas' first chapter, titled "First Words," begins with a distinct lack of clarity: "In nineteen question-mark question-mark my silent grandfather came to the United States" (2001, 3). Her

Barbadian grandfather haunts this text and skulks through its shadows with an uncanny ability to unsettle her and thus also readers. The figure of the grandfather is typically silent beyond comprehension, and when he does speak, what he says appears to only make matters worse.[5] *Body Toxic* commences with vague indications of time ("nineteen question-mark question-mark") instead of with coordinates and orientation: there are no maps, no timelines, nothing to grasp onto. Her memoir is deliberately slippery and diaphanous.

Body Toxic not only begins with a lack of specificity of time and space but Antonetta perpetually refuses to grant the reader perspective. In literary representations of embodied risk, materiality – especially when compromised – is often expressed as a crisis in representation. The natural state of bodies is disrupted, and as a result the stories they tell engage in a kind of civil disobedience, defying chronological order and traditional narrative structures. As Stacy Alaimo eloquently points out, a cross-section of US literature "dramatize[s] the onto-epistemological ruptures that occur when people must contend with the invisible dangers of risk society" (2010, 72).

For Antonetta the break with reality and known structures of understanding probably began in utero, caused both by a hereditary predisposition to mental illness and environmentally induced mania and depression. Antonetta stopped using street drugs at age seventeen and a year later she was on a list of prescription drugs that she complains have "less truth in advertising" (2001, 206). The street drugs at least gave her the sense that she could control how she felt and what the letdown would be: "I'd quit street drugs at seventeen, and began facing the drugs I could not control. My brain chemicals, and the chemicals given by legal prescription. Before I had swallowed a mind, a place to be and a way to be: *goofy pills, silly-cybin, ups, downs*. I missed that – the absoluteness of the claim, of the follow-through" (2001, 206, emphasis in the original). The prescription drugs she ingests leave her feeling like a blundering version of herself. Though people remark that she seems like a different person and mean it as a compliment, she feels that the drugs she takes for manic depression make her not herself: "when I say 'myself' I lie by simplification" (2001, 207). Antonetta believes that the drugs are reducing the breadth of her emotional register, but I read her observation also as a comment about the lack of "separation and separation and separation" between her interior and the exterior, between her body and its surroundings, and between the toxicity we note in pills and that which we cannot identify and is already in us.

The caginess of Antonetta's text is not haphazard, and it cannot be fully attributed (as some wish it to be) to her transition from poet to prose author. She continually refuses to accept her readers as allies, not trying to win them over or hand them what Dana Phillips might term a "quintessential ecocritical experience" (2003, 5). In Phillips's musings about environmental critic Lawrence Buell – whom he rightly names the "de facto spokesman" of ecocriticism, the study of literature of the environment and of literature linking humans to their physical surroundings (2003, 5) – Phillips comments that one of the most powerful ideas that Buell adopted from risk theory, environmental history, and sociology (among other disciplines) is that ecocriticism is a rapidly shifting field that responds to a demand for answers but does not offer them in expected ways, or even at all. In a similar way, Antonetta's text refuses reduction to a story of "good" nature versus "bad" humans. The murkiest moments of her memoir are those during which she tries to distinguish truth from fiction and good from bad. Her ambivalence appears to be the result of a disconcerting history of psychosomatic violation and deep shame. Although one could say that the passages in *Body Toxic* that create consternation in the reader are due to post-modern pastiche and an authorial penchant for poetry over prose, in the end it is content rather than form that creates the sense that the world has become unhinged.

Bodies in "anti-place"

Environmental Justice in Contemporary US Narratives recognizes the immense potential in recent movements that question the human-constructed and oppositional spaces between human and nonhuman, inner and outer, and us and them. I note an emerging trend in ecocritical and environmental justice movements to explore how humans by and large unwittingly contribute to their own disenfranchisement while feeling as if they are actually improving their existence. It is this false sense of self-legitimization and security that propels some of the most harmful and partisan environmental practices. While we are undercutting the possibility of a healthy and happy future for humans and other species and harming the ecosystems of our planet, we feel as if we are actually doing our part to mitigate risk and govern our own future and the future of those around us. *Environmental Justice in Contemporary US Narratives* analyzes texts that overturn notions of bound and predetermined risk, or of predictable and manageable outcomes. Instead, I detect a trend in literature and films that actually aim to reschematize troubling dualisms (between mind and body, for example) and thus also the audiences' understanding of their participation in the production of – and contact with – different types of harm.

Antonetta's memoir is particularly interesting because it lays bare the contradictory relationship that humans have to their bodies. The management of risk in the form of exposure to toxins has increasingly been framed as a question of individual choice and ability. We are theoretically able to control the food we eat, the water we drink, the location of the house we buy and the purity of its surrounding elements (air and water), the car we drive, the paint we use, and so on. People are beginning to realize the lack of control that we have over our individual exposure to risks, but we are more reluctant to conceptualize this lack of control as a collective undertaking.[6] Such an ideological shift – from notions of individual exposure to ideas of collective exposure – requires a change in how we think of communal harm and thus also responsibility.[7] I would argue that particularly for US citizens, the right to privacy trumps most other rights. Other cultures and languages do not have the same understanding of the words "personal" and "private"; instead, those words often connote a private company or something that is for individual use.[8] Part of what becomes disempowering about the spatialization of a model that clearly delineates between personal and communal is that it will always by definition become a battle of a few individuals against a larger collective. It is a predetermined and failed model of discourse on risk and injury, which translates to an autonomous and personal battle, or what Wendy Brown has argued are wounded identity attachments that rule out the possibility of alternative futures and subjects as "potentially in motion" (1995, 75; see also 52–76). We cannot shake the lingering sense of victimization attached to our individual bodies, even if a number of injured bodies come together. Brown identifies potential in the possibility of reclaiming emotional attachments and sentiments as connected to agency. That agency relies on the understanding that identity is "deconstructable" and not "fixed"; it is not completed or wholly formed (1995, 75).

The public is evermore beginning to doubt answers that have clear boundaries and clean edges. Feigning control over anthropogenic catastrophes such as nuclear waste in the soil and water is exactly what has led to the continued tragedy of the Toms River region – Antonetta's childhood stomping grounds. According to Beck, risk is no longer spatially or temporally constrained; instead, it is disseminated through global threats such as nuclear war and global warming. Beck suggests that the main challenge for nation-states in a new global order is their inability "*to feign control over the uncontrollable*" (2002, 41; emphasis in the original). Toms River is located in Ocean County, which in turn is in the middle of New Jersey's shoreline and was the subject of one cover-up after another for a period of sixty years. In 2001 three companies – Ciba Specialty Chemicals Corporation, Union Carbide Corporation, and United Water Resources, Inc. – reached an agreement with sixty-nine families for an undisclosed amount and with a no-fault clause. The settlement came days before a report was set to go public about whether or not cases of childhood cancer in the region were linked to polluted groundwater from dump sites and plants (Avril and Moroz 2001; State of New Jersey Department of Public Health 2001; Sucato 2001).

Antonetta's memoir tests our ability to differentiate between our bodies and our waste, and it becomes clear that in economic terms we privilege and support the health of our waste over that of other human bodies, especially if we think that our own bodies are not made vulnerable by our waste. When describing her grandmother's conservative child-rearing practices in stark contrast to said grandmother's skinny-dipping revelry, Antonetta writes:

> (Every morning first thing my grandmother crossed the gravel road. As she crossed the road her spirit rose and kited out of her life. She threw off her cotton shift and the hydraulic system that was 1930s women's underwear, and skinnydipped for a long time in Barnegat Bay. Still her children weren't allowed to use the words "pregnant" or "God.")
>
> Separation and separation and separation.
>
> (*Body Toxic*, 11)

While her grandfather "had little feeling for nature" and Antonetta "never knew him to go outside without a reason" (2001, 5), her grandmother wanted to give the family a sense of a countryside existence. Maybe her grandfather knew that the great outdoors in which he had "jury-rigg[ed]" two cottages (land that was available only because of the economic collapse of 1929) was not the best place to explore (2001, 11). Antonetta's tone implies that he somehow knew or is at fault for trying to take advantage of the economic destitution of others: her grandfather habitually arrived "on the heels of disaster" (2001, 10), but the disease clusters that later surfaced in the surrounding area were something he could not have predicted, especially since according to his granddaughter he did not like going outside. Certainly, he could not connect and quantify the different kinds of disaster around him. As numerous reports and exposés have since revealed, he was unknowingly putting the family on a sure path of exposure to radioactive waste.

Startling and more recent revelations demonstrate that much of the toxic matter we fear is already a part of our bodies, not something that can be expunged and exported. Antonetta's grandmother feared illness but did not believe in its hold over the physical body and was expert at separating body from mind and sickness from health. Antonetta's grandmother and mother (a "quasi-Christian Scientist") firmly believed in the docetic body and thus made distinctions between two worlds: one in which the body is material, the other in which it is not (2001, 60). As Stephanie LeMenager explains, Antonetta groups together a blind faith in industrial progress with an unquestioning belief in Antonetta's family's version of the docetic body: "Like Mark Twain, Antonetta recognizes Mary Baker Eddy's faith as deeply complicit with American ideologies of progress" (2014, 192). Antonetta names people who worked at Ciba-Geigy and Denzer and Schafer who were also Christian Scientists and who, according to Antonetta, believed in a split between the material and immaterial. To Antonetta's mind, it was the people in power at the companies that recklessly dumped hazardous waste who believed that, like Christ's body at times, their bodies were immaterial and impervious to earthly hazards. It was the same group of people who believed "we lived in two different dimensions," who were able to pour "sludges in the ground we drank from and the river we swam in" (2001, 61).

The splintering of matter from bodies is key to Antonetta's memoir, as she alternates between thinking that the body is phantasmal or illusory, to feeling its weight when undergoing various bouts of identifiable illness. Her writing reminds us of the same belief that we see in many ecocritical texts and more widely in public discourse about climate change: that we have lost the right to live in a good and clean world, "I love my grandmother's religion: I believe it in a way and yet I believe I'm sick. Maybe we did live bodiless. Maybe by treating ourselves as impregnable we've somehow renounced the privilege, incarnating ourselves slowly in the world we've fouled" (2001, 61). As further proof of how we have laid waste to our world as an inhabitable space for humans, Antonetta recalls the movement to collect physical evidence from human bodies (baby teeth). People were seeking to understand if there was a connection between Oyster Creek's nuclear reactor in Ocean County and the cancer clusters later discovered in the surrounding areas (2001, 25). The rounding up and mailing of "old baby teeth" (2001, 25) for the Radiation and Public Health Project – also known as the Tooth Fairy Project – mixes fantasy with the grotesque in uncomfortable ways. The gothic nature of much of Antonetta's memoir, which commingles idyllic childhood dreams with gut-wrenching moments of harsh violence, keeps both dreams and violent moments contained to the penumbra of reality. This cannot have happened, we think – not here in the United States, and certainly not to average people. Antonetta toys with the readers' hope that this is a story about degenerates who have received a just punishment, not a tale of environmental and corporate injustice. She shares events that are hard for us to look at and she dares us to look away.

The connection of one's body to one's natural and national borders is a global phenomenon, but it is particularly tied to the bodies of US citizens. Arjun Appadurai writes that the lines between "American bodies, American cultural glitz, and the known power of the American state" are elastic (2006, 120). American studies scholars have long wondered about the borders of American identity, and with increased focus on global terrorism such questions gain urgency. Not only are US bodies linked to national borders, but they are also, as Appadurai points out, imaginatively subsumed into the fabric of US imperialism. Imagine how difficult life is for Antonetta, who feels that her body is perpetually violated and deemed useless. Antonetta states that her family emigrated and found an "anti-place," and that her mixture of Barbadian and Italian ancestry has robbed her of the chance to be either American or normal. She writes that her family found "an America that seemed less like a place than an anti-place, a not-Barbados, not-Europe, not Asia or Africa. . . . Not this, not that" (2001, 3).

The sense of an anti-place is inseparable from her sense that her family's dreams of America have been violated, as have the bodies and minds of their progeny. Antonetta's brother, Mark, also "became one" (that is, he was diagnosed as bipolar), and Antonetta's "being also a diagnosed manic-depressive" further disgraces her in her family's eyes. But it is her cousin, Helen, who disappoints the Barbadian side of the family most by leaving "the husband her mother selected for her in order to live with one of her patients, a man with thirty-odd personalities" (2001, 45). Nobody in the family is allowed to exhibit signs of mental or physical illness, much less act in ways that fly in the face of the dream of success that Antonetta's grandfather clung to after he arrived to America. Similarly, "Dan," the Amazon.com reviewer, needs to racialize and invalidate Antonetta's right to be ill because it threatens his sense of control over his personal risk and familial safety.

By denying the legitimacy of Antonetta's story, Dan treats it as a combination of mistruths and "junk science" (Dan 2004). His response exposes three points of intervention for *Environmental Justice in Contemporary US Narratives*. All three are based on my main premise: that we need to urgently consider the forms of individual harm and violence leveled against human bodies on an everyday basis in the United States and to consider how these forms have been shaped by US industrialization and conservation efforts since World War I. The first point of intervention is that as imagined by the writers, artists, and directors whose work I read, corporeally anchored moments of contact and interaction with foreign bodies – not just with human bodies but also with toxins, pathogens, and parasites – disrupt accepted notions of US citizenship and challenge US neoliberal ideologies. The second point of intervention is that the renderings of palpable harm, I argue, imply that what hovers inside and below official ideology of US progress is a disturbing history of violent colonial and corporeal domination. Recent debates about representing the body at the cellular level as both biological and abiological matter lead to a third intervention in the material turn. I identify a common tactic of subversion: the reclamation of disfigured and sick bodies in these texts serves as a trope for the larger project of artists and activists, in which the markedly foreign body becomes a revisionist subtext in the narrative of the US body politic. Nonnormative bodies are synecdochic of the ecological destruction inherent in rampant – and markedly American – global capitalism.

The material turn

A number of texts in *Environmental Justice in Contemporary US Narratives* center on bodies in space that labor to have a right to be recognized in that space and also for the surrounding space to be read as a part of their somatic makeup. As Serenella Iovino and Serpil Oppermann poignantly state in their introduction to *Material Ecocriticism*, "bodies, both human and nonhuman, provide an eloquent example of the way matter can be read as a text" (2014, 6). Narratives of climate change, human rights, food justice, and environmental justice evermore converge at the level of the body and of "things." The recent revival of material studies, or "new materialism," reinforces the importance of an ongoing discourse on how our lives take shape in harmony with our surroundings, sometimes in tension with them, but always in relation to and with them. The emerging conversations on human agency and objects is creating a shift from thinking of the "less-than-human" world to the "more-than-human" world as a universe that demands further consideration. David Abram first coined the term "more-than-human" world (1996, 5–7) in his writings on ontology, nature, and the work of (among others) René Descartes, Martin Heidegger, Edmund Husserl, and Maurice Merleau-Ponty. His description of nonhuman agency, based in large part on French existentialist Merleau-Ponty's work, is arguably the first example of eco-phenomenology. Much has developed since 1996 in the "more-than-human" world as people's awareness of its relevance was necessarily heightened on the heels of natural disasters, environmental inequity, oceanic and air pollution, climate refugees, wealth disparity, health crises, and the near certainty of human extinction in the not-too-distant future.

Materiality as a discourse requires that we think about the enmeshed ways in which the somatic and nonsomatic and the biological and abiological all interact, and it has continued to gain traction since the 1990s. Feminist critic Elizabeth Grosz argues that Western thought has been underwritten by a conception of somatophobia, a fear of the body and its materiality (1994, 5).[9] Grosz employs Merleau-Ponty's work ([1945] 1962) and posits that the experiences of the lived body are key to knowledge formation. Grosz's dialectic of corporeal feminism, similar to Judith Butler's (1993), concerns itself with performativity and the inscription of the body as meaning-making. Butler, more than Grosz, is interested in materiality insofar as it seems constricting to postmodern feminism. As Stacy Alaimo and Susan Hekman note in their introduction to *Material Feminisms*, Butler's two most relevant books to materiality studies (*Gender Trouble*, 1990; *Bodies That Matter*, 1993), are more of a "retreat from materiality" than an engagement with the body as matter (2008, 3). Alaimo and Hekman eruditely add that although postmodernists react negatively to material ecofeminism and new materialism as a misreading of the poststructuralist blueprints of Gilles Deleuze and Michel Foucault, Deleuze and Foucault "do, in fact, accommodate the material in their work" (2008, 3). Butler, along with philosophical inquiries like those of Deleuze, Foucault, and Luce Irigaray, created the perfect foundation for neo-materialism, or new materialism, to become its own discourse. Strikingly, the mid-1990s is also when Manuel De Landa (1995) and Rosi Braidotti (1994, 2000) began to use different versions of "new materialism" as a term in order to think through posthumanism, subjectivity, and ontology.[10] These related but independent publications on how objects might be as theoretically rich as subject and subjectivity were the precipice of the material turn. The post-Cartesian interpretations and expression of bodies (human and nonhuman) mark a new moment of thinking of the body as networked matter, matter that is interrelated to objects and biological matter on the other end of the dermal divide. Bruno Latour, Donna Haraway, Andrew Pickering, and Karen Barad engage in similar theoretical projects of what Haraway might refer to as the "material-discursive" or Barad as the agential realism made up of "intra-actions." Barad proposes "intra-action" as a neologism that "signifies the mutual constitution of entangled agencies" (2007, 33). As opposed to "interaction," which signifies "separate individual agencies," Barad envisions an emergent discourse of possibility in the treatment of the "more-than-human" as crucial to our understanding of humanity and a kind of ethical corporeality.

The threshold between the body and its surroundings, especially the "polluted" external world, is a matter of much interest to the writers I discuss in this book. Their renderings of toxic and intoxicated bodies not only force the national body politic to grapple with the waste of its excesses, but they also articulate an emerging politics of disruption. Stacy Alaimo's definition of the "trans-corporeal" challenges accepted representations of human bodies and examines how the body interdigitates with its environment (2010, 2). Jane Bennett argues that matter holds vitality and can act as an influential force (2010, 94). She observes that the nonhuman runs "parallel" to the human because "the image of dead or thoroughly instrumentalized matter feeds human hubris and our earth-destroying fantasies of conquest and consumption" (2010, xi). The models of the trans-corporeal (Alaimo) and the vitality of things (Bennett) interact in productive ways and push ecofeminist thinking to directly address new materialism as the radical yet logical next step in exploring the agency of objects that we have hitherto ignored.[11] Alaimo revisits the genealogy of new materialism and notes that even though object-oriented ontology (OOO), "speculative realisms," and "new vitalisms" (2014, 193) are all forms of "thing theory" that in some ways advance the case for new materialism, it is actually at the crossroads of ecofeminism and materialist studies that material ecocriticism was formulated.

Most of the writers, artists, and directors in my book find visibility in the least visible and least legible bodies, which are normally occluded from society's vision. The politics of perception and reception gain importance for environmental scholars and activists. We are at a precarious time of information overload, and environmental destruction is an ominous subject that tests our limits of empathy. In a field that appears to be vision deficient and that finds other forms of apprehension and expression similarly challenging, it might be time to reconsider not only that which is invisible but also more largely undetectable. In their introduction to *New Materialisms*, Diana Coole and Samantha Frost point out that the "reprisal of materialism must be truly radical" (2010, 3) and that in order for new materialism to resonate and gain traction, it must concurrently shift from subjectivity to "subject objectivity and material reality" (2010, 2). Coole and Frost's collection highlights the relevance of new materialism to discourses of agential corporeality, ones that do not depend solely on subjecthood but rather subject objectivity. The material turn beckons humans to reimagine their relationship to pollution as a self-induced part of our cellular existence, but this turn also offers a new lens through which material agency has potentially transformative powers.

Interrogating texts

Environmental Justice in Contemporary US Narratives does not ignore the colonial and imperial overtones of the roots of American studies, but it builds on a new area of research: it looks at US texts through an ecological lens and uses them to investigate the criticisms of elitism leveled against the ecocritical movement within American literary studies. For example, Steinbeck's elegiac *The Grapes of Wrath* ([1939] 1976) mourns a preindustrial time in US farming, while Cherríe Moraga's play *Heroes and Saints* (1994) tackles the ills of a postindustrial American landscape. These divergent narratives of industrial agribusiness are significant in their differences. Steinbeck writes of a period when World War I, the Homestead Act, and ecological damage combined to produce the Dust Bowl, which Rolland Dewing refers to as the "most extreme natural event in 350 years" (2006, 5). My book aims to show that such moments of natural disaster are inherently global and universal, and by definition also homologous. Many of the texts discussed in this book grapple with the fierce struggle between retaining state and somatic boundaries and the concurrent traversal of both by corporate-sponsored environmental hazards.

In tackling issues of globalization, corporate interests, and government complicity, *Environmental Justice in Contemporary US Narratives* foregrounds the biopolitical violence that accompanies the corporate-driven division of global capital inside and outside of the United States. Historian T.J. Jackson Lears writes extensively about the antimodern push against the "efficient control of nature under the banner of improving human welfare" (1981, 7). The natural and unnatural catastrophes discussed in this book indicate the way in which we continue to rationalize violence and harm as an inescapable part of life. In the twenty-first century in particular, the avoidance of risk has instead become its cause. Beck distinguishes between personal and public risk in meaningful ways. Identifying modernization as itself the vessel of risk, Beck proposes that in premodern times there were risks like those that Christopher Columbus took on, which "were personal risks" and "not global dangers like . . . nuclear fission" (1992, 21). Risks are a consequence of the ebbs and flows of modernization and "are politically reflexive" (1992, 21). Beck suggests that humans are secure in their knowledge of the mastery of nature, and thus they have become insecure and highly susceptible to risk. Increased production has hitherto been a sign of success, but the mining of nature has led to a false sense of security.[12]

As the theatrical nature of any nation's attempt to contain and control risk increases along with messages to the public that we can control and mitigate risk, so too do the sophistication of creative responses by activists and artists deepen. Andrew Szasz states that particularly in the United States people are privileging personal over shared risk and consuming products in a manner that ignores the inherently communal nature of events such as global warming and toxic dumping. Szasz's diagnosis that modern urbanites are participating in a race to purchase products and use methods of "inverted quarantine" (2007, 18) speaks to the fear and paranoia that enmeshed materiality brings when it is accompanied by environmental degradation.

The authors, directors, and artists I discuss in *Environmental Justice in Contemporary US Narratives* attempt to communicate risk to those who consider themselves to be free of it. Fictional stories based on the nonfiction of environmental injustices possess the power to move people in ways that statistics and risk assessment reports cannot. Postcolonial critics – Elizabeth DeLoughrey and George Handley (2011, 14), and Rob Nixon (2005, 2011, 3–39), to name a few – express a well-founded anxiety that US ecocriticism will present environmental concerns as originating in the United States and being dominated by US researchers. My aim in this book is to broaden the treatment of US-centric ecocriticism through readings of stories about bodies. The texts in my book depict global and planetary risks in ways that go far beyond national boundaries, demonstrating that ecocriticism and the environmental humanities already think and act globally.

Environmental Justice in Contemporary US Narratives is chock-full of bodies that do not obey and that behave in unexpected ways, and their creators (the writers and directors who give life to the bodies through stories about them) are asking their audiences to reconsider their understanding of the place of the body in relation to its environments. Oppositional constructs like "body" and "environment" actually encourage self-reflexive forms of violence. Bodies are sorted as clean or dirty, healthy or ill, and the tipping point for such divisions appears to be a murky set of coordinates on a spectrum that rapidly shifts. In an essay titled "The Ecocritical Insurgency," Buell suggests that if the twentieth century was indeed defined by what W.E.B. Du Bois termed "the problem of the color line," (quoted in Buell 1999, 699) then surely, writes Buell, "the twenty-first century's most pressing problem will be the sustainability of earth's environment" (1999, 699). Priscilla Solis Ybarra traces and builds on the lineage from Du Bois to Buell, and ecocriticism at large, and "extends Buell's observation: the most pressing problem of the twenty-first century may be that racism, homophobia, and sexism continue alongside – and are exacerbated by – the shrinking sustainability of the natural environment" (2009, 176). Yes, as Ybarra suggests, human life on earth is becoming less sustainable. Yes, "racism, homophobia, and sexism," as well as speciesism, are strengthened by the human-created problem of unequal access to clean resources.

All of the above are supported by a xenophobic mentality that has been so deeply ingrained in our political systems that we hardly notice our own participation in it. Samuel Huntington's ideas about the clash of civilizations (1996) expose a teleology of the modern nation-state that easily enables predatory environmental practices because it reduces space for dissent. Huntington's work further elucidates why the "separation and separation and separation" that Antonetta notes is such a successful modus operandi in the United States and for other first-world powers. As Rita Raley writes, in unpacking what it means to protest the neoliberal binary of "friend and enemy," Huntington's theory teases out how the "imaginary of the new world order maintains territorial divisions as metaphysical" ones and thus "naturalizes" lines like the US–Mexico border (Raley 2009, 37).[13] With that naturalization and the acceptance of the present as inevitable comes a type of personal and political paralysis that is as debilitating as it is undetectable.

The undetectable nature of the naturalization of false inevitabilities gives way to fear: both the fear that leads to a retrenchment behind false borders and the fear of what would happen without those borders. *Environmental Justice in Contemporary US Narratives* begins and ends by discussing the public's response to ideas of bodies as being inseparable from their environment. The public responds with great doubt and fear to ideas of individual and communal exposure to – and responsibility for – planetary ills and risks. This fear often manifests itself as a fear of other bodies, leading us to read the bodies of others as representing illness, aberrance, difference, impurity, and contagion. All of these things are seen as different from the qualities we assume that healthy and good bodies possess. Here, the majority fears that a minority will overtake it. As Appadurai lyrically states, "minorities do not come preformed" (2006, 42). In fact, in the spirit of Huntington, and with the hindsight of post-9/11 US politics, Appadurai goes on to say that minorities are not preformed but "produced in the specific circumstances of every nation and every nationalism" (2006, 42). I find it telling that he considers a minoritarian practice or movement to be "the major site for displacing the anxieties of many states about their own minority or marginality (real or imagined) in a world of a few megastates, of unruly economic flows" (2006, 43). If, as Appadurai writes, minorities are "metaphors and reminders of the betrayal of the classical national project" (2006, 43), then we can stretch our imaginations enough to see that what we apprehend as minority bodies operate in the same way.

National conservation and laboring bodies

The writers, artists, and directors discussed in this book engage in imaginative and subversive methodologies to turn our attention to a material corporeality. *Environmental Justice in Contemporary US Narratives* focuses on post-1929 works that attempt to highlight the ills of a system gone awry. Taking first the Roaring Twenties and then the Great Depression as temporal markers, I argue that the New Deal policies that followed the Great Depression significantly shaped present-day understandings of our relationship to the outdoors. While the early twentieth century appeared to be closing the gap between US citizens and their natural resources, it in fact fostered a strained and profit-driven connection between people and the land. In the United States after World War I, "conservation" became synonymous with "cultivation," and therefore it also distanced humans from their surroundings. President Calvin Coolidge ushered the United States through the Roaring Twenties – a decade of excess, materialism, grand industry, and the development of farming and agribusiness in ways that the world had never imagined. In a stark departure from his predecessors, Coolidge overhauled the touchstone of America's symbolic agrarian backbone: the yeoman farmer. The most patriotic behavior was defined as the most prodigious and the least individual, and farming became a way to network capital and create a stronger national economy (Bentley 1998; Carruth 2013). This great boom was followed by a huge crash in both the stock markets and the quality of America's landscape. The New Deal era is remembered as a time that stood apart in US history, one when private citizens worked toward the public good. The inauguration of Franklin D. Roosevelt (FDR) as president in 1933 was followed by the so-called one hundred days of dramatic legislation that included the National Recovery Act and the formation of the Public Works Administration. It marks a moment when US ideology connected conservation to natural resources and the development of these resources to improve the living standards of those closest to them.[14] Rural areas and their inhabitants – the people closest to the land – became a symbol of unity in a fractured time.

Environmental Justice in Contemporary US Narratives is unique both because of its approach to environmental justice media and because it takes up new efforts by academics to strengthen the ties between literature and the social sciences.[15] Many of the following chapters examine literary and visual manifestations of natural resources and the manner in which national and cultural boundaries are forcibly mapped onto them. Environmental literature labors to present on the page both the scope and sense of nature – that is, to communicate sights, smells, sounds, tastes, and touch in their entirety. In *Ecology Without Nature*, ecocritic Timothy Morton writes extensively on what he terms "eco-mimesis," which is "above all a practice of juxtaposition" (2007, 143). Eco-mimesis conflates the representation of things/nature with the things themselves and is another way of querying and overturning traditional ecocriticism through "*dark ecology*" (2007, 143, emphasis in the original). Since Morton coined it, dark ecology has been used to deepen and expand forms of ecocriticism to move beyond juxtaposition and metaphor and into what Morton later termed "the mesh" (2010, 15), requiring a "radical openness to everything" (2010, 15) and demanding that critics pay particular attention to the interpenetration not only of things but also of philosophies of thought. In their coedited volume *Material Ecocriticism*, Iovino and Oppermann point to the necessary turn away from dead and flat metaphors and the necessary embracement of "anthropomorphizing matter" in order to close the gap of human perceptions between subject and object, person and thing: "We are well aware that 'stories' or 'narratives,' if applied to matter might be read as metaphor . . . anthropomorphism can even act against dualistic ontologies and be a 'dis-anthropocentric' stratagem" (2014, 8). This is a crucial pursuit for environmentalists worldwide as they attempt to communicate the erosion of the ozone or deforestation, as well as microscopic harm.

Environmental literature threatens to destabilize the foundation of US citizenship in complex and as-yet-unexplored ways; it makes visible not only deep-seated class-based strife but also the roots of US capitalist-driven progress that has quietly mutated into ecological violence. In the epilogue to *Slow Violence and the Environmentalism of the Poor* (2011), Rob Nixon uses the case of the Maldives to demonstrate the problem of the public's perception of violence. Next to a 2009 photograph of then president Mohamed Nasheed holding an underwater cabinet meeting to draw attention to the dark future of his country because of global warming, Nixon poses two related questions: first, how do countries facing immediate repercussions from environmental pollution make up for the "drama deficit of climate change," and second, how do smaller "minnow" nations like the Maldives gain a powerful global voice to "render visible the slow violence" that threatens to destroy them (2011, 264)?

Scholars and activists have recently begun to grapple with the idea that unrepresentable, nonvisual – indeed, unphotographable – violence and harm will go unnoticed. In American studies, argues Nixon, the environmental justice movement has remained subordinate to the general greening of the humanities, which privileges a US-based agrarian sense of the environment (2011, 235). But I wonder whether working with US-based texts necessarily furthers the agenda of an elitist greening of the humanities. In her wildly popular *The Shock Doctrine: The Rise of Disaster Capitalism*, Naomi Klein suggests a theory and history of "disaster capitalism," in which a "fundamentalist version of capitalism" grows at an exponential rate only when preceded by "shock" (2007, 6).

In the literature before us, the trope of tangible scarring of the earth accompanied by intangible shifts in psychosomatic intelligence is repeated again and again. The shock to a land, whether by natural or unnatural causes (such as Hurricane Katrina or the United States's invasion of Iraq, respectively), goes hand in hand with the swift manipulation of the land's crippled state for capitalistic economic gain. Klein argues that these surreal moments become an opportunity for the public mining of personal disasters and that the stories of these disasters are often told through a group of families sharing their grief or images of dead animals (take, for example, the image of a pelican covered by crude oil). The stories are rarely, if ever, communicated in terms of collective harm, and almost never in terms of state-driven violence. Elizabeth Kolbert avers that her well-known *Field Notes from a Catastrophe* was about "watching the world change" and was written "to convey, as vividly as possible, the realities of global warming" that she connects absolutely to human interference (2006, 2). Here, too, personal stories are used to give perspective to national disasters, but they are offered as unscientific memories to balance dry data and obscured dates. Yet again we are faced with a question of framing – in terms, as Nixon has pointed out – both of national boundaries and spatiotemporal ones.

Environmental justice and American studies

This book and works like it are nodes that form a network to demonstrate how US-centered texts have an important role to play in recalibrating the conversation on ecocriticism, environmental justice, and literature through a specifically materialist lens. Ecocriticism and environmental justice have become increasingly intertwined. Buell refers to this as the "second wave" of interest from the field (2005, 22–3). The first wave proffered romanticized idealizations of a pure or true natural beauty, while the second wave queries both the relationship between urbanization and pollution and the permeable membranes between humans and nature. The green movement was initially considered to attract only the elite and predominantly whites, but second-wave ecocriticism – with its increased attention to environmental justice, deep ecology, toxicity, and the different meanings of "the natural" – works against monolithic configurations of nature.[16]

While the green movement is still considered by many to be a hierarchical, top-down movement, the shift in American studies toward transnational concerns is changing this dynamic. Joni Adamson and Scott Slovic respond to such concerns in their 2009 coauthored introduction to a special issue of *MELUS*. They identify a "*third* wave of ecocriticism, which recognizes ethnic and national particularities and yet transcends ethnic and national boundaries" (2009, 6; emphasis in the original).[17] Critics are increasingly taking note of people like Leo Marx and using the relationship between literature and the environment to narrativize and clarify much of what is going on in our contemporary moment.[18]

The complaint by many ecocritics that American studies has turned its back on ecocritical concerns since its inception should be dispelled by the earlier work of figures like poetry specialist F.O. Matthiessen and Marx. Marx identified a nineteenth-century allegiance to the pastoral in a time of rapid industrialization and modernization (Adamson and Ruffin 2013). Matthiessen's coinage of the term "American Renaissance" (1941) has proven controversial because of his focus on canonical (that is, white male) writers and his exclusion of Emily Dickinson and Edgar Allan Poe. Finally, American studies is not a narrowly nationalistic field. Rather, it is informed by and includes studies of the global South and its practitioners are well aware of the hazards of thinking of all things in terms of how America affects them. The environmental justice movement is a vibrant part of an ongoing dialogue in American studies between ecocriticism and more traditional literary studies. As someone who worked at the *Journal of Transnational American Studies* for a number of years, I am particularly sensitive to the dangers of co-optation of American studies, then transnational American studies, and finally global studies as different versions of American exceptionalism.

A quick glance at the website of the Natural Resources Defense Council (n.d.) demonstrates the trajectory of the environmental justice movement from the 1960s to the 1980s, and the way in which the movement was a reaction to the tacit complicity of the government in cases of toxic dumping, dangerous labor conditions, and the denial of a voice to the most disenfranchised. The environmental justice movement was spurred on by the zeitgeist of the civil rights movement and began as an antiracist call for equal human rights to a clean environment. While Buell has pointed out that environmental justice has become an "increasingly heterogeneous movement" (2005, 1), debates continue about whether it is centered on the United States or whether it is becoming more transnational. Whereas the romanticized notions of bucolic nature as inherently pure and just are now thought of as outdated, even earlier grassroots movements tended to ignore the common ground between man and nature while constructing a paradigm of man versus nature. Raymond Williams astutely argues that "the idea of nature is the idea of man" (2005, 56). Man constructs nature, Williams continues, because "it allows us to look, with unusual clarity, at some quite fundamental interpretations of all our experiences." In other words, all "that was not man" became nature (2005, 56). We can now recognize this as furthering the anthropocentric view that humans are the peacekeepers of nature. Writing on death in the Anthropocene, Roy Scranton explains why his individualistic story is actually a planetary one. He eloquently observes that "climate change is too big to be reduced to a single narrative" (2015, 24) – but, like many of us, he attempts to do just that. If we do away with the idea of a natural backdrop to the stories of humanity (à la Williams), thus dispensing with nature as something on which we can project our hopes and fears and the complexities of our lives, then we have to step back and consider the idea that nature is not monolithic, not a narrative that we can co-opt and control, and not something that humans can remake in their likeness. Environmental justice critiques are exploratory as they cover complicated terrain and include stories that do not seem like ones anybody would want to hear. But there is an audience for the stories, and that audience is growing.

Transnational American studies

One aim of *Environmental Justice in Contemporary US Narratives* is to tie the transnational vein in American studies to the ecocritical one both inside and outside the field. More than an international approach to American studies, the "transnational turn" was coined by Robert Gross (2000) and defined as the undoing of an American imperialist gaze. Gross likens a transnational perspective to "looking through the reverse lens of a telescope" (2000, 384). American studies scholars like Stefan Brandt, Winfried Fluck, and Ingrid Thaler generally agree that transnational American studies began to grow in the 1990s with the end of the Cold War (please see Fluck, Brandt, and Thaler 2007). International voices within the discipline cite transnational American studies as the answer to complaints that American studies reinforces the idea of American exceptionalism and is solipsistically concerned only with domestic affairs. American studies scholar Alfred Hornung contends that transnational American studies "is by definition political" (2005, 69). Although scholars have written eruditely about the reversal of the gaze back into the United States from outside its physical borders, the material turn is a fairly recent movement that gives us a wider vantage point – one that is not a reversal but an interrogation (see, for example, Rowe, Robinson, and Hornung, n.d.).

While American studies has been faithfully revising its aims and working to rebut the claim that it echoes US imperialism, its transnational turn has also worked to expose international ties to the manipulation of human and nonhuman resources in the interest of US corporate gain. Shelley Fisher Fishkin's call for a "transnational turn" (2005, 17) in American studies has been accepted, and scholars are thinking through what that might look like in the future. In Emory Elliott's American Studies Association (ASA) presidential address, he similarly lauded transnational American studies as a step toward "thoughtful citizenship" that increased diversity both inside and outside US borders (2007, 6). Six years later, Priscilla Wald's presidential address to the ASA not only partially answered Fishkin's call, but it also generated a new one: for scholars across the humanities to address an "increasing turn in American studies from the familiar grounding terms of the citizen and the nation to the human and networks" (2012, 186). Using the real-life biomedical history of Henrietta Lacks and Foucault's notions of biopower, Wald further interrogates the threshold of American studies by welding together the pieces of Lacks's story (institutionalized US racism, class inequity, and capitalist greed in the name of science) to suggest that the "distribution of power through which the state regulates life is a form of violence" (2012, 191). Citing Johan Galtung's work on "structural violence" (1969, 171) – the institutionalized violence that lives beneath the surface of things – Wald wonders about endemic and veiled violence in the United States, and she employs Galtung's term to whittle away at the binary distinction between natural and unnatural disasters (2012, 190–3).

Indeed, the multivalent entanglements between what is deemed to be at fault for natural catastrophes and what buttresses everyday, systemic violence in the United States lie at the heart of Wald's exploration of structural abuses of power. In the introduction to their edited volume, Joni Adamson and Kimberly Ruffin delineate the lag time in American studies and beyond from the early nineteenth century until Hurricane Katrina (2013, 2–3). Adamson and Ruffin's volume is a testament to the work being done to continue the greening of the humanities while drawing attention to global discourses of race, class, and gender. Even critics who tried to avoid US-based work while researching global environmentalism have found it important to query the way that Americans have framed their relationship to nature. Ursula Heise questions "whether localism is indeed a necessary component of environmental ethics, as much as U.S.-American ecodiscourse leads one to believe," or if it is a product of US-specific traditions (2008b, 9). Using her experiences with German culture as a contrast to US culture, Heise finds that there is, indeed, something singular about the American conception of environmental concerns as radiating out from the local to the universal.

The turn to the material and the theoretical may have been identified as a new phenomenon in American studies or literary studies more generally, but scholars have long been working through the ties we build between the human and nonhuman. We find ourselves looking ahead to the remainder of the twenty-first century and beyond, wondering what the future holds and how we can shape it. If the twentieth century was, as Evelyn Fox Keller has called it, the "century of the gene" (2000), then how are we to conceive of the twenty-first? A number of theorists from various academic disciplines – including Sarah Franklin (2007), Ian Hacking (2006), Donna Haraway (1991), N. Katherine Hayles (1999), Keller (2000), Paul Rabinow (1996), and Nikolas Rose (2007) – have made important headway in studying the emerging dialogue on postgenomic subjects. New discoveries at the molecular level have opened up possibilities for a different understanding of the subject, one that moves away from genetic predetermination and is instead, as Rose suggests, "probabilistic not deterministic, open, not closed" (2007, 161). This discursive shift away from genetic determinism delineates postgenomics as an opportunity for the redefinition of life itself. Franklin, an anthropologist, cautions that in the postgenomic sciences of agriculture and tissue engineering, "the questions of what the biological *is* has become inextricable from what the biological *does* or can be made to do" (2007, 33; emphasis in the original).

This is precisely why critics such as Wald and Franklin are looking at case studies such as Henrietta Lacks and Dolly (the cloned sheep) – because they make clear the manner in which a focus on end results and futuristic, probabilistic invention ignores a politically and ecologically fraught present and past. What happens to a word like "bioethics" when the definition of the "biological" includes abiological matter and ceases to equate "life" with the image of a newborn (human) baby? As Alaimo points out, the shift from "scientific" and "objective" writings like those of Rachel Carson (1951, 1962) to personal, "materialist memoirs" delineates "a sea change of sorts – a broad consciousness or, at least, an anxious, nearly conscious awareness – that late twentieth- and early twenty-first-century citizens may not imagine ourselves as separate from the risky environments we inhabit" (2010, 95). The very idea of citizenship becomes contested territory. Alaimo implies a type of global citizenship whose subjects are aware of their shared materiality and thus their shared vulnerability and culpability. The ideology of global citizenship obscures the very disparate ways in which notions of citizenship have developed, particularly in the United States. Given the country's colonial histories and geographic isolation, American citizenship is intensely complicated. Post-1918 American environmental politics, American liberalism, and New Deal conservation policies have collectively shaped the contours of our sense of entitlement and belonging to a US landscape.

Material fictions

Germane to this book is the lively discourse in the environmental humanities on the nature of materiality and somatic-centered narratives, and the ongoing debates about how to communicate truths to readers and viewers – particularly truths that traverse national boundaries. Heise concludes *Sense of Place and Sense of Planet* by addressing the drama deficit of terms like "global warming" and she states that "imagining how such planetary transformation might affect particular places and individuals, therefore, amounts to a paradigmatic exercise in 'secondhand nonexperience'" (2008b, 206). She indicates that if people can be mobilized through "secondhand nonexperience" they might be able to form transnational communities through an idea of shared – if only imagined – risk. Heise underscores the fact that environmental movements seek anchors and roots in places: "certain features recur across a wide variety of environmentalist perspectives that emphasize a sense of place as a basic prerequisite for environmental awareness and activism" (2008b, 33). *Environmental Justice in Contemporary US Narratives* identifies one such anchor as an attachment to bodies and corporeal borders rather than land-based locations. Thus, this book is a response to the charges of elitism that are made against any US-based ecocritical ventures. While we might argue that US bodies are marked by first-world privilege and thus reinforce ideas of elitism within the greening of the humanities, the texts I discuss in this book argue for a collective, transnational questioning of structures of power and violations of human rights.

Environmental Justice in Contemporary US Narratives traces the sense of first-hand experience that is possible through reading materially inflected fiction and argues for the centrality of the body in US texts, films, and other artworks of the twentieth and twenty-first centuries. Through their disruption of traditional knowledge systems, these works reveal the porous and uncontainable nature of the environment and lend agency to both human and nonhuman actors. Significantly, they all imaginatively represent the immaterial as material on the page and on the screen. The writers, directors, and activists I discuss in the book demand that we take seemingly disparate fictions about food production, labor, and ecology and add them to the larger commentary on contemporary global flows of capital and US politics of belonging. From the works of John Steinbeck to those of Karen Tei Yamashita (1997), fictional renditions of American culture collectively offer a powerful commentary on US environmental practices and biopolitical citizenship. While literature is often seen as reactionary – that is, responding to shifting political landscapes – in this book I highlight the manner in which it can shape public opinion about humans' place in the world and our complicated relationship to it.

Chapter 2, "Laboring Bodies," takes as its starting point John Steinbeck's Depression-era writing. Steinbeck's *The Grapes of Wrath* ([1939] 1976) is a well-known work of US literature about the labor movement and a touchstone of literary history, but its deep ecological implications are less often considered. If we examine this novel together with Steinbeck's coauthored scientific travel narrative *Sea of Cortez* ([1941] 2009) and its later reworking, *The Log from the Sea of Cortez* ([1951] 1995), the shift in focus from the land to the sea and in genre from fiction to nonfiction demonstrate Steinbeck's prescient – and ethically fraught – environmentalism. I argue that *Sea of Cortez* and *The Grapes of Wrath* work together in significant and exciting ways to reveal both Steinbeck's nostalgia for preindustrial agriculture and his anticipation of Cold War anxieties that are linked to notions of national scientific progress in oceanic spaces. Steinbeck's sea writing alternates between complicity with, to criticism of, human meddling in the environment, and perhaps because of this it has been unfairly ignored in ecocritical discourse. Taken together, *The Grapes of Wrath* and *Sea of Cortez* articulate a sharp critique of the forced separation between humanistic and scientific study, and between the ways readers apprehend fiction and nonfiction.

Chapter 3, "Embodied Consumption," presents an ecocritical, postcolonial reading of Bich Minh Nguyen's memoir, *Stealing Buddha's Dinner* (2007). Through examinations of Laura Ingalls Wilder's *Little House on the Prairie* series (1932–43), which was a leitmotif of Nguyen's childhood, I show that the intoxicating culinary and literary discourse Nguyen longs to be part of as a child becomes a toxic landscape of alienation. Her simplistic reading of homesteading obscures its real purpose: to settle uncivilized territories and claim land that was seen by whites as US territory that had not yet been developed as such. In many ways, Nguyen's romanticized version of American life was necessitated by the fact that to fit in she needed seamless stories of growth and success, even if those stories and their complexities eventually required her to exit their plots. Nguyen's experiences of growing up as a Vietnamese refugee and immigrant in the 1980s in Grand Rapids, Michigan, center on her longing for assimilation. Her interactions with nature and the surrounding environment are almost exclusively through fiction. She admires the connection between local, small-scale food production and consumption in the texts she reads, but this connection does not exist in her real surroundings. The intoxicating falseness of American junk food and the contrived narratives of US expansionism and imperialism lead Nguyen down an unsettling path of processed identity. In pursuit of the ghostly tracks of displaced indigenous peoples that are obscured by tales of fictional pioneer families, she tries to eat her way into existence and map herself onto the heartland of America. Through her food choices she dissociates herself from both nature and her cultural roots. Although at first Nguyen imagines that if she eats like the pioneer families she reads about she will be Americanized from the inside out, she becomes uncomfortable with the colonial and ecological implications of her eating practices. In this chapter, I wed ecocritical discourse to debates about indigeneity and ethnicity in the United States.

Chapter 4, "Toxic and Illegible Bodies," turns to the voice of technologically poisoned female bodies across genres (drama, novels, and documentary films) and asks how bodies speak. Steinbeck's *The Grapes of Wrath* immortalized California's San Joaquin Valley, but one might argue that it is returned to a state of mortality by Moraga's 1992 play, *Heroes and Saints* (1994). This is a postmodern play based on the cancer cluster in 1978–88 in McFarland, California. In following the thread of the human body and its interaction with nature from Steinbeck to Moraga, and from the earlier part of the twentieth century to its end, we see that the body as matter takes on new significance in Moraga's play and revises the relationship between humans and nature so that discourse about workers' rights becomes a cry for environmental justice and women's rights. In examining first-person accounts of toxic poisoning, archival footage of protests, and US fiction, this chapter navigates the uneven terrain of race and environmental justice in the San Joaquin Valley. I pair Moraga's work with Ruth Ozeki's *My Year of Meats* (1998) and employ them as a frame through which to look at the nature of corporeal representation in disease-based narratives. Ozeki's popular fiction is based on the real-life poisoning of humans by the hormone diethylstilbestrol (DES). DES is a plant-based synthetic estrogen that was widely used in women and livestock to produce supposedly healthy pregnancies and offspring. Whereas in Ozeki's work environmental degradation becomes a background to human suffering caused by the ingestion of medications and meat, in Moraga the sinister and scientifically unknowable nature of chemical poisoning is underlined.

Chapter 5, "Bodies on the Border," focuses on stories of ill and chemically charged bodies that indicate not only the permeable nature of the human form but also the inverse relationship between visibility and harm that has been increasingly expressed since the mid-twentieth century. By putting Alex Rivera's science fiction film *Sleep Dealer* (2008) in dialogue with Karen Tei Yamashita's *Tropic of Orange* (1997), I examine literary and visual manifestations of natural resources and the manner in which national and cultural boundaries are violently mapped onto them. These works address such realities as the North American Free Trade Agreement (NAFTA) and the Department of Homeland

Security's continuing efforts to build a wall between the United States and Mexico. In both *Tropic of Orange* and *Sleep Dealer* environmental degradation and corporate greed manifest themselves most clearly along the border. Both works attempt to make audiences ask themselves why violence against certain bodies is accepted and who dictates its distribution. Representations of nature in film and literature within the framework of post-9/11 US politics of national security and globalization reveal that the fluid mediums of water and air defy the logic of uniform, normalized borders and corporatization. But there are real and material dangers to the manifestation of bodies as flesh: the very bodies that take a stand against US imperialism and ecological degradation are symbolically subjected to violent and painful confrontations. The creators of these texts and films do not avoid issues of race, gender, and speciesism. The multiple disturbing ruptures, when bodies are violated or violate our conception of reality, lead us to question our complacency about what has been peddled by powerful heads of industry to the public as inevitable consequences of the growth of global capital. The directors, writers, and activists in my book employ imaginative and subversive methodologies to focus our attention on material corporeality. My coda, "Environmental Interplay" examines new manners of environmental protest and engagement that is no longer purely reactive but rather proactive, ambivalent, and playful.

Notes

1 The ideas in this paragraph will be fleshed out throughout this chapter. They owe much to the work of Joni Adamson (Adamson, Evans, and Stein 2002; Adamson and Ruffin 2013), Stacy Alaimo (2010), Lawrence Buell (1998, 2005), Elizabeth DeLoughrey and George B. Handley (2011), Mary Douglas (1966, 1986), Cheryll Glotfelty (1996), Donna Haraway (1991), Ursula Heise (2008b), Carolyn Merchant (1980), Rob Nixon (2005 and 2011), Andrew Szasz (2007), and Julie Sze (2002, 2007). These thinkers have helped shape my work, and their research continues to move forward in surprising and creative ways.

2 For two cutting-edge meditations on climate change, activism, and the possibilities inherent in the use of shame and hope, see Jacquet (2015) and Shewry (2015). I do not think it is a coincidence that both books have to do with oceanic spaces and liquidity, which lend themselves to imagining a more malleable future of change. I was delighted to see a draft version of Una Chaudhuri's paper on oceanic performance (2015). Chaudhuri deftly handled the complexities of converting sea spaces into places of protest that reject anthropocentric ownership of both the ocean and its creatures.

3 As of January 6, 2016, Antonetta's *Body Toxic* had fifteen customer reviews on Amazon.com, including the one by "Dan." Another reviewer was equally incensed by what he or she refers to as the "flagrant errors in her [Antonetta's] geography and chronology" and goes on to post that Antonetta writes about things that "could not have occurred." The review is titled "Antonetta Is Talent-Less and This Book Is Full of Lies" (Customer 2001).

4 I thank Robert Nixon for suggesting that I read *The Meadowlands.*

5 One discussion of Antonetta's interactions with her grandfather is particularly confusing. In the chapter titled "The Jersey Devil," she writes that she doubts she can remember things exactly as they were, but she describes her naked grandfather trying to get her into bed with him. According to Antonetta, he "threw the covers back. Then I saw nude skin and my head blurred. Time became space and swam past me physically, through and

around" (2001, 170). The traumatic implications of this passage are many and I do not give it the full attention it calls for in my reading.

6 Bruno Latour suggests that people have always expanded the borders of the sciences to extend into the humanities, and the borders of intuition to extend into the place of factual evidence (1993). Latour proposes that these expansions are a kind of miscalculation. See also Latour's *Politics of Nature* (2004), where he more fully develops a discourse on nature as an assemblage of agency and continues to query the human–nature divide.

7 For an erudite discussion of the commons and its connection to the field of American studies, see Adamson and Ruffin (2013, especially pages 3–5).

8 In Modern Greek, for example, a language I grew up speaking, it is rare to use the words "private" and "personal" to refer to not sharing something (either material or immaterial).

9 Elizabeth Grosz's introductory chapter briefly outlines a definition of somatophobia (1994, 5). She argues that Western philosophy, working from a Cartesian mind/body duality, has regarded the body as a type of threat to reason.

10 See for example, Manuel De Landa's "The Geology of Morals: A Neomaterialist Interpretation" (1995) and *A Thousand Years of Nonlinear History* (1997); see also Rosi Braidotti: *Nomadic Subjects: Embodiment and Sexual Difference in Contemporary Feminist Theory* (1994) and her essay, "Teratologies" (2000); lastly, Braidotti's interview in *New Materialism* (2012) and the work in general in that collection give a good overview of new materialism and the freshest developments.

11 For more on new forms of material agency and discourse on vital matter, see Dana Phillips and Heather Sullivan's coauthored introduction to *ISLE* (2012). It speaks further to the central importance of new materialism in studies of waste, agriculture, and aquaculture; their special issue is one of a growing number of publications that draw attention to environmental concerns, ecocriticism, and new materialism. See also Rick Dolphijn and Iris van der Tuin's *New Materialism: Interviews & Cartographies* (2012), a collection of interviews and writings that feature groundbreaking research on inanimate versus animate agency. Finally, Andrew Pickering's book (1995) on the production of scientific knowledge and "the mangle" of intersections emphasizes the importance of interdisciplinarity and how ontology is a coauthored undertaking.

12 Beck argues that "in contrast to all earlier epochs (including industrial society), the risk society is characterized essentially by a *lack* . . . the sources of danger are no longer ignorance but *knowledge*; not a deficient but a perfected mastery over nature" (1992, 183; emphasis in the original).

13 I must thank Giles Gunn for encouraging me to audit a course on globalization that thoroughly discussed Huntington's ideas. Similarly, it was in teaching a section of Rita Raley's course on "Narratives of War" that I was walked through Carl Schmitt's work and the genealogy of which he is a part, and for that I will be forever in her debt.

14 For a thorough analysis of how FDR's legislative actions in his first one hundred days as president defined this period as a critical one in the terms of future presidents, see Badger (2008).

15 Rob Nixon makes a similar argument – that the "less developed . . . bridgework between environmental literary studies and the social sciences" needs further development. See also Alaimo (2010), Buell (1998, 2005), Dimock (2006), Heise (2008b), and Houser (2014).

16 In Buell's categorizing of first- and second-wave ecocriticism, he allows for existence of more waves in the future. Cheryll Glotfelty writes: "Ecocriticism has been predominantly a white movement. It will become a multi-ethnic movement when stronger connections are made between the environment and issues of social justice, and when a diversity of voices are encouraged to contribute to the discussion" (1996, xxv). There is ample evidence that ecocriticism has indeed become a more diverse movement.

17 Parts of this paragraph and the previous one are taken from Athanassakis (2009).

18 Marx's classic *The Machine in the Garden* (1964) has remained in print and is of great importance to American studies scholars and ecocritics alike.

References

Abram, David. 1996. *The Spell of the Sensuous: Perception and Language in a More-Than-Human World*. New York: Vintage Books.

Adamson, Joni, Mei Mei Evans, and Rachel Stein, eds. 2002. *The Environmental Justice Reader: Politics, Poetics, and Pedagogy*. Tucson: University of Arizona Press.

Adamson, Joni, and Kimberly N. Ruffin, eds. 2013. "Introduction." In *American Studies, Ecocriticism, and Citizenship: Thinking and Acting in the Local and Global Commons*, edited by Joni Adamson and Kimberly N. Ruffin, 1–17. New York: Routledge.

Adamson, Joni, and Scott Slovic. 2009. "The Shoulders We Stand On: An Introduction to Ethnicity and Ecocriticism." *MELUS* 34 (2): 5–24.

Alaimo, Stacy. 2010. *Bodily Natures: Science, Environment, and the Material Self*. Bloomington, IN: Indiana University Press.

———. 2014. "Oceanic Origins, Plastic Activism, and New Materialism at Sea." In *Material Ecocriticism*, edited by Serenella Iovino and Serpil Oppermann, 186–203. Bloomington, IN: Indiana University Press.

Alaimo, Stacy, and Susan Hekman. 2008. "Introduction: Emerging Models of Materiality in Feminist Theory." In *Material Feminisms*, edited by Stacy Alaimo and Susan Hekman, 1–19. Bloomington, IN: Indiana University Press.

Antonetta, Susanne. 2001. *Body Toxic: An Environmental Memoir*. New York: Counterpoint.

Appadurai, Arjun. 2006. *Fear of Small Numbers: An Essay on the Geography of Anger*. Durham, NC: Duke University Press.

Athanassakis, Yanoula. 2009. "LA and TJ: Immigration, Globalization, and Environmental Justice in *Tropic of Orange* and *Sleep Dealer*." *Journal of American Studies in Turkey* 30 (1): 89–110.

Avril, Tom, and Jennifer Moroz. 2001. "Toms River Families Settle Cancer Claims a Mediated Deal Covers 69 Families That Blamed Companies for Their Children's Illnesses: Suits Are Pending in Separate Cases." *The Inquirer*, December 14. http://articles.philly.com/2001-12-14/news/25307892_1_cancer-claims-families-separate-cases.

Badger, Anthony J. 2008. *FDR: The First Hundred Days*. New York: Hill and Wang.

Barad, Karen. 2007. *Meeting the Universe Halfway: Quantum Physics and the Entanglement of Matter and Meaning*. Durham, NC: Duke University Press.

Beck, Ulrich. 1992. *Risk Society: Towards a New Modernity*. Translated by Mark Ritter. London: Sage.

———. 2002. "The Terrorist Threat: World Risk Society Revisited." *Theory, Culture & Society* 19 (4): 39–55.

Bennett, Jane. 2010. *Vibrant Matter: A Political Ecology of Things*. Durham, NC: Duke University Press.

Bentley, Amy. 1998. *Eating for Victory: Food Rationing and the Politics of Domesticity*. Urbana and Chicago: University of Illinois Press.

Braidotti, Rosi. 1994. *Nomadic Subjects: Embodiment and Sexual Difference in Contemporary Feminist Theory*. New York: Columbia University Press.

———. 2000. "Teratologies." In *Deleuze and Feminist Theory*, edited by Ian Buchanan and Claire Colebrook, 156–72. Edinburgh: Edinburgh University Press.

———. 2012. "The Notion of the Univocity of Being or Single Matter Positions Difference as a Verb or Process of Becoming at the Heart of the Matter: Interview with Rosi

Braidotti." In *New Materialism: Interviews & Cartographies*, edited by Rick Dolphijn and Iris van der Tuin, 19–37. Ann Arbor, MI: Open Humanities Press.

Brown, Wendy. 1995. *States of Injury: Power and Freedom in Late Modernity*. Princeton, NJ: Princeton University Press.

Buell, Lawrence. 1998. "Toxic Discourse." *Critical Inquiry* 24 (3): 639–65.

———. 1999. "The Ecocritical Insurgency." *New Literary History* 30 (3): 699–712.

———. 2005. *The Future of Environmental Criticism: Environmental Crisis and Literary Imagination*. Malden, MA: Blackwell.

Butler, Judith. 1990. *Gender Trouble: Feminism and the Subversion of Identity*. New York: Routledge.

Butler, Judith. 1993. *Bodies That Matter: On the Discursive Limits of Sex*. New York: Routledge.

Carruth, Allison. 2013. *Global Appetites: American Power and the Literature of Food*. New York: Cambridge University Press.

Carson, Rachel. 1951. *The Sea Around Us*. Oxford: Oxford University Press.

———. 1962. *Silent Spring*. New York: Houghton Mifflin.

Chaudhuri, Una. 2015. "Ocean Oriented Ontologies: Interspecies Performance in Anthropocenic Waters." Paper presented at the Human-Animal Studies Seminar, Columbia University, New York, November 10.

Coole, Diana, and Samantha Frost. 2010. "Introducing the New Materialisms." In *New Materialisms: Ontology, Agency, and Politics*, edited by Diana Coole and Samantha Frost, 1–46. Durham, NC: Duke University Press.

Customer. 2001. "Antonetta Is Talent-Less and This Book Is Full of Lies." *Customer Review of Body Toxic: An Environmental Memoir* by Susanne Antonetta. http://tinyurl.com/gsc2lkq.

Dan. 2004. "Sounds Like Nonsense to Me." *Customer Review of Body Toxic: An Environmental Memoir* by Susanne Antonetta. https://www.amazon.com/Body-Toxic-Environmental-Susanne-Antonetta/product-reviews/B000H2MXXI/ref=cm_cr_getr_d_paging_btm_next_2?ie=UTF8&pageNumber=2.

De Landa, Manuel. 1995. "The Geology of Morals: A Neomaterialist Interpretation." *World-Information Institute*. http://www.t0.or.at/delanda/geology.htm.

———. 1997. *A Thousand Years of Nonlinear History*. New York: Zone Books.

DeLoughrey, Elizabeth, and George B. Handley, eds. 2011. "Introduction: Toward an Aesthetics of the Earth." In *Postcolonial Ecologies: Literatures of the Environment*, edited by Elizabeth DeLoughrey and George B. Handley, 3–39. Oxford: Oxford University Press.

Dewing, Rolland. 2006. *Regions in Transition: The Northern Great Plains and the Pacific Northwest in the Great Depression*. Lanham, MD: University Press of America.

Dimock, Wai Chee. 2006. *Through Other Continents: American Literature across Deep Time*. Princeton, NJ: Princeton University Press.

Dolphijn, Rick, and Iris van der Tuin, eds. 2012. *New Materialism: Interviews & Cartographies*. Ann Arbor, MI: Open Humanities Press.

Douglas, Mary. 1966. *Purity and Danger: An Analysis of the Concepts of Pollution and Taboo*. London: Routledge.

———. 1986. *Risk Acceptability According to the Social Sciences*. New York: Russell Sage Foundation.

Edelstein, Michael R. (1988) 2004. *Contaminated Communities: Coping with Residential Toxic Exposure*. Boulder, CO: Westview.

Elliott, Emory. 2007. "Diversity in the United States and Abroad: What Does It Mean When American Studies Is Transnational?" *American Quarterly* 59 (1): 1–22.

Fagin, Dan. 2013. *Toms River: A Story of Science and Salvation*. New York: Bantam.

Fishkin, Shelley Fisher. 2005. "Crossroads of Cultures: The Transnational Turn in American Studies – Presidential Address to the American Studies Association, November 12, 2004." *American Quarterly* 57 (1): 17–57.

Fluck, Winfried, Stefan Brandt, and Ingrid Thaler, eds. 2007. "Introduction: The Challenges of Transnational American Studies." In *Yearbook of Research in English and American Literature* (REAL), 23. http://tinyurl.com/zngjuro.

Franklin, Sarah. 2007. *Dolly Mixtures: The Remaking of Genealogy*. Durham, NC: Duke University Press.

Galtung, Johan. 1969. "Violence, Peace, and Peace Research." *Journal of Peace Research* 6 (3): 167–91.

Glotfelty, Cheryll. 1996. "Introduction: Literary Studies in an Age of Environmental Crisis." In *The Ecocriticism Reader: Landmarks in Literary Ecology*, edited by Cheryll Glotfelty and Harold Fromm, xv–xxxvii. Athens: University of Georgia Press.

Gross, Robert. 2000. "The Transnational Turn: Rediscovering American Studies in a Wider World." *Journal of American Studies* 34 (3): 373–93.

Grosz, Elizabeth. 1994. *Volatile Bodies: Toward a Corporeal Feminism*. Bloomington, IN: Indiana University Press.

Hacking, Ian. 2006. "Genetics, Biosocial Groups, and the Future of Identity." *Daedalus* 135 (4): 81–95.

Haraway, Donna. 1991. *Simians, Cyborgs, and Women: The Reinvention of Nature*. New York: Routledge.

Hayles, N. Katherine. 1999. *How We Became Posthuman: Virtual Bodies in Cybernetics, Literature, and Informatics*. Chicago: University of Chicago Press.

Heise, Ursula K. 2008a. "Ecocriticism and the Transnational Turn in American Studies." *American Literary History* 20 (1–2): 381–404.

———. 2008b. *Sense of Place and Sense of Planet: The Environmental Imagination of the Global*. Oxford: Oxford University Press.

Hornung, Alfred. 2005. "Transnational American Studies: Response to the Presidential Address." *American Quarterly* 57 (1): 67–73.

Houser, Heather. 2014. *Ecosickness in Contemporary U.S. Fiction: Environment and Affect*. New York: Columbia University Press.

Huntington, Samuel P. 1996. *The Clash of Civilizations and the Remaking of World Order*. New York: Simon and Schuster.

Iovino, Serenella, and Serpil Oppermann. 2014. "Introduction: Stories Come to Matter." In *Material Ecocriticism*, edited by Serenella Iovino and Serpil Oppermann, 1–17. Bloomington, IN: Indiana University Press.

Jacquet, Jennifer. 2015. *Is Shame Necessary? New Uses for an Old Tool*. New York: Pantheon.

Kamsler, Victoria. 2002. "The Body Toxic: An Environmental Memoir by Susanne Antonetta (Review)." *Ethics and the Environment* 7 (2): 194–6.

Keller, Evelyn Fox. 2000. *The Century of the Gene*. Cambridge, MA: Harvard University Press.

Klein, Naomi. 2007. *The Shock Doctrine: The Rise of Disaster Capitalism*. New York: Metropolitan Books.

Kolbert, Elizabeth. 2006. *Field Notes from a Catastrophe: Man, Nature, and Climate Change*. New York: Bloomsbury.

Latour, Bruno. 1993. *We Have Never Been Modern*. Translated by Catherine Porter. Cambridge, MA: Harvard University Press.

———. 2004. *Politics of Nature: How to Bring the Sciences into Democracy*. Translated by Catherine Porter. Cambridge, MA: Harvard University Press.

Lears, T.J. Jackson. 1981. *No Place of Grace: Antimodernism and the Transformation of American Culture (1880–1920)*. New York: Pantheon.

LeMenager, Stephanie. 2014. *Living Oil: Petroleum Culture in the American Century*. Oxford: Oxford University Press.

Marx, Leo. 1964. *The Machine in the Garden: Technology and the Pastoral Ideal in America*. Oxford: Oxford University Press.

Matthiessen, F.O. 1941. *American Renaissance: Art and Expression in the Age of Emerson and Whitman*. Oxford: Oxford University Press.

Merchant, Carolyn. 1980. *The Death of Nature: Women, Ecology, and the Scientific Revolution*. New York: HarperCollins.

Merleau-Ponty, Maurice. (1945) 1962. *Phenomenology of Perception*. New York: Routledge.

Moraga, Cherríe L. 1994. *Heroes and Saints*. In *Heroes and Saints and Other Plays*, 85–149. Albuquerque, NM: West End Press.

Morton, Timothy. 2007. *Ecology without Nature: Rethinking Environmental Aesthetics*. Cambridge, MA: Harvard University Press.

———. 2010. *The Ecological Thought*. Cambridge, MA: Harvard University Press.

Natural Resources Defense Council. n.d. "Environmental Justice." http://www.nrdc.org/ej/.

Nixon, Rob. 2005. "Environmentalism and Postcolonialism." In *Postcolonial Studies and Beyond*, edited by Ania Loomba, Suvir Kaul, Matti Bunzl, Antoinette Burton, and Jed Esty, 233–51. Durham, NC: Duke University Press.

———. 2011. *Slow Violence and the Environmentalism of the Poor*. Cambridge, MA: Harvard University Press.

Nguyen, Bich Minh. 2007. *Stealing Buddha's Dinner: A Memoir*. New York: Viking.

Ozeki, Ruth. 1998. *My Year of Meats*. New York: Penguin.

Phillips, Dana. 2003. *The Truth of Ecology: Nature, Culture, and Literature in America*. Oxford: Oxford University Press.

Phillips, Dana, and Heather Sullivan. 2012. "Material Ecocriticism: Dirt, Waste, Bodies, Food, and Other Matter." In *Material Ecocriticism*, edited by Heather Sullivan and Dana Phillips, Special Issue of *Interdisciplinary Studies in Literature and Environment* 19 (3): 445–7.

Pickering, Andrew. 1995. *The Mangle of Practice: Time, Agency, and Science*. Chicago: University of Chicago Press.

Rabinow, Paul. 1996. *Essays on the Anthropology of Reason*. Princeton, NJ: Princeton University Press.

Raley, Rita. 2009. *Tactical Media*. Minneapolis: University of Minnesota Press.

Rivera, Alex, dir. 2008. *Sleep Dealer*. Los Angeles: Maya Entertainment. DVD.

Rose, Nikolas. 2007. *The Politics of Life Itself: Biomedicine, Power, and Subjectivity in the Twenty-First Century*. Princeton, NJ: Princeton University Press.

Rowe, John Carlos, Greg Robinson, and Alfred Hornung. n.d. "Featured Articles: Three Articles on Transnationalism and American Studies." American Studies Association. http://www.theasa.net/project_eas_online/page/project_eas_online_eas_featured_article/.

Scranton, Roy. 2015. *Learning to Die in the Anthropocene: Reflections on the End of a Civilization*. San Francisco: City Lights.

Shewry, Teresa. 2015. *Hope at Sea: Possible Ecologies in Oceanic Literature*. Minneapolis: University of Minnesota Press.

State of New Jersey Department of Public Health, Environmental and Occupational Health Surveillance Program. 2001. "Evaluation of Childhood Cancer: 1996–2000." http://www.nj.gov/health/eohs/dovertwp.shtml.

Steinbeck, John. (1939) 1976. *The Grapes of Wrath*. Reprint, New York: Penguin.
———. (1951) 1995. *The Log from the Sea of Cortez*. Reprint, New York: Penguin.
Steinbeck, John, and Edward F. Ricketts. (1941) 2009. *Sea of Cortez: A Leisurely Journal of Travel and Research*. Reprint, New York: Penguin.
Sucato, Kristy. 2001. "What's Wrong in Toms River?" *New York Times*, December 16. http://www.nytimes.com/2001/12/16/nyregion/what-s-wrong-in-toms-river.html?pagewanted=all.
Sullivan, Robert. 1998. *The Meadowlands: Wilderness Adventures on the Edge of a City*. New York: Doubleday.
Szasz, Andrew. 2007. *Shopping Our Way to Safety: How We Changed from Protecting the Environment to Protecting Ourselves*. Minneapolis: University of Minnesota Press.
Sze, Julie. 2002. "From Environmental Justice Literature to the Literature of Environmental Justice." In *The Environmental Justice Reader: Politics, Poetics, and Pedagogy*, edited by Joni Adamson, Mei Mei Evans, and Rachel Stein, 163–80. Tucson: University of Arizona Press.
———. 2007. *Noxious New York: The Racial Politics of Urban Health and Environmental Justice*. Cambridge, MA: MIT Press.
Wald, Priscilla. 2012. "American Studies and the Politics of Life." *American Quarterly* 64 (2): 185–204.
Wilder, Laura Ingalls. (1932) 2004. *Little House in the Big Woods*. Reprint, New York: HarperCollins.
———. (1933) 2004. *Farmer Boy*. Reprint, New York: HarperCollins.
———. (1935) 2004. *Little House on the Prairie*. Reprint, New York: HarperCollins.
———. (1937) 2004. *On the Banks of Plum Creek*. Reprint, New York: HarperCollins.
———. (1939) 2004. *By the Shores of Silver Lake*. Reprint, New York: HarperCollins.
———. (1940) 2003. *The Long Winter*. Reprint, New York: HarperCollins.
———. (1941) 1971. *Little Town on the Prairie*. Reprint, New York: HarperCollins.
———. (1943) 1971. *These Happy Golden Years*. Reprint, New York: HarperCollins.
Williams, Raymond. 2005. "Ideas of Nature." In *Nature: Thinking the Natural*, edited by David Inglis, John Bone, and Rhoda Wilkie, 47–62. London: Routledge.
Yamashita, Karen Tei. 1997. *Tropic of Orange*. Minneapolis: Coffee House.
Ybarra, Priscilla Solis. 2009. "Borderlands as Bioregion: Jovita González, Gloria Anzaldúa, and the Twentieth-Century Ecological Revolution in the Rio Grande Valley." *Multi-Ethnic Literature of the US (MELUS)* 34 (2): 175–89.

2 Laboring bodies

> Is a tractor bad? Is the power that turns the long furrows wrong? If this tractor were ours, it would be good – not mine, but ours. We could love that tractor then as we have loved this land when it was ours. But this tractor does two things – it turns the land and turns us off the land. There is little difference between this tractor and a tank. The people were driven, intimidated, hurt by both. We must think about this.
>
> John Steinbeck, *The Grapes of Wrath*

An August 2007 *New York Times* article citing Arvin (in Kern County, California) as having "the nation's worst air" describes the city of 20,000 as the ultimate petri dish of smog and disease. Each year, Arvin had only seventy-three days of air quality rated acceptable by the Environmental Protection Agency, and residents claim that the air "smells toxic" (Associated Press 2007). Kern County sits in a basin and is encircled by mountains, trapping its own pollutants in the immediate area. Worse yet, as hazardous substances produced within its boundaries do not move (generated by diesel fumes, waste lagoons, hydraulic fracturing, feed lots, tractors, and other agricultural activities), Arvin also absorbs contaminants from Los Angeles, San Francisco, and Sacramento. John Steinbeck's *The Grapes of Wrath* ([1939] 1976) immortalized California's San Joaquin Valley, and the town of Weedpatch (or the Weedpatch Camp) featured prominently as a haven for migrant workers and community organizers. The *Sacramento Bee*'s Sam McManis (2013) points out that although the Arvin Federal Government Camp is the highlight of the Dust Bowl Festival, it remains an unincorporated town southeast of Bakersfield. The Dust Bowl Festival is an annual event funded by the Lamont Chamber of Commerce and dedicated to the unique culture of the migrant workers that were in the Arvin Camp and settled that region of California. Steinbeck's fictional Weedpatch Camp served as the epicenter of civil unrest and subversive action and is now ironically a hotbed of toxicity and respiratory ailments. Eerily, Steinbeck understood long ago the interconnectedness of one type of pollution and violation to another, identifying Weedpatch as something extraordinary. His writing foreshadows the remarkable intensity of combined human and environmental violations as they traverse both human-constructed and natural frontiers.

Steinbeck's Depression-era writing solidified his reputation as a social agitator and commentator on class disparity, but at the time that he wrote *The Grapes of Wrath* ([1939] 1976) he was already troubled by the domination of nature by humans. Steinbeck's writing on the dangers of industrialized agriculture and the hardships faced by farmers fleeing the Dust Bowl received a mixed reception. While he wrote about the labor movement and is more often connected to California's Central Valley and to its coastal enclaves, especially Monterey, the public is not as well informed of his intense friendship with marine biologist Edward F. Ricketts and how his influence moved Steinbeck to think of waterways in a new light. Steinbeck's concerns over corporate control of natural resources on land began to extend to the sea. In fact, through his interaction with and in the water off of Baja California, Steinbeck's own philosophical limitations are exposed and he begins to question firm definitions of the kind of matter that *matters*. Stephen C. Trombulak writes that Steinbeck's passion for marine biology and specimen collection was "ignited" by his friendship with Ricketts, and it came at a time when Steinbeck was "thoroughly disappointed, and somewhat worn down, by the critical attacks" (2012, 3) on *The Grapes of Wrath.*[1] *Sea of Cortez*, the collective and coauthored efforts of Steinbeck and Ricketts ([1941] 2009) is, as Trombulak states, part "natural history and travel narrative" (2012, 4) but it is also indicative of the kind of ethical quandaries Steinbeck faced when participating in the harpooning of manta rays and watching vessels even larger than the *Western Flyer* trawl the sea.

Steinbeck's environmental concerns gain urgency in the years between the publication of *The Grapes of Wrath* ([1939] 1976), the coauthored scientific travel narrative *Sea of Cortez: A Leisurely Journal of Travel and Research* ([1941] 2009), and later *The Log from the Sea of Cortez* ([1951] 1995). These three works, taken together, reveal Steinbeck's evolving environmental philosophy shifting toward a more careful consideration of humanity's impact on spaces of land and sea. Steve Mentz – who works in new maritime studies, or thalassology – proposes the term "blue humanities" to outline the study of oceans and seas "as organizing principles" (2009, 101). Historian Thomas Bender explains how the use of waterways in early "contact" or "discovery" or "invasion" of the Americas "redefined" space because "movement across oceans made possible entirely new global networks of trade and communication" (2006, 15–16). Bender's acknowledgment of the importance of liquid space is accompanied by the understanding that "beyond the ocean was an unknown, often terrifying space" or a "kind of anti-world" (2006, 16). Along with obsessive expansion and the race to find new territories and resources comes a natural fear of the unknown. Hence we see that the initial moments of "discovery" of the Americas by European settlers were haunted by a paranoid desire to control oceanic boundaries: both fluid lines mapped onto spaces of water and the line that separates the surface from the world below it. Although Steinbeck's sea writing demonstrates a certain complicity with human meddling in the environment, it also contains a critique of interference with nature. In fact, Steinbeck and Ricketts were looking to the water for connections with and answers about the land.

Steinbeck's depiction of California's landscape and the relationship of labor to land exposes the period from 1929 to 1939 as a disruptive force on the American psyche. During these ten years, natural disaster became synonymous with national financial ruin. The physical world was tied to fiscal shifts, and the impulse to conserve and preserve US landscapes was presented to Americans as an opportunity to contribute to US domestic and international financial prowess. In the paradigmatic work that secured his reputation as a leading environmental historian, Donald Worster ([1979] 2004) argues that not only are the Great Depression and the Dust Bowl intertwined phenomena, but 1930s New Deal policies proffered errant economic and irresponsible ecological policies that created the Dust Bowl: " . . . the same society produced them both, and for similar reasons. Both events revealed fundamental weaknesses in the traditional culture of America, the one in ecological terms, the other in economic" ([1979] 2004, 5). Worster rightly points out something that becomes crystal clear in Steinbeck's writing: in an increasingly capitalist and neoliberal framework, we more easily oscillate between language of the ecological, physical, and somatic to language of the financial and economic.

Steinbeck composed *The Grapes of Wrath* between June and October of 1938.[2] In this compressed and productive five-month period, he kept a journal of his challenges and triumphs – his fears, concerns, and hopes for the novel. Both his next book, *The Moon Is Down* ([1942] 1995), and *Working Days* (his personal journal) reveal how Steinbeck's unease about the proto-fascist anti-worker movements in Salinas, California, reinforced his support of Franklin Delano Roosevelt (FDR); his wife, Eleanor Roosevelt; and the later war effort. However, *Sea of Cortez* presents not only escapist fantasies of reckless exploration but also a meditation on deeper questions about imminent war and violence. Steinbeck employs the border regions of seascapes both as a canvas onto which he can project his creativity and as a metaphorical checkpoint at which he has to consider the dangers of anthropogenic impacts on marine ecosystems. Steinbeck grows uncomfortable with human intervention, i.e., industrial capitalism, in nature and even, I argue below, with New Deal policies of preservation and social justice.

The sanctity of marine ecosystems was not Steinbeck's foremost concern, but it played a major part in shaping his personal views and in his professional development. Steinbeck began attending Stanford University in 1919, but he came and went for six years, taking odd jobs in between stints at college and sporadically studying literature and journalism. In 1923 he completed a summer course on field zoology at the Hopkins Marine Station in Pacific Grove, California. His own discovery of Monterey Bay as a nonhuman and delicate habitat had a great impact on him. His writing in *Sea of Cortez* has a different and less subtle tone than the writing of Rachel Carson in her seminal book *The Sea Around Us* (1951). One reviewer, M.R. Levitas, took particular note of the authors' different approaches and dismissed *The Log from the Sea of Cortez* as "unworthy of its predecessors" (1952, 374). Levitas noted that although

Steinbeck's book was intended "for both average readers and marine biologists, it is hard to say which the current *Log* will appeal to less" (1952, 374). *Sea of Cortez* was composed ten years before *The Sea Around Us* and was indeed less about respecting marine habitats and more about the experience of maritime exploration. But as this chapter demonstrates, Steinbeck and Ricketts recorded their findings, collected specimens, and pondered the meaning of biological life on earth; the result was the 1941 coauthored travelogue, *Sea of Cortez*. It explores early ideas of sustainability at sea, environmental health, and the interconnectedness of the human body and other bodies.

Overproduction on the Great Plains and the accompanying ecological costs could not have been far from Steinbeck's thoughts as he set out to sea in 1940 on the *Western Flyer*. His focus had to shift from land to sea and to the liminal space between them. Although class-based strife is not the focus of *Sea of Cortez*, in it, as in much of Steinbeck's other work, he gestures toward the cause of capitalist-driven progress that crescendos into ecological violence. It is precisely the transition from civic-minded New Deal liberalism to injurious capitalism that Steinbeck queries through the most complex passages in *Sea of Cortez* (hereafter *SC*). The sea is a place for problematizing oversimplified and politicized rhetoric regarding the production of land for agribusiness and the relationship between the materiality of the human body to other bodies, both biological and abiological.

My book at large investigates how twentieth-century material narratives of bodies and stories about places that should be heralded as signs of progress actually work to undermine such sites of capitalist and corporate advancement. More than using nature as a metaphor for the human condition in modernity, the stories of human interaction with the environment (and their mutual influence) link the manner in which we view the environment to the ways we understand American identities. Greg Garrard argues that US ecocritical writing "about the countryside emphasizes a working rather than an aesthetic relationship with the land," whereas British romanticists had a more removed and "sublime" understanding of the outdoors (2004, 54). Indeed, in this book laboring bodies act as a wedge that opens exploratory avenues to closely consider US notions of nature and environmentalism. Yet workers' rights are not a teleological end point for the texts at hand; instead, they are one manner of accessing an evolving understanding of materiality.

Musings on land

Steinbeck's *The Grapes of Wrath* (hereafter *GW*) depicts the plight of the Joad family as its members join thousands of other Dust Bowl farmers migrating west in search of opportunity. From the book's beginning, the detailed descriptions of the earth and its parched state reveal the author's interest in land defined by state lines. As the novel continues, however, Steinbeck questions the wisdom of the division of land across state and even national lines and its subsequent overproduction by the agricultural industry. In the book's first paragraph, the narrator describes an Oklahoma landscape, which is portrayed ominously, as if it is poised to decide the fate of the Joads:

> To the red country and part of the gray country of Oklahoma, the last rains came gently, and they did not cut the scarred earth. The plows crossed and recrossed the rivulet marks. The last rains lifted the corn quickly and scattered weed colonies and grass along the sides of the roads so that the gray country and the dark red country began to disappear under a green cover. . . . The surface of the earth crusted, a thin hard crust, and as the sky became pale, so the earth became pale, pink in the red country and white in the gray country. (*GW*, 3)

Clouds of dust cover the landscape, and the desperate exodus of the Joad family begins. Following the Great Depression, thousands of displaced farmworkers traveled west, and this led to tensions between native Californians and Anglo American workers looking for economic opportunity.

Steinbeck's writing on the laboring classes is considered a classic work of literature about the labor movement, but it is less often considered in terms of its deep ecological implications. In Steinbeck's (1936) series *The Harvest Gypsies*,[3] he addresses tensions between migrant and native California workers and he enumerates the many accusations leveled against the former. Steinbeck notes that the migrants are thought of as filthy vessels of disease and debauchery: "the migrants are hated for the following reasons, that they are ignorant and dirty people, that they are carriers of disease, that they increase the necessity for police and the tax bill for schooling in a community, and that if they are allowed to organize they can, simply by refusing to work, wipe out a season's crop" ([1938], 1996). The last scene in *The Grapes of Wrath* ends in the ambivalent description of Rose of Sharon smiling as she breast-feeds a starving man. She treats him like a baby, cradling his head to her breast and stroking his hair: "She looked up and across the barn, and her lips came together and smiled mysteriously" (*GW*, 581). The mysterious smile has been read in a myriad of ways, but Steinbeck's choice to keep Rose of Sharon's last act ambiguous could be seen as an extension of his own ambivalence about the future of the US agricultural industry and US liberal ideologies more generally.

The deep anxiety in this Depression-era work reveals that the failings of the American dream are not just those related to the economic collapse of the Great Depression. While Steinbeck's novel has been called an activist novel in the vein of other great naturalist and realist works of the time, he is also beckoning readers to reconsider their spiritual relationship to the almighty dollar and to the earth. *The Grapes of Wrath* begins with Tom Joad's return to Oklahoma after serving a four-year prison sentence for manslaughter. While heading home to the family farm he meets Jim Casy, a preacher who left narrow constraints of preaching because he considered all aspects of life and the world to be holy. Casy continues to believe in the Holy Spirit, but above all else he believes in loving all humans. Finding his farm abandoned, he is told by a neighbor that the farmers have been displaced by tractors, or what is commonly referred to as being "tractored out" (*GW*, 12) and here we see the first hint of the struggle between man and machine. The tractors repeatedly represent the bank, while the bank itself represents a larger struggle between the proletariats and the system.

Steinbeck's interest in the California landscape became a point of contention among researchers: some of them interpret it as an extension of a colonial drive to dominate the land, while others see it as a harbinger of his later ecocritical writing. California's mythos as a land of opportunity and agricultural fecundity is a double-edged sword. It is expected to provide equally and endlessly as a kind of utopia, especially when juxtaposed with the Oklahoma landscape at that time. Such a depiction lends itself to the kind of ferocity with which developers approach natural resources and the labor forces used to extract them. Literary scholar Morris Dickstein argues that Steinbeck's early work had "little connection to social protest" because what drove Steinbeck was "his feeling for the land" and a sense of adventure (2004, 113–14). Certainly, the connection the characters exhibit with the land is one of spiritual communion, as in the case of Casy. His spiritual awakening and alternative belief system involves turning his back on organized religion and cultivating a holistic attitude toward the earth. For him, this connection translates into activism and finally self-sacrifice. In a pivotal scene, Casy is beaten and killed by the Tulare police, who mistake him for the leader of the workers' strike. Called a "red son-of-a-bitch" by the officers, he is killed by a white pick handle that is smashed into his head with a "dull crunch of bone" (*GW*, 495). He is portrayed as a communist agitator for talking "so much," and the contrasting colors of red and white – our final image of him – echo the accusations that social justice activists are communists (*GW*, 494). Casy's belief in equality leads to his lethal beating and leaves a strong impression on Tom Joad. California, the land of opportunity and natural bounty, becomes a landscape of privatized wealth and public violence.

The troubling dissonance between a naturally peaceful nature and its unnatural and violent cultivation is reinforced by Steinbeck's treatment of scientific advancements in agriculture. In his chapter on spring, Steinbeck pens one of the most poignant and beautiful passages about the fertile valleys in California while also presenting dark undertones of harmful technological interference. The narrator begins by meditating on the grapevines: "The spring is beautiful in California. Valleys in which the fruit blossoms are fragrant pink and white waters in a shallow sea. Then the first tendrils of the grapes, swelling from the old gnarled vines, cascade down to cover trunks" (*GW*, 445). The narrator progresses from a description of the bountiful land to "the men of chemistry" who help protect crops against diseases and pests, for "behind the fruitfulness are men of understanding with knowledge and skill . . . endlessly developing the techniques for greater crops. . . . These are great men" (445–46). Yet these great men who "drive the earth to produce" are applying mixtures of chemicals to it, so that if the men were to try to make wine from the rotten grapes, the smell from the fermenting process would be "not the rich odor of wine, but the smell of decay and chemicals" (447). The chapter ends with a famous quote, referring to the starving workers and economic depression together, warning that the system must change or there will be an uprising: "In the souls of the people the grapes of wrath are filling and growing heavy, growing heavy for the vintage" (449).

Steinbeck presciently investigates the relationship of technology and the development of nature for profit. Capitalistic interests in industrial agriculture are symbolized by the machines and "the bank," which is a "monster" (*GW*, 43). The monstrosity of greed and unbridled exploitation of the land is summarized by the tenants or squatters on the land who are being forced out by the plows. The plows "go through the dooryard," and the bank is "the monster" that "isn't like a man" (*GW*, 43). In fact, the bank becomes a part of the mythology of westward expansion, equivalent to "Indians" and "snakes": "The tenants cried, Grampa killed Indians, Pa killed snakes for the land. Maybe we can kill banks – they're worse than Indians and snakes" (*GW*, 43). The tenants acknowledge a generational colonialism tied to ideas of Manifest Destiny and the tilling of "virgin" lands. In their rhetoric of fighting back they deploy colonial symbolism. The racial overtones of their version of how the Midwest was settled is made more interesting not by the parallel drawn between Native Americans and snakes (a common trope) but by the accusation leveled against the bank: that it is a far worse enemy than past "impediments" to US expansion. The bank is synecdochically used to refer to a particularly American brand of capitalism, one that touts progress but that diminishes the quality of life, one that depends on a palimpsest of oppression and that readily exploits humans and nature. The tractor and the bank are contrasted with the pristine beauty of a California spring, pitting technology against nature.

Oceanic expeditions

Government legislation under New Deal policies was part of an effort to assert control over nature and prevent future natural disasters. Steinbeck writes that humans are "related inextricably to all reality" and that all things are "bound together by the elastic string of time" (*SC*, 217). Nascent ideas of a holistic and communal responsibility are prevalent in Steinbeck and Ricketts's *Sea of Cortez*. They used waterways as an imaginative frontier through which to process ideas of conservation and cultivation. Public intellectuals like Steinbeck were discovering and growing uncomfortable with the New Deal neoliberalism they had once embraced and were attempting to recalibrate their principles. Steinbeck and Ricketts's *Sea of Cortez* articulates a sharp critique of the forced separation between humanistic and scientific study, and between readers' approaches to fiction and nonfiction:

> The design of a book is the pattern of a reality controlled and shaped by the mind of the writer. This is completely understood about poetry

> or fiction, but it is too seldom realized about books of fact. And yet the impulse which drives a man to poetry will send another man into the tide pools and force him to try to report what he finds there. Why is an expedition to Tibet undertaken, or a sea bottom dredged? Why do men, sitting at the microscope, examine the calcareous plates of a sea-cucumber, and, finding a new arrangement and number, feel an exaltation and give the new species a name, and write about it possessively?
>
> Steinbeck and Ricketts ([1941] 2009)

In this quote from the introduction to *Sea of Cortez* Steinbeck and Ricketts indicate the fault lines we draw between reality and imagination and criticize the human impulse to record and thereby make real. The human "impulse" is to imagine that by putting something into writing it becomes real and quantifiable. Steinbeck extends this point in a passage on counting the spines of the Mexican sierra fish. He writes that there is one truth – or untruth – in laboratories and a different "relational reality" (*SC*, 2) when you directly encounter the fish. In the laboratory, "you have recorded a reality which cannot be assailed" while it also holds "many lies" (2–3). Yet out of these two experiences together, he suggests, there might "emerge a picture more complete and even more accurate than either alone could produce" because the "facts" need a "story" and the "story" is shaped by "facts" (4). Steinbeck compares expeditions to Tibet to those to the bottom of the sea, yet these are two dramatically different occurrences for anthropocentric humans. Encountering "alien" ecosystems at the sea bottom is an unwieldy experience that proves confusing for both Steinbeck and Ricketts. Steinbeck inadvertently reveals the bifurcated approach that he and Ricketts take to the conquest of peaks versus those of watery valleys: seeing Tibet is an expedition unto itself, but exploring the sea includes its dredging and the extraction of its bounty.

The year 1940 was a memorable one for Steinbeck. It was the year that he and Ricketts set out on a six-week expedition to the Gulf of California. Steinbeck's marriage to Carol Henning was ending, but his friendship with Ricketts was deepening, as was his fascination with both animate and inanimate marine life (Astro 1973, 19). Supported by a crew of four, Steinbeck and Ricketts sailed the sea and wrote *Sea of Cortez*. The book is an unabridged version of the later and more popular *The Log from the Sea of Cortez* ([1951] 1995). It is widely believed that the attack on Pearl Harbor just two days after *Sea of Cortez*'s publication (on December 5, 1941) virtually guaranteed its obscurity.

Wartime and periods of national crisis, even those that are caused by reckless consumption, are not times to reflect on a nation's use – especially its overuse – of its natural resources. Words that might have been heard as a prophetic warning fell on the deaf and busy ears of US citizens dealing with the crisis of war. But ten years later the truncated version of the text, crediting Steinbeck alone as the author, proved to be a commercial success. Both works contain the same 270-page narrative section. The main differences between them are that the 1951 version includes Steinbeck's preface about Ricketts, who had died; the removal of Ricketts's name as an author; and, most notably, the elimination of Ricketts's catalogue of species. The catalogue consists of 327 pages of directions on how to prepare specimens, images of specimen slides, a list of references, and an annotated catalogue of more than five hundred invertebrate species.

The omission of the most scientific sections of the original work indicates that the commercially minded editors at Viking Press were interested in stories about the sea, not data from it – or that they at least believed the public would like Steinbeck as a rakish explorer but not as a scientist. The genre of *Sea of Cortez* is confusing: the work is part biological field notes, part travel narrative, part marine species catalogue, and part philosophical treatise. Indeed, the narrative voice of *Sea of Cortez* at times suggests the imperialistic wanderings of a rogue and his pals, exploring the sea and its bounty in troubling ways. The sometimes Darwinian, sometimes masculinist discourse eclipses the more complicated and schismatic passages that I unpack in this chapter. Such an unpacking requires a recognition that the overall tone of *Sea of Cortez* (and especially *The Log from the Sea of Cortez*) is what Mary Louise Pratt might deem imperial discourse cloaked as natural history (2007, chapter 3). Although a segment of critics would consider *Sea of Cortez* just one such imperial escapade as natural history, Steinbeck and Ricketts's moments of trepidation complicate the reductiveness of a Conrad-esque gloss.

Steinbeck's chatter in the narrative log drowns out the voice of science in Ricketts's catalogue. Yet archival research demonstrates that Steinbeck took a number of ideas and passages verbatim from Ricketts's journals although he is listed as the sole author of *The Log from the Sea of Cortez*. Richard Astro convincingly argues this point in his biography of Steinbeck and cites a joint memorandum to Viking Press's editorial board signed by Steinbeck and Ricketts that acknowledges the full extent of the two men's collaboration and coauthorship: "in several cases parts of the original field notes were incorporated into the final narrative, and in one case a large section was lifted verbatim from other unpublished work" (quoted in Astro 1973, 13). Both the original version and the preface to the second version suggest a lack of difference between science and fiction. In fact, both versions intimate that science might be telling more stories about other forms of life than Steinbeck, the ultimate storyteller.

The arc of this particular story, from the failure of *Sea of Cortez* to the success of *The Log from the Sea of Cortez*, is particularly significant to the state of the humanities today. Ecocritics are committed to drawing attention to the tethered nature of the sciences and the humanities (although they are often seen as firmly divided) and to increasing the conversations between the disciplines and outside the walls of institutions of higher education. The publication history of *Sea of Cortez* and *The Log from the Sea of Cortez* and the stark difference in their popularity further supports the idea that there is fertile ground for collaboration between disciplines and offers opportunities for us to rethink our approach. In the end it is the "narrative" section of an earlier publication that brings attention to its scientific counterpart while simultaneously eliminating the name of that material's author (Ricketts). Furthermore, as Astro (1973) and

Susan Shillinglaw (1997) have pointed out, Steinbeck borrowed liberally and verbatim from Ricketts's journal, so the narrative portion is scientific in origin. In an era when the humanities are being asked to quantify their work and justify their value, how do these two facets of the same voyage shed light on the value of narrativizing experiences between the human and nonhuman for a wider audience?[4] Viking's choice to focus on the narrative in *The Log from the Sea of Cortez* and the book's resulting commercial success reveal a human need to search for meaning in the imaginary, exotic, and liminal space between the shore and sea. That same need to externalize and exoticize life at sea is at the core of Steinbeck's struggle when he witnesses overt violence and the disruption of marine life.

Steinbeck and Ricketts's *Sea of Cortez* anticipates later work in the fields of human ecology and environmental studies long before those disciplines and terms existed. *Sea of Cortez* differs from Steinbeck's other works that focus on the culture of coastal California. Unlike *Cannery Row* ([1945] 1992), for example, *Sea of Cortez* grapples with the littoral zones between sea and land. It, also, to a lesser but important degree, extends its reach into the deep sea. Scientist Wesley Tiffney Jr. explains that at the time of their collaboration "neither Ricketts nor Steinbeck would [have] recognize[d] the terms 'environment,' 'environmentalist,' or 'environmental scientist' as they are used today" (1997, 3). The writing is doubly fascinating because it outlines the contradictory relationship humans have to their surroundings and to their bodies.

Steinbeck's relationship to nature, even in *Sea of Cortez*, reveals a fascination with alien life forms. While some might argue that it is precisely the otherworldliness of these creatures that leads to a feeling that humans are entitled to colonize oceanic spaces while harvesting their resources, his feelings of entitlement and awe are intertwined and separating them is nearly impossible. Historian John Gillis contends that works like Daniel Defoe's *Robinson Crusoe* ([1719] 2001), Herman Melville's *Moby-Dick* ([1851] 1967), and Carson's *The Sea Around Us* (1951) as well as Steinbeck's collaboration with Ricketts indicate "humankind's mental and imaginative turn to the sea" (2013). Gillis argues that our main challenge is a global uncertainty about how to coexist with the inhabitants of the sea and how to live in a sustainable and peaceful way. Certainly if we are considering a US-based, Westernized view of oceanography, the works listed above show the evolution of thinking about the fusion of humanistic and scientific study.

To romanticize and even exoticize the past is a compelling yet flawed endeavor. Imagining that our ancestors cohabitated with inferior life in bodies of water ignores differences in scale and complications of modernity. Carson's treatise on the importance of the ocean, *The Sea Around Us* (1951), was published in the same year as Steinbeck's more successful narrative of his voyage to Baja California. During the time of Carson's writing, new ideals of conservationism developed and shifted into something closer to our modern-day notions of environmentalism. FDR's galvanization of conservationism as tied to US federal politics came on the heels of what was dubbed the "New

Conservation" movement. The uneven distribution of wealth was to be combated by an evening up of the cultivation of resources, and the agricultural industry was at the epicenter of the government's calculations. The compelling idea that land-based conservation policies would achieve national economic equilibrium caught on.

The amazement of Steinbeck, Ricketts, and their crew at their encounters with marine life in the waters off Baja California can be read as both productive and destructive: "We at least have kept our vulgar sense of wonder. We are no better than the animals; in fact in a lot of ways we aren't as good. And so we'll let the book fall as it may" (*SC*, 69). While the ocean is a space where the imagination has traveled unbounded, humans are now recognizing that the space is bounded and finite, and wholly at the mercy of human recklessness. Systemic violations of human rights and the environment lend meaning to the eerie descriptions of the barren land in *The Grapes of Wrath* and the bountiful but misunderstood sea of *Sea of Cortez*.[5] Steinbeck's determination to demonstrate that it was corporate-driven agricultural mismanagement – not a freak natural drought – that created the Dust Bowl exhibits his understanding that there is no real line between natural and unnatural disasters.

The Dirty Thirties and neoliberalism

I begin with John Steinbeck's writing, so emblematic of the Great Depression, because it marks the beginning of a new era of government interest in the preservation, development, and mining of nature. As political and economic historian Jason Scott Smith points out, the flow of federal money during the New Deal era was in large part directed toward the "public good": "On average, between 1933 and 1939 over two-thirds of federal emergency expenditures went toward funding public works programs" (2009, 1). The Great Depression, New Deal liberalism, and the public works legislation and policies that followed 1929 significantly altered the American state. Renewed interest in nation building after the Great Depression led to a wider chasm between man and nature. Nature became a powerful resource that could be developed through agriculture and hydroelectric power, and a space to which Americans could flock and marvel at the great outdoors.

The 1937 recession was a turning point when many of the original new ideas of liberal thought were absorbed into an amalgamation of New Deal policies. Historian Alan Brinkley suggests that the current understanding of liberal ideologies stems from post-New Deal disenchantment and war: "This new liberalism focused less on the broad needs of the nation and the modern economy than on increasing the rights and freedoms of individuals and social groups. . . . It has also attempted to expand the notion of personal liberty and individual freedom for everyone" (1995, 10). Brinkley highlights the manner in which the sense of personal freedom, so foundational to the formation of the United States, gradually became privileged over the collective good that many of the New Deal policies sought to promote. Yet, as Smith points out, recent studies suggest that the infrastructure developed through public works projects solidified "gendered and racial boundaries," thus laying the foundation for the modern American welfare state (2009, 15). Voters against New Deal policies were deemed conservative, whereas those in favor were known as liberals – but the meanings of these designations have changed dramatically in the last seventy to eighty years. New Deal liberalism might make the modern liberal cringe, with its emphasis on the private rights of citizens.

FDR remarked in a 1931 speech (made when he was governor of New York State, before his election as president) that one of the country's biggest problems was the lack of balance between "urban and rural" living (1938a, 487), and his suggested solution was a state-driven "intensive development of the good land" (1938a, 489). Thus began the shift toward federal conservation efforts and resource management in the name of the public good. The US landscape was seen as a source of endless development, where even acts of conservation became part of a larger national agenda to develop the identity of US citizens as progressive, advanced, and separate from people of other nations – especially through their relationship to the natural world. FDR's administration effectively sutured the notion of national success to a robust agricultural industry. The1920s farm crash was cited as an example of the type of catastrophe the United States would face if the federal government did not intervene. Historian Sarah Phillips points to FDR's agenda to "raise rural living standards directly" (2007, 63). The equitable distribution of profit would come from the development of rural areas and the redistribution of wealth garnered by harnessing and harvesting natural resources. FDR's policies hinged on the promise that the industrialization and demarcation of the rural landscape would directly benefit the urban one.

The context of the 1930s is key to understanding the sociopolitical backdrop that preceded Steinbeck's maritime writing. In his elegiac Dust Bowl fiction, Steinbeck yearns for a simpler time in US farming; he expresses great anxiety about scientific practices and the inevitable risks that come with progress. Public uproar over the Great Depression – and the mining of natural and fiscal disaster – became a platform for state-driven funneling of private capital toward the public good. Steinbeck attempts to record the ephemeral memories of widespread poverty and suffering. His message is that the mistakes of the past – that is the man-made disaster of the Dust Bowl and the economic collapse – should not be repeated. Alan Brinkley points to the complexities of the transmutations of liberal ideologies in Steinbeck's time (during and after FDR's presidency). Brinkley argues that New Deal "liberalism" was transformed into "a potent justification for a rapidly expanding capitalist world" (1995, 9). Ironically, what started as a movement against the disenfranchisement of the masses became a justification for neoliberalism's machinations.

Steinbeck's name conjures up images of barren landscapes and abandoned farms, as well as the iconic and ironic beauty of California's agriculture and its fertile San Joaquin Valley. It is nearly impossible to read Steinbeck and ignore his interest in the environment and how technological advances in agriculture affected American workers during and after the Great Depression. *The Grapes of Wrath* can be read as a sociological treatise, protest fiction, an American classic, and a masterpiece of modernism. Rarely, however, is Steinbeck recognized for his interest not only in the land but also the sea. While his Dust Bowl fiction defines him, his marginal musings on waterways offer some of the most cutting-edge thinking on socially constructed divides between human and nonhuman matter and the equally deep class lines between rich and poor, "native" and "migrant." The Dirty Thirties were brought on by human meddling as much as by nonhuman phenomena.

Animals as more than interludes

The images of parched prairies, swirling dust, and destitute humans and animals were foremost in Steinbeck's thoughts as he set out to sea. Steinbeck is admired for being well ahead of his time in terms of his break from traditional notions of environmentalism as the preservation of cultivated land and *Sea of Cortez* demonstrates his growing understanding and unease that his adventures at sea interfered with marine habitats. Even in his writings predating *Sea of Cortez* one can see Steinbeck is searching for ways to make the connections between animals and humans deeper than one simply being a reflection of the other. Steinbeck's use of animals and his animation of matter (dirt and dust) point to an earlier attempt to think through the artificial divides between nonhuman and human, thing and being.

The challenges of making palpable mankind's dirt – that is, the offshoot of soil erosion and overproduction in the Midwest – may be what drives Steinbeck to construct his biological interludes, or the in-between chapters in *The Grapes of Wrath* that focus on animal life. In a 1934 letter to his friend George Albee, Steinbeck responds to Albee's inquiry as to what he "wants." Citing his self-proclaimed lack of ambition, Steinbeck calls himself a "stupid, slothful animal" and an "organism" without designs for the future: "In fact as an organism I am so simple. . . . I don't want to possess anything, nor to be anything. I have no ambition" (Steinbeck, *A Life in Letters*, [1975] 1989, 92–93). Steinbeck's description of himself as an organism is an interesting choice of words. He reveals his understanding of biological matter as dominating life and with that understanding comes a sense of the need to strive for the communal good – even if the motivation he ascribes to himself is "no ambition." While Frederick Hoffman acknowledges Steinbeck's "curiosity" about the biological world, he dismisses it as a "self-indulgent" way to advance plots and offer shallow animal-man parallels: "Though Steinbeck has the curiosity of his scientists, he has neither the need nor the desire for their disciplines. The curiosity is thus essentially self-indulgent" (1951, 149). Together, *Sea of Cortez* and *The Log from the Sea of Cortez* serve as a lens through which such critiques can be studied and challenged: Steinbeck's treatment of the biological seems less "self-indulgent" and in fact less anthropocentric than one might expect. Josephine Levy challenges Hoffman's assessment of Steinbeck as anthropocentric but she does not overturn or question the issue of speciesism. Levy writes that Steinbeck's novels build a world in which humans are "inseparable from biological realities and relationships with nonhuman animals" (1994, 66). But Steinbeck's renderings of human life in relation to animal life indicate an interest in trans-species relations and a curiosity about different ways of relating to the earth, here literally meant as topsoil. Just as Steinbeck works to reveal the connection between production and consumption, he also implies a connection between humans and their surroundings. Hoffman's dismissive attitude of Steinbeck as an armchair biologist pervades much of the criticism surrounding his work. If Steinbeck's writing is imbued with animal imagery as a metaphor for the basic drives of mankind, that imagery is also an indication of his view that the nonhuman world is sacred.

Steinbeck's writing is full of animal imagery and symbolism, and he has been accused of both sentimentality and a dependence on animalism – the use of animals to symbolize the basic drives of humans. While these drives are often the negative parts of human nature and lead to violence and isolation from the community, they are also an indication of his fascination with the biological world and its relation to humankind. Levy explains how Steinbeck's use of animal imagery goes beyond literary interests in animalism, but I see his interchapters as some of the most persuasive passages, demonstrating a fusion between humans and animals and human and nonhuman matter.

Steinbeck's interchapters – the short vignettes and interludes that interrupt the Joads' narrative – frequently center on the biological world in a time of abandonment and catastrophe. They demonstrate the magnitude and reach of the issues that face the Joad family. By continually pulling the reader out of the micro narrative of the Joad family and into the macro world of larger economic and environmental issues, Steinbeck subtly invites readers to consider the deeper implications of minutiae, and how small decisions can have a cumulative effect of long-term harm. In effect, Steinbeck is pointing to the web of life that connects living and nonliving beings and how minutiae create our environment in ways we cannot begin to imagine. Especially poignant are the passages on the land turtle traversing the land. Starting in chapter 3, the narrator gives great attention to the "old" turtle's "yellow toe nails" and "humorous eyes," as well as the way in which the human world invades the animal kingdom (*GW*, 21). While trying to cross the highway, the turtle meets two vehicles. The driver of the first is a "forty-year-old woman" who turns her car to avoid hitting the turtle, but the second vehicle is a "light truck" whose "driver saw the turtle and swerved to hit it" (*GW*, 21). The turtle spins and finds itself again by the side of the road, where it recovers and – nonplussed – continues on its journey.

The interchapters also allow Steinbeck to emphasize humans' connection to the land and the generational occupation of land as an important aspect of American identity. Ursula Heise argues that a positive sense of "local autonomy" and "self-sufficiency" can "only be achieved through prolonged residence in one place" (2008, 30–1). This view seems to drive Steinbeck's schematization of man's relationship to land – and "man" here is the Anglo-Saxon American settler turned migrant, who built a connection to land in the Midwest and now seeks that same connection in the West. Such a connection is accrued through colonial domination and imperialist agendas of westward expansion. The conquest of land becomes the cultivation of it, then the settling of it, and finally the ownership and privatization of it. In *The Grapes of Wrath* the reader is presented with conflicting ideas of what constitutes a moral relationship to the land. Steinbeck's biological interludes do more than offer a parallel to human existence; they also query the morality of humanity and the political, economic, and personal decisions being made. They effectively require that we think about the sanctity of life in a manner that privileges the abiological over the biological, and the animal over the human.

In his articulate analysis of Depression-era texts, James Miller posits that, together with other 1930s ethnographic texts, *The Grapes of Wrath* captured an American vanishing past that ironically served to justify capitalism's future. Miller writes that "the Joads are more than mere victims; they stand as objectified embodiments of a 'living history,' the fragmentary, human records of a larger, 'ruined' heritage that, while decimated, stubbornly refuse to disappear" (2004, 381). Miller contends that the push to represent the present as a "vernacular past" was not an effort to represent the outskirts of society and its hardships; rather, these works are meant to "imbue capitalism's rationalized and articulated operations with a tangible sense of historicity, a palpable and authenticating texture of 'pastness'" (2004, 373).

Employing John Brinckerhoff Jackson's theory of the "necessity for ruins" in modern American times – that is, the influence of the "junk" of a past era on contemporary life (1980, 90) – Miller extends Jackson's theory and applies it to the work of Steinbeck and his contemporaries. Miller argues that the push to represent the present this way was meant to legitimize the corporate capitalist transition in the United States by offering depth and historicity to something that was for all intents and purposes depthless. Thus, according to Miller, the story of the Great Depression and environmental disaster becomes a justification for New Deal liberalism driven by the machinery of capitalism. The Oakies, then, represent a past on which the United States will build its future. But this logic is troubling from an ecological perspective because the technological and environmental future that Steinbeck describes is harrowing. Steinbeck is pushing against the tide of capitalist-driven profit by shaping large systems of consumption and production into intimate articulations of biological, laboring bodies.

The conflict between Steinbeck's notions of nationalism and anthropocentricism comes to a head as he is forced to consider the cost of collecting samples from the sea and how a wider audience will receive this when he translates his experiences to the page. Clifford Gladstein and Mimi Gladstein present multiple instances of the *Western Flyer*'s crew's environmentally irresponsible practices, including Steinbeck's blasé attitude toward destroying segments of the El Pulmo coral reef and the senseless harpooning of manta rays and a tortoise-shell turtle by a crew member named Tiny (1997, 170–1). Although Gladstein and Gladstein include a note underlining the differences over time in what are considered to be acceptable practices of marine biology, it is likely that some of Steinbeck's contemporaries would have been disturbed by the extermination of marine life: "Steinbeck and Ricketts were following correct procedures for good marine biological collecting of the 1930s. They lacked the . . . equipment for a more judicious collection behavior" (1997, 175). Yet Steinbeck, at least, appears reluctant to wholly blame such instances on a lack of equipment. While he argues that on their own animals register as relevant, as a whole animals are only "commas in a sentence," but then contradicts himself when pointing out that "man is related to the whole thing" (*SC*, 216–17). Steinbeck's troubled relationship to animals is twofold. – He is torn between treating them as individuals versus treating them as an entire species, and he is also troubled by the differing perspectives on sea creatures versus land creatures. All of this contributes to a waning sense of ethics in his journal entries.

In *Sea of Cortez* the moments of trepidation over how marine life should be treated stem from Steinbeck and Ricketts's dim understanding that they are participating in the destruction of sea and animal life while trying to document and preserve it. The lack of commentary on issues like the harpooning of manta rays for sport or the removal and destruction of coral reefs indicate Steinbeck's growing awareness of the tension between scientific study and the conquest of oceanic spaces. This silence disrupts a US nationalistic attitude that cultivation is progress and that human colonization of nonhuman spaces that clutters the Anthropocene in the mid-twentieth century is further proof of US prowess.

The interconnectedness of things does not escape the crew of the *Western Flyer*, but the philosophy of holism has its shortfalls, as Steinbeck notes: "The rare animal may be of individual interest, but he is unlikely to be of much consequence in any ecological picture . . . the extinction of one of the rare animals, so avidly sought and caught and named, would probably go unnoticed in the cellular world" (*SC*, 216). The killing of the individual animal is justified as not ultimately counting as violence because the animal is one of many, and because humans do not recognize the effects of the eradication of species in the "cellular world," an oceanic world in which an animal is so tiny and so foreign to human eyes that it does not register as an animal. Steinbeck's word choices are particularly interesting when we consider *Sea of Cortez* from a materialist perspective. His recognition that the "cellular world" is dramatically different from the human world in scale while nonetheless being governed by the same principles of life and death reads like a forced reconciliation of his impulse to explore with his desire to preserve.

The Grapes of Wrath and *Sea of Cortez* indicate a change in Steinbeck's view of the government's investment in both the exploitation and the preservation of nature. As I wrote about earlier, FDR led the wave of conservation and management efforts as part of federal agenda to shape the identity of US citizens. Steinbeck and Ricketts note the gap between the government's wishes for a robust economy and its wishes for an equally healthy environment and wonder how that gap will be closed. Steinbeck's turn from the novelistic (*The Grapes of Wrath*) to the scientific travelogue (*Sea of Cortez*) exposes his contradictory sentiments. In *The Grapes of Wrath*, nature takes on anthropomorphic qualities, and the dust in particular becomes a sinister force that literally and figuratively commingles with humans. The dust is an inescapable part of the domestic space in the tightly sealed homes that it invades: "Now the dust was evenly mixed with the air, an emulsion of dust and air. Houses were shut tight, and cloth wedged around doors and windows, but the dust came in so thinly that it could not be seen in the air, and it settled like pollen on the chairs and tables, on the dishes" (*GW*, 5). Steinbeck maps the invisible dirt, a result of man's greed and mismanagement of nature, directly into the visible space of the home and anticipates later movements that challenge dichotomies between human flesh and its surroundings. Biological and abiological matter seem to merge in the domestic space when the untamable parts of nature fuse with human bodies. The bodily contours of the human are revealed to be permeable, a revelation that indicates Steinbeck's understanding that it is more than just US financial health that is affected by changes in nature.

Steinbeck's detailed descriptions of the ravaged earth betray his concerns about how natural resources are managed and abused by state and federal governments at the expense of the people. Importantly, scientific advancements and human tampering with nature trigger and create ecological imbalance. The mixed reception of his 1962 Nobel Prize in literature indicates the way that Steinbeck balanced the roles of social agitator and formidable modernist. Critics note that part of Steinbeck's drive to show human suffering was motivated by the documentary photography of FDR's New Deal Farm Security Administration in 1937 (the agency was renamed after its creation as the Resettlement Administration in 1935).[6] Steinbeck seemed to be highlighting the connections between scientific and agricultural progress. His anxieties about these connections are expressed in a muted and perhaps convoluted fashion, first in *Sea of Cortez* and later in *The Log from the Sea of Cortez*. If the ecological implications of Steinbeck's Dust Bowl fiction have been lost over time, then certainly the equally important contributions of his expedition with Ricketts have been all but forgotten and they must be recovered: drawing attention to *Sea of Cortez* and the preface and changes to *The Log from the Sea of Cortez* from new angles are a step toward that recovery.

"Manself" and organisms

> The last clear definite function of man – muscles aching to work, minds aching to create beyond the single need – this is man. To build a wall, to build a house, a dam, and in the wall and house and dam to put something of Manself, and to Manself take back something of the wall, the house, the dam; to take hard muscles from the lifting, to take clear lines and form from conceiving. For man, unlike any other thing organic or inorganic in the universe, grows beyond his work, walks up the stairs of his concepts, emerges ahead of his accomplishments.
>
> John Steinbeck, *The Grapes of Wrath*

In Steinbeck's *The Grapes of Wrath* it seems that "Manself" is meant to triumph in challenging times by the sweat of his brow and the work of his laboring muscles.

The divide between Manself (between the individual and the world) is built on man's ability not only to be industrious but also to build and create things with his hands. According to the masculinist logic of the passage above, man first builds things "beyond the single need" and puts something of himself – "Manself" – in those things. This anthropocentric faith in humans' ability to cultivate a maturity or wisdom "beyond" their work exhibits the dualistic thinking that the narrator of *The Grapes of Wrath* alternately praises and disdains, albeit unwittingly. Furthermore, it creates an ironic relationship between Manself and the world, or between the individual and the world. Manself brings something back from this experience in his very body, and in so doing "emerges ahead of his accomplishments." Descriptions like these stand in stark contrast to those of the tractors. Steinbeck's attention to animals and their relationship to the earth serve as further evidence that he was intensely interested in the mixing of biological and abiological matter.

While Steinbeck may have written *The Grapes of Wrath* in a nostalgic mood, the manner of work and human connection to abiological matter presented in the book are paramount in the balance between nature and humans. Jonathan Ebel argues that Steinbeck's championing of Manself represents "expressions of faith in Manself over and against recognizable bureaucracies" and that while the tide of modernization and "progress" in the United States meant that "power" sits in "the bureau" for Steinbeck, "authority rests in the calloused hands of hard-working, desperately poor people" (2012, 528). Ebel senses a deep irony in Steinbeck's portrayal of man in relation to bureaucracy, but there is more to the passage quoted above than a push against the bureaucratic. Certainly the narrator is proposing a type of hierarchical progress based on man's ability to reason, and this is how he will emerge "ahead" of his past successes. But a key component of this description is that it betrays the divide the narrator constructs between organic human (biological) matter and inorganic nonhuman (abiological) matter.

Steinbeck's chapters on the government-sponsored and migrant-run Weedpatch Camp give the reader a momentary reprieve from the series of calamities facing the Joads and demonstrate Steinbeck's antibureaucratic views. Ma Joad is impressed by the sanitary conditions and running water in the camp, while Tom is relieved to find out that the police there are elected by the people. In fact, the people running the camp are "jus' fellas" like the Joads (*GW*, 369). Tom meets Timothy and Wilkie Wallace in the camp, and they take him to their boss, Mr. Thomas, in the hope that he can also give work to Tom. Mr. Thomas is upset to have to give them a five-cent pay cut but explains that as a member of the Farmers' Association, he has no choice. The paradisal experience of a community-run camp where people work to help each other and food is abundant is disrupted by these invasions from the outside world. Mr. Thomas claims that if he pays the men more it will cause unrest, and the Farmers' Association is planning to send agitators into the camp to start a riot to get the police to evict the migrants.

The Farmers' Association considers the camp to be a zone of "red agitators" (*GW*, 379) with communist sympathies. But life in the camp is not as uniform as it first appears. When members of the Ladies' Committee come to visit the Joads, an especially "religious" woman, Mrs. Sandry, tells Rose of Sharon that there are "scandalous things" happening in the camp and that she needs to be careful and "better watch out for that there baby" by keeping herself and her belly out of sin (*GW*, 398). Mrs. Sandry is most worked up about the dances and the "stage play" the camp people put on: "They ain't but a few deep down Jesus-lovers lef'. Every' Sat'dy night when that there strang ban' starts up an' should be a-playin' hymnody, they're a-reelin' – yes, sir, a-reelin'. They's clutch-an'-hug, I tell ya" (396–97). She complains of debauchery and concludes that "the devil was jus' a-struttin' through this here camp" (397). She warns that there are few "lamb-blood folks" – followers of Jesus – left in the camp and that God is punishing sinners: "He's awready smoked two of 'em out" (*GW*, 398). The punishment for one young pregnant mother was a bloody miscarriage and banishment from the camp. Mrs. Sandry later suffers a "visit" from "the sperit" and collapses while behaving like an animal: "Her eyes rolled up, her shoulders and arms flopped loosely at her side, and a string of thick ropy saliva ran from the corner of her mouth. She howled again and again, long deep animal howls" (412). While the reader is sure to dislike her because of her threats toward Rose of Sharon, Mrs. Sandry's collapse nonetheless seems extreme and disturbing in its animalism. But above all else her disruption of the Joads' reprieve from violence is alarming because it comes from within the camp.

Mrs. Sandry's character is doubly disturbing because she tries to unravel the unity in the camp by invoking Jesus as her ally. Her pernicious rhetoric preys on young people like Rose of Sharon, a young pregnant woman representing the next generation. As Jonathan Ebel comments, "Sandry and her transgressive Protestantism threaten multiple New Deal ideals from within" (2012, 533). Her attack from within is not only the ultimate betrayal, but Steinbeck's construction of her as degenerating into a howling, animalistic state depicts her style of spirituality – in which she tries to move people toward religion by shaming them – as being on par with insanity. Although the novel's portrayal of animals is largely positive, with Steinbeck allying the laboring bodies of his workers with those of animals, here the image of a howling human is meant to be read negatively, as pure craziness.

Unrest outside the camp increases, and the migrants begin to trade important information in the form of stories, folk music, and reports. A migrant described simply as "the tubby man" tells of a worker being thrown into jail for daring to question the integrity of a system in which farmers and workers are being exploited while big business thrives. When Timothy Wallace asks how a working man was incarcerated for vagrancy, the "tubby man" explains that nobody who questions authority has rights: "You know a vagrant is anybody a cop don't like. An' that's why they hate this here camp. No cops can get in. This here's United States, not California" (*GW*, 430). The self-governed camp is configured as a geopolitically independent oasis free of unjust governance. J.T. Jackson Lears (1981) writes that the restructuring of the US economy from agriculture to agribusiness concurrently restructured spaces of industrial production into spaces of entertainment and leisure. The natural landscape on which sites of production sat were meant to be returned to a more natural state via human help; modern technology and aesthetics would make pastures more pastoral and natural. It would seem that Steinbeck is disagreeing with the very New Deal policies he was known to support – policies that were instituted with the same goals in mind of helping displaced and destitute workers. The most urgent challenge FDR faced in his first term as president was to address the economic depression. And part of the New Deal's legacy was a number of agencies that were formed to enact deep social and economic change.[7]

The camp is a space where the telling of subversive stories is important. Near the end of their time at the camp, Tom hears the story of Akron rubber workers who took up arms in a thinly veiled act of protest. The "mountain" people who made up the majority of the workforce joined the workers' union and the "storekeepers and legioners an' people like that . . . get . . . yellin', 'Red!' An' they're gonna run the union right outa Akron. Preachers git a-preachin' about it, an' papers a-yowlin'" (*GW*, 443). In response, the mountain men "marched through town" with their rifles, claiming they were going to a turkey shoot on the other side of town, and then marched back peacefully (*GW*, 444). This story is significant because it shows a different type of protest: one that used the threat of numbers, a visible demonstration of the power of Manself. Human bodies form a collective that mimics the power structure against which they are fighting – that is, an authoritarian government. While the mountain men are armed, they do not seem to have the intention to use their weapons. Rather, their form of protest is an exhibition of mass and masculinity, with people descending from the mountains to enact a kind of renegade justice.

In 1937 Chester Davis, codirector of the Agricultural Adjustment Bureau, wrote to his colleagues that there was little hope of an economic recovery in the United States: "There is little reason to expect a 'natural' upturn in the near future. The recession could be severe and prolonged if government does not intervene" (quoted in Brinkley 1995, 30). Government intervention is proposed as a remedy for the unruly American socioeconomic landscape. Environmental disasters in the United States seemed to come hand in hand with economic ones, and the New Deal's policies were meant both to address such disasters and to generate jobs while protecting and restoring valuable resources. While many scholars have understood New Deal reforms as having wide-ranging impacts, Jason Scott Smith proposes that there was a "public works revolution" that solidified the powerful role of government agency in the new American state: "This revolution helped justify the role of the state in American life. . . . New Dealers remade the built environment that managed the movement of people, goods, electricity, water, and waste" (2009, 3). As Smith convincingly retraces the shifts in the economic and political landscape from 1933 to 1956, he argues that the New Deal set a precedent for federal authorities to shape the nation's future and its policies on the ground of providing future economic security. Sweeping reforms were not only meant to save the country from staggering unemployment; they were also used to mask the political motivations behind government-sponsored economic reforms. The infrastructure put in place by the New Deal created a blueprint for the postwar economic growth of the military-industrial complex and the continued relationship between the welfare state and New Deal American liberalism.

Dust Bowl environmentalism

In 1932, the year that FDR accepted the Democratic Party's presidential nomination, memories of World War I were fresh in the United States; the country was reeling from the 1929 stock market crash, which spurred the Great Depression; and ecological disasters loomed large. In a 1932 speech, after becoming president, FDR spoke the words that would define government policy and shape a collective national consciousness. He promised government intervention to help mitigate the effects of the Depression, marketing his solution as "a new deal for the American people" that involved the calculated cultivation and preservation of the country's natural resources (1938b, 659). This spirit of hope and community was what seemed to fuel Steinbeck's earlier support of politics. Steinbeck's sense of allegiance later morphed into disappointment and his attempts to illustrate the realities of migrant life was met with resistance and distrust.

Literary critic Arthur Mizener calls Steinbeck's talent into question, accusing him of harping on the past and of attracting public support for little more than sociological observations. Mizener states that to reread Steinbeck's writing in the 1960s is to be reminded that "our feelings are no longer under the special influences that affected them strongly in the thirties" (1962). While recently released documents from the Nobel Prize's selection committee reveal internal strife and frustration with the list of names of possible prize winners (Flood 2013; Itzkoff 2013), Steinbeck nonetheless won, and his writings continued to garner praise over time. Mizener's article implies that in 1962 the United States had moved beyond sentimentally when considering civil injustice and government accountability, yet the civil rights movement reached its crescendo a few years later – proving that in fact US citizens were far from done considering the plight of everyman. Steinbeck's contemporaries referred to him as a "New Deal Democrat," and the epithet became a part of his private and public persona. His championing of workers' rights led some people to consider him an anti-American agitator with little artistic talent.

Steinbeck's and Ricketts's anxieties about the abuse of land due to industrialization crystallize in chapter 27 of *Sea of Cortez*. Interestingly, the reckless overfishing of shrimp by Japanese dredge boats catalyzes their discomfort, whereas their own interactions with individual animals (like a porpoise and manta rays) do not affect them the same way. After setting sail with a shrimp-boat owner, Captain Corona, the *Western Flyer* dropped anchor in a cove near Pajaro Island. Not far from the cove the crew came upon the Japanese shrimp fishers that the local fishermen had identified as engaging in irresponsible behavior. The "Japanese fishing fleet" consisted of six ships along with a "large mother ship of at least

10,000 tons . . . farther offshore" (*SC*, 247). There were twelve boats in the fleet, and they were doing a "systematic job" of "scraping the bottom clean," resulting in "not only taking every shrimp from the bottom, but every other living thing as well" (*SC*, 247). The fleet "cruised slowly along in echelon with overlapping dredges," and "not even the sharks got away" (*SC*, 247). Such descriptions ascribe a sinister and alien-like quality to the Japanese and reinforce Steinbeck's sense that these were "good men, but they were caught in a large destructive machine, good men doing a bad thing" (249). The sheer mass and variety of fish is both awe-inspiring and horrifying, as one imagines the heart of the ocean emptying as the dredge boats are "scraping the bottom clean" to get the "many tons of animals" (247) that Steinbeck witnesses spilling onto the deck.

The top-down benefits of environmental degradation (in which the concentration of resources at the top is achieved by depleting those at the bottom) manifests itself in the sea, yet resource depletion does not fully develop in Steinbeck's writing as being directly related to either his own expedition or to the greedy machinations that led to soil erosion in the Midwest. But Steinbeck is unapologetic about the same mentality to collect and "rush" in an "indiscriminate" manner because it resulted in the "discovery" of new species: "once on board the boat again we could re-collect, going over the pieces of coral and rubble carefully and very often finding animals we had not known were there" (*SC*, 78). Diving "again and again for perfect knobs of coral" (*SC*, 79) is on a different scale than the sweeping fishing practices of larger vessels, but it is in effect a similar act of destroying nonhuman life for human gain, something that Ricketts and Steinbeck viewed as immoral.

The crew of the *Western Flyer* believes that the delicate ecological balance being disrupted together with the "intense energy" of the Japanese will exterminate the shrimp of the region: "The disturbed balance often gives a new species ascendancy and destroys forever the old relationship" (*SC*, 249). Continuing to meditate on disturbances to the ecosystem, Steinbeck writes: "We in the United States have done so much to destroy our own resources. . . . With our own resources we have been prodigal, and our country will not soon lose the scars of our grasping stupidity. But here, with the shrimp industry, we see a conflict of nations, of ideologies, and of organisms" (250). He sees the interconnectedness of such acts as affecting the "welfare of the whole human species" (250), but on the very next page begins the disturbing section where Tex and Tiny harpoon manta ray after manta ray, getting excited when they killed "one of the largest rays" that "came to the bitt and struck with a kind of groaning cry, quivered, and went limp" (252). The crew pulls the harpoon up but finds "only a chunk of flesh," and Tiny is "heart-broken" not because he feels sadness for the acts of senseless violence or the "groaning cry" of the ray (252), but because he wanted to take pictures to prove to their friends in Monterey that he had speared one (252–53). How Steinbeck did not see this as another instance of "good men doing a bad thing" is puzzling in light of his tender portrayal of animals elsewhere in his writing. While the difference in scale is one reason for the oversight, it is not reason enough. These moments of aphasia in the face of complex ethical matters reveal an underlying struggle: how do you decentralize the human in an anthropocentric world? Once you do so, the damaging implications of this sea adventure become glaringly obvious.

As a US-based narrative that articulates connections between the inner body and the outer world, *Sea of Cortez* directly questions the definitions of citizenship and political ecology. By disrupting traditional knowledge systems, both *Sea of Cortez* and *The Log from the Sea of Cortez* delineate the porous and uncontainable nature of the environment and lend agency to both the human and nonhuman; significantly, their abiding legacy is to imaginatively represent "immaterial" matter as material on the page. The lively discourse in the environmental humanities evermore centers on how to raise awareness about the monetization of ecosystems for capitalistic endeavors. The legitimization of abiological and nonhuman matter, or what we more often see referred to as more-than-human matter, creates possibilities for ecocriticism as more than narrative and anthropomorphizing mechanism.

Bringing order to the sea

Steinbeck's tilling of the soil, so to speak, as he wonders about the wisdom of US progress in terms of industrialized agriculture takes center stage in *Sea of Cortez*. Lears argues that a push against the modern defines the twentieth century: "The antimodern impulse stemmed from revulsion against . . . the systematic organization of economic life for maximum productivity . . . the drive for efficient control of nature under the banner of improving human welfare" (1981, 7). It was this "maximum productivity," undergirded by scientific research, that troubled Steinbeck as he set off to sea.

Between the twenty-nine sections of the narrative portion of *Sea of Cortez* and the photographs is a five-page section titled "A Note on Preparing Specimens" (*SC*, 272–77). The mix of clinical and sentimental prose throughout the narrative stops here, where the advice includes directions on how specimens are "best killed" and anesthetized (273). Constantly remarking on the delicacy of marine life, the instructions regarding flatworms warn that they "are hard to collect, hard to handle, and hard to preserve," and the reader will have great difficulty with "pelagic invertebrates" because of their "extreme softness" (274). The thin borders between marine life as sport and as sustenance (not to mention as scientific specimens) are made clear in statements like this one regarding the Mexican sierra fish: "Simply fried in big hunks, it is the most delicious fish of all" (155). Marine life is a source of food, adventure, and scientific discovery. However, it is also a source of discord and tension as the crew of the *Western Flyer* questions the varying fishing practices they observe and environmental ethics in that realm become increasingly murky.

The blurred line between knowledge and domination of nature is highlighted: the scientific act of acquiring knowledge also entails the destruction of biological life and great risk that marine habitats will be mislabeled and misunderstood. The five-page section on preparing specimens concludes with a point that "cannot be over-emphasized," advice to label specimens immediately after their collection: "Each label should include the date, the exact place, the depth, and a number added which will agree with the number in the collecting notes. . . . The label should be placed *inside* the jar with the animal" (*SC*, 276–7; emphasis in the original). Steinbeck and Ricketts warn that the mislabeling of specimens has caused "ridiculous situations" and multiple "errors" (*SC*, 276–7). This sliver of insight into the tension between science and ecology and between practice and theory appears between the narrative and photographic sections.

One cannot help but connect Steinbeck's representations of microcosms like those in *Sea of Cortez* to an effort to eradicate the hierarchy of the abiological over the biological, which he saw as interrelated with the hierarchy of the wealthy over the poor, and the powerful few over the disempowered masses. Commenting on the boundaries of human understanding of the tides of nature and extinction, violence, and war, Steinbeck and Ricketts write that "the limitation of the seeing point in time, as well as in space, is a warping lens" (*SC*, 264). Ironically, it is the attempt to gain the perspective of time and space through the collection of specimens that is most destructive to the marine habitats that Steinbeck and his crew encounter.

The desire to archive and preserve leads to the "ridiculous situations " (*SC*, 276) and multiple sites of trauma in *Sea of Cortez*. The killing and cataloguing of marine life in the name of scientific progress eerily echoes the uncanny presence of the tractors in *The Grapes of Wrath*. The books were published only two years apart, yet Steinbeck's blind spots in his travel narrative indicate that the shift from fiction to nonfiction entailed a lack of self-awareness. Following the photographic reproduction of specimens in *Sea of Cortez* is the introduction to the "Annotated Phylectic Catalogue," in which Ricketts and Steinbeck express their attempt to organize the chaos of nature: "This is an attempt to bring order to a subject previously unordered, and to shed light onto a field that has been dark" (*SC*, 285). Order will be brought through the taxonomy of specimens, the use of Latin, and the presence of a bibliography and a glossary. The "light" shed into the darkness of the sea comes at the cost of the destruction of nonhuman lives, and this is the disturbance in Steinbeck's field of vision, the tractor writ large on the body of the sea.

While not without their complications as ecocritical texts, *Sea of Cortez* and *The Log from the Sea of Cortez* express Steinbeck's opposition to the endless mining of nature. When national borders are transposed onto bodies of water or schools of fish, the untenable manner in which countries mine natural and human resources is made clear. At sea, Steinbeck more plainly sees the bleeding of one type of border into another and it galvanizes him to think about American policies. What previously seemed like individual and geographically isolated choices now clearly have collective repercussions on a global scale. The value of stories might seem unquantifiable, but in the arc of the commercial success of *The Log from the Sea of Cortez* one understands that narrative matters immeasurably.

The *New York Times* article on the pollution and despair in Arvin, California, was written seventy-five years after Steinbeck's fictional Weedpatch Camp drew attention to the region's uniqueness. Arvin was once the seat of civil disobedience; later it became the epicenter of disease and toxicity. On land, Steinbeck recognized that it was "good men" doing a "bad thing" that led to human suffering and ecological ruin. At sea, however, metrics and ethics become opaque. It is at sea that one can clearly identify an early version of environmentalism that pushes Steinbeck and Ricketts to reconsider firm divisions between land and sea, and between the ethical and unethical.

Although Steinbeck's Dust Bowl fiction lacks a certain rebellious tone because it is set within US borders, his sea-based writing directly questions the ethics of environmental depletion and the cataclysmic implications of harvesting marine life. As I previously noted, M.R. Levitas, Steinbeck's unimpressed contemporary, judged *The Log from The Sea of Cortez* as "unworthy of its predecessors" and unappealing to general and specialized audiences alike (1952, 374). In the same article, Levitas wrote that although *The Log from the Sea of Cortez* would be a disappointment, "the ocean has always provoked the imagination of sailors, poets, scientists, and seaside lovers on a moonlit night. Placid and turbulent, its whisperings have lisped the enticements of mystery" (1952, 374). He cites "two brilliant and successful attempts at providing the layman with some answers to the riddle of the sea – Thor Heyerdahl's *Kon-Tiki* and Rachel Carson's *The Sea Around Us*" (1952, 374). Levitas contrasts these two works to Steinbeck's *Sea of Cortez*, which – like them – "attempts to" make "the sea more meaningful." Most relevant to this chapter is the way that Steinbeck is rendered irrelevant because he cannot offer "meaningful" answers to the "riddle of the sea," whereas the other two authors apparently can. Yet Steinbeck views the sea less as a riddle to be solved, and more of a reflection of the machinations of agribusiness. Oceanic space is a place to ponder the human body as materiality and its relationship to other material and immaterial bodies, and the limitations of humans at sea. For this reason, *The Log from the Sea of Cortez*, with its self-critical comments about the absurdity of an "attempt to 'clean up' biology" (*LSC*, 58) with phyletic catalogues, does make the sea more meaningful. The bodily contours of the human are porous in *Sea of Cortez* and provide, I contend, a vision of "natural disasters" not simply as environmental catastrophes but as events that yoke financial, social, and ecological phenomena.

Notes

1 Steinbeck was known as a protest writer and thus was frequently criticized for sacrificing artistry to serve sociological and moral ends; his Dust Bowl fiction depicts the hardships of many families as they migrate west in search of opportunity and an escape from starvation. Marilyn Wyman identifies Steinbeck's crucial role in translating to the wider public the sense of disorientation of the white laboring class and the anxieties this migration produced as it "threatened the very stability of the American political discourse" (2005, 37).

2 For insights into Steinbeck's reasoning and innermost thoughts, his personal journal, *Working Days* (1989), is a critical source of information in addition to his major works.
3 *The Harvest Gypsies* was originally published in seven parts in the *San Francisco News* on October 5–12, 1936. Two years later the Simon J. Lubin Society published *The Harvest Gypsies*, with a new eighth chapter, as *Their Blood Is Strong* (1938).
4 Commenting on the collaborative investigations of ecology, literary critic Neil Browne considers *Sea of Cortez* as a "precursor" to current ecocritical materialist investigations into "how science and literature can inform each other" (2007, 59).
5 Stacy Alaimo writes that the exoticization of seascapes is a double-edged sword with both costs and benefits for environmental activists: "The pervasive trope of the oceans as alien may alienate humans from the seas, but it may also suggest that sea life hovers at the very limits of what terrestrial humans can comprehend" (2012, 477).
6 Morris Dickstein groups Steinbeck as somebody who did the same type of ethnographic, documentary work as the Farm Security Administration's photographers: "Steinbeck became one of the key witnesses to those years of social trauma and suffering" (2004, 112). Peter Valenti adds that the interchapters of *The Grapes of Wrath* employed visual rhetoric with a sense of urgency reminiscent of the aims of the Farm Security Administration's documentary photographers, most notably Dorothea Lange (1997, 98–103).
7 These agencies were often known by their acronyms: the Works Progress Administration (WPA), the Civilian Conservation Corps (CCC), the Public Works Administration (PWA), the Farm Security Administration (FSA), the National Recovery Administration (NRA), and the Agricultural Adjustment Agency (AAA).

References

Alaimo, Stacy. 2012. "State of Suspension: Trans-Corporeality at Sea." *ISLE* 19 (3): 476–93.

Associated Press. 2007. "Seeking Relief Where the Air Is Deemed the Dirtiest." *New York Times*, August 12. http://www.nytimes.com/2007/08/12/us/12smog.html?_r=0.

Astro, Richard. 1973. *John Steinbeck and Edward F. Ricketts: The Shaping of a Novelist*. Minneapolis: University of Minnesota Press.

Bender, Thomas. 2006. *A Nation Among Nations: America's Place in World History*. New York: Hill and Wang.

Brinkley, Alan. 1995. *New Deal Liberalism in Recession and War: The End of Reform*. New York: Vintage.

Browne, Neil F. 2007. *The World in Which We Occur: John Dewey, Pragmatist Ecology, and American Ecological Writing in the Twentieth Century*. Tuscaloosa: University of Alabama Press.

Carson, Rachel. 1951. *The Sea Around Us*. Oxford: Oxford University Press.

Defoe, Daniel. (1719) 2001. *Robinson Crusoe*. Reprint, New York: Simon and Schuster.

Dickstein, Morris. 2004. "Steinbeck and the Great Depression." *South Atlantic Quarterly* 103 (1): 111–31.

Ebel, Jonathan H. 2012. "Re-Forming Faith: John Steinbeck, the New Deal, and the Religion of the Wandering Oklahoman Author(s)." *Journal of Religion* 92 (4): 527–35.

Flood, Allison. 2013. "Swedish Academy Reopens Controversy Surrounding Steinbeck's Nobel Prize." *The Guardian*, January 3. http://www.theguardian.com/books/2013/jan/03/swedish-academy-controversy-steinbeck-nobel.

Garrard, Greg. 2004. *Ecocriticism*. New York: Routledge.

Gillis, John R. 2013. "The Blue Humanities: In Studying the Sea, We Are Returning to Our Beginnings." *Humanities: The Magazine of the National Endowment for the Humanities* 34 (3). http://www.neh.gov/humanities/2013/mayjune/feature/the-blue-humanities.

Gladstein, Clifford Eric, and Mimi Reisel Gladstein. 1997. "Revisiting the Sea of Cortez with a 'Green' Perspective." In *Steinbeck and the Environment: Interdisciplinary Approaches*, edited by Susan F. Beegel, Susan Shillinglaw, and Wesley N. Tiffney Jr., 162–75. Tuscaloosa: University of Alabama Press.

Heise, Ursula K. 2008. *Sense of Place and Sense of Planet: The Environmental Imagination of the Global*. Oxford: Oxford University Press.

Hoffman, Frederick J. 1951. *The Modern Novel in America 1900–1950*. Chicago: Henry Regnery.

Itzkoff, Dave. 2013. "No Wrath but Some Discontent When Nobel Prize Was Awarded to Steinbeck." *New York Times*, January 4. http://artsbeat.blogs.nytimes.com/2013/01/04/no-wrath-but-some-discontent-when-nobel-prize-was-awarded-to-steinbeck/?_r=0.

Jackson, John Brinckerhoff. 1980. *The Necessity for Ruins and Other Topics*. Amherst: University of Massachusetts Press.

Lears, J.T. Jackson. 1981. *No Place of Grace: Antimodernism and the Transformation of American Culture (1880–1920)*. New York: Pantheon.

Levitas, M.R. 1952. "Steinbeck All at Sea." In *John Steinbeck: the Contemporary Reviews* (American Critical Archives), edited by Joseph R. McElrath Jr., Jesse S. Crisler, and Susan Shillinglaw, 374–5. New York: Cambridge University Press.

Levy, Josephine. 1994. "Biological and Animal Imagery in John Steinbeck's Migrant Agricultural Novels: A Re-Evaluation." *Between the Species* 10 (1): 66–70. http://digitalcommons.calpoly.edu/bts/vol10/iss1/15/.

McManis, Sam. 2013. "Discoveries: Weedpatch Camp." *Sacramento Bee*, October 13. http://www.sacbee.com/entertainment/living/travel/article2579379.html.

Melville, Herman. (1851) 1967. *Moby-Dick*. Reprint, New York: Bantam Dell.

Mentz, Steve. 2009. *At the Bottom of Shakespeare's Ocean*. New York: Continuum.

Miller, James. 2004. "Inventing the 'Found' Object: Artifactuality, Folk History, and the Rise of Capitalist Ethnography in 1930s America." *Journal of American Folklore* 117 (466): 373–93.

Mizener, Arthur. 1962. "Does a Moral Vision of the Thirties Deserve a Nobel Prize?" *New York Times Book Review*, December 9, 43–5.

Phillips, Sarah T. 2007. *This Land, This Nation: Conservation, Rural America, and the New Deal*. New York: Cambridge University Press.

Pratt, Mary Louise. 2007. *Imperial Eyes: Travel Writing and Transculturation*. New York: Routledge.

Roosevelt, Franklin D. 1938a. "Address before the Conference of Governors on Land Utilization and State Planning. French Lick, Ind." June 2, 1931. In *The Public Papers and Addresses of Franklin D. Roosevelt. Vol. One: The Genesis of the New Deal: 1928–1932*, 485–95. New York: Random House.

———. 1938b. "'I Pledge You – I Pledge Myself to a New Deal for the American People.' Address Accepting the Presidential Nomination at the Democratic National Convention in Chicago." July 2, 1932. In *The Public Papers and Addresses of Franklin D. Roosevelt. Vol. One: The Genesis of the New Deal: 1928–1932*, 647–59. New York: Random House.

Shillinglaw, Susan. 1997. "Introduction: A Steinbeck Scholar's Perspective." In *John Steinbeck and the Environment: Interdisciplinary Approaches*, edited by Susan F. Beegel, Susan Shillinglaw, and Wesley N. Tiffney Jr., 8–13. Tuscaloosa: University of Alabama Press.

Smith, Jason Scott. 2009. *Building New Deal Liberalism: The Political Economy of Public Works, 1933–1956*. New York: Cambridge University Press.

Steinbeck, John. (1937) 1993. *Of Mice and Men*. Reprint, New York: Penguin.

———. (1938) 1996. *The Harvest Gypsies [Their Blood Is Strong]*. San Francisco: Simon J. Lubin Society. In *John Steinbeck: The Grapes of Wrath and Other Writings 1936–1941*, edited by Robert DeMott and Elaine Steinbeck, 990–1027. New York: Library of America.
———. (1939) 1976. *The Grapes of Wrath*. Reprint, New York: Penguin.
———. (1942) 1995. *The Moon Is Down*. Reprint, New York: Penguin.
———. (1945) 1992. *Cannery Row*. Reprint, New York: Penguin.
———. (1951) 1995. *The Log from the Sea of Cortez*. Reprint, New York: Penguin.
———. (1975) 1989. *Steinbeck: A Life in Letters*. Edited by Elaine Steinbeck and Robert Wallsten. Reprint, New York: Penguin.
———. 1989. *Working Days: The Journals of the Grapes of Wrath 1938–1941*. Edited by Robert DeMott. New York: Viking Penguin.
Steinbeck, John, and Edward F. Ricketts. (1941) 2009. *Sea of Cortez: A Leisurely Journal of Travel and Research*. Reprint, New York: Penguin.
Tiffney Jr. Wesley N., Susan Shillinglaw, and Susan F. Beegel. 1997. "Introduction: A Scientist's Perspective." In *Steinbeck and the Environment: Interdisciplinary Approaches*, edited by Susan F. Beegel, Susan Shillinglaw, and Wesley N. Tiffney Jr., 1–7. Tuscaloosa: University of Alabama Press.
Trombulak, Stephen C. 2012. "One Hundred and One Natural History Books that You Should Read Before You Die: John Steinbeck's *The Log from the Sea of Cortez*." *The Journal of Natural History Education and Experience* 6: 1–3. http://naturalhistorynetwork.org/journal/articles/7-john-steinbecks-the-log-from-the-sea-of-cortez/.
Valenti, Peter. 1997. "Steinbeck's Ecological Polemic: Human Sympathy and Visual Documentary in the Intercalary Chapters of *The Grapes of Wrath*." In *Steinbeck and the Environment: Interdisciplinary Approaches*, edited by Susan F. Beegel, Susan Shillinglaw, and Wesley N. Tiffney Jr., 92–112. Tuscaloosa: University of Alabama Press.
Worster, Donald. (1979) 2004. *Dust Bowl: The Southern Plains in the 1930s*. Oxford: Oxford University Press.
Wyman, Marilyn. 2005. "Affirming Whiteness: Visualizing California Agriculture." *Steinbeck Studies* 16 (1–2): 32–55.

3 Embodied consumption

> The Ingallses were the epitome of American. They memorized the Declaration of Independence, knew an inexhaustible number of hymns and American folk songs, and took pride in being "free and independent." They had big, "Westward Ho!" ideas about migration, property, and ownership. They built homes everywhere they landed, frying up salt pork in their iron skillet in hand-built hearths across the plains. They had such confidence in the building, such righteous belief in the idea of home, in the right to land, in the life of farming.
>
> Bich Minh Nguyen, *Stealing Buddha's Dinner*

> The real wealth of our country, its productive capacity, its great manufacturing plants, its far-reaching railroad system, its mighty commerce, and its agriculture did not come into being all at once, but is the result of a vast multitude of small increments brought about by long, slow, and laborious soil. Whatever a few individuals may do, the Nation as a whole and its great subdivisions of industry, transportation, commerce, and agriculture can increase by no other method. The percentage of yearly returns upon all the property of this country is low, but in the aggregate it is a stupendous sum. Unless all past experience is to be disregarded, notwithstanding its present embarrassments, agriculture as a whole should lead industry in future prosperity.
>
> Calvin Coolidge, "Address before the Annual Convention of the American Farm Bureau Federation, Chicago, Ill., December 7, 1925"

Bich Minh Nguyen writes that for the iconic Ingalls family, who appear in Laura Ingalls Wilder's *Little House on the Prairie* ([1935] 2004) and many sequels, going west and "conquering" the land is a national duty. The backbone of American identity is thus demonstrated by self-sufficiency, productivity, and by following the spirit of Manifest Destiny. The mythology of the United States continues to include the ideas of defiant individualism, a strong work ethic, and the tilling of soil that led to America's national and global prosperity. The archetype of the covered wagon and a pioneer family endures, as do those of the cowboy and the gold prospector. These powerful symbols are the scaffolding on which high-school curricula are built, on which presidential addresses rely, and on which much of the world bases its definition of Americans.

President Calvin Coolidge's 1925 speech to the Farm Bureau Federation reveals the fabric of the story of US expansion. While stereotypical images of America continue to include scenes of prairies and individual families braving the elements, Coolidge's speech indicates a sharp deviation from that past: now is the time for the "vast multitude of small increments" (that is, small farms) to drive other industries and become the source of rapid economic growth and expansion. There is actually little room for the Ingalls family and their commitment to self-sufficiency and small-scale production. In fact, one major reason why Nguyen's memoir is packed with leitmotifs from America's earliest days as a nation is because of the palpable sense of adventure and hardship that she culls from books about US colonial times. The Ingallses needed to produce enough food to feed themselves and keep their land. On its face, farming seemed to be a step toward both individual success and national pride. This perspective is radically different from Coolidge's speech, which calls for farmers to value industry over individualism.[1]

In 1925 Coolidge anticipates a major shift in the United States: that farming become a global business and catapult the country to prosperity such as it had never seen before. As Allison Carruth notes, "the speech captures a new dimension of the American national imaginary . . . according to which food and agriculture propel, rather than offer a retreat, from modernity" (2013, 1). Coolidge makes a calculated departure from the ideas of his predecessors. He dismisses the ideal of the yeoman farmer, the agrarian mythos of a single-family farm, and the notion that such farms are the backbone of US prosperity. And as Carruth persuasively argues, this moment is the beginning of a postindustrial and technocratic "*food system*" (2013, 1–2; emphasis in the original) that confronts the intellectual divide "of agricultural history from food studies" (2013, 2).

Yet here we are in a moment when that "system" is first created, at once distancing itself and nonetheless employing the myths of the American farmer. Jeffersonian democracy emphasized the tenets of Thomas Jefferson, George Washington, and Benjamin Franklin using the symbol of the yeoman farmer, and a rustic existence to set a course for success.[2] Subsequent criticisms of Coolidge's laissez-faire ideology point out that it paved the way for the Great Depression and caused undue suffering for farmers. Coolidge's aggressive plan to turn farming into a great industrial enterprise both auspiciously announces the arrival of a new era and predicts a future trajectory with the certainty of a president who will direct it. Under closer examination, his celebratory statement that "whatever a few individuals may do, the Nation as a whole and its great subdivisions of industry, transportation, commerce, and agriculture can increase by no other method" (1925) takes on a darker undertone in its unilateral push for prosperity through absorption.

The previous chapter in *Environmental Justice in Contemporary US Narratives* announces the arrival of global US industrial agriculture. John Steinbeck's *The Grapes of Wrath* ([1939] 1976) and his coauthored scientific travel narrative *Sea of Cortez* ([1941] 2009) interrogate the complexities of scientific and industrial progress first at land and then at sea. *The Grapes of Wrath*, a seminal text on the human cost of the US economy's 1929 collapse, articulates what the overproduction of land through large-scale economic and industrial change can do to a country's infrastructure. Steinbeck is firmly convinced that the industrialization of farming and the national for-profit development of nature led to the destruction of the Great Plains and the hardships of migrant workers in California. Chapter 4 considers two works written in the 1990s, Ruth Ozeki's *My Year of Meats* (1998) and Cherríe Moraga's *Heroes and Saints* (1994), which outline the connections between human manipulation of large-scale food systems and the resulting costs and risks. While working on twentieth-century US narratives about the connections of the human to the environment, I noticed a number of missing bridges that are crucial to an understanding of something that is taken for granted: the United States was destined to be a global leader in both the production and consumption of meat and grains. Mary Douglas emphasizes the agency inherent in gastronomic exchange: "If food is to be treated as a code, the message it encodes will be found in the pattern of social relationships being expressed" (1972, 61). Douglas's statement signals the importance of food choices not only in everyday life but also in terms of their deeper sociohistorical implications. This chapter is an attempt to bridge the divide between the stories coming from the earlier part of the twentieth century and those coming from the latter part of it by looking at a text that questions the logic of the postindustrial US foodscape and landscape. For the sake of clarity, I refer to the persona created by Nguyen to represent the younger version of herself in the memoir as Bich, and the author as Nguyen. Nguyen's *Stealing Buddha's Dinner* (2007) is unusual in that it reads as a paean to American culture while concomitantly questioning that culture's foundation.

Midwestern foodscapes

Nguyen's memories of growing up as a Vietnamese American immigrant and refugee in the 1980s in Grand Rapids, Michigan, are largely expressed as memories of yearning for American junk food. *Stealing Buddha's Dinner* is an elegiac ode to Nguyen's thwarted desires to mimic colonial food practices and thus become more American than anybody in her school; ironically, she equates her Americanness with her participation in consuming iconic US junk food such as Twinkies, Pringles, and Kit Kats.[3] She later reflects that through her food choices she alienated herself from her family's own cultural history and also from the ecological implications of her consumption habits. Nguyen oscillates between seeing herself as the child of a political refugee (and inhabiting a refugee subjectivity) and seeing herself as an immigrant. Her writing is an attempt to make the connections between the books that fed her childhood fantasies of being "American" and the intense estrangement she felt from those same books as an adult.

Writing about these tensions in her memoir gives Nguyen a chance to make sense of seemingly dissonant impulses: on the one hand, to become "the whitest girl possible" (2007, 163), and on the other hand, to understand that to do so would mean removing herself from her family's version of an assimilation story. Nguyen's culinary bildungsroman is based on moments of discord between British and US notions of female perfection that she encounters through reading. Nguyen experiences these ideals as continued neocolonial attempts to control her body. Her first novel, *Short Girls* (2009), picks up many threads from her memoir and also discusses post-9/11 immigration to – and ethnicity in – the United States. In this chapter I focus on her memoir, in part because the genre of memoir lends itself to the kind of interpretive leaps necessary to make sense of the apparently nonsensical.

While young Bich admires an array of literary characters, she is especially struck by Ma Joad in Steinbeck's *The Grapes of Wrath* ([1939] 1976) and the Ingallses in Wilder's Little House books (written in 1932–1943 but set in the 1870s–1880s). The plot progression of both the migrant workers in *The Grapes of Wrath* and the Ingallses relies on humans' struggles with the natural elements and a national pride that comes from survival. Significantly, Steinbeck and Wilder both began writing the works that I discuss in the period between the two world wars, and both explored the theme of staking a claim to land and to the limits of agricultural production. In her research on World War II propaganda, Amy Bentley connects advertising campaigns to the war effort around the theme of food: "it defined these aims in private, individualistic terms that dignified and promoted consumption" (1998, 3). A good citizen was told to consume more and thus become a better American.

Nguyen's writing straddles the genres of the bildungsroman and memoir in unique ways; her hybrid model takes the developmental narrative of the bildungsroman and transforms it within memoir through the exploration of materiality and racial melancholia. Querying the "flatten[ing]" of Asian American texts, Stephen Hong Sohn suggests that "twentieth-century narrative texts by American authors of Asian descent generally fall into two aesthetic and formal categories: autobiography/memoir or the ethnoracial bildungsroman (or some variation that melds those two literary genres" (2014, 4). Sohn convincingly writes that given the historical, "dehumanizing" (2014, 4), and racialized renderings of Asians in US fiction, "self-representation is of paramount importance" (2014, 4–5). Nguyen's modes of self-representation simultaneously unsettle expected narratives of US history and those of Asian American memoirists.

Using the classic bildungsroman model as a prism through which to refract the complexities of *Stealing Buddha's Dinner*, I contend that Nguyen both engages and subverts the tradition in ways that adapt the bildungsroman to a US setting and ultimately reveals the form's failure. In broad terms, the bildungsroman is a novel of growth in which the (traditionally male) protagonist moves from youth to maturity and is socialized into a heteronormative type of nationally inflected subjectivity. Prompted by repeated failed encounters with the traditional bildungsroman, Bich begins to imagine new forms of ethical citizenship. A postcolonial understanding of self and society seems bound to cause friction within the bildungsroman tradition. While Bich does not reverse the bildungsroman process, her body – influenced by her choices in fiction – deconstructs the forms of selfhood resulting from the underlying mixed messages of US multiculturalism in the 1980s. The modernist bildung blueprint is a process of subject formation; the protagonist begins as an unformed locus of shifting desires and ends with a more fully rendered and mapped subjectivity. When Nguyen, reflecting on her past, understands that she deviated from that blueprint she questions its sanctity.

Here we have a subject who saw the US bildungsroman at an earlier stage in her life as the epitome of perfection: Bich naturalized and disseminated the norms of sociohistorical structures of belonging (systems of class, race, gender, and self-sufficiency), and in so doing she considered them to represent her dream of being a normal American girl. Yet as she matures, she can no longer hold all of the conflicting notions of being a good citizen together. They unravel before her eyes, and she has to let go of the idea that her fantasies can exist harmoniously, or that they ever did so. The mechanization of agriculture is disturbingly laid bare (at the Jiffy Hotel, for example, or when she reads Steinbeck and connects his work to the strike of the United Farm Workers). So too is the freakishness of the speed, scale, and impersonal nature of the global production of food – food that Bich once imagined as being particular to America and Americans, like the Ingallses and the Joads. The complexities of local food production and the violence inherent in clearing the land to create homesteads (in the case of the Ingallses) and large-scale farms (in the case of the Joads) occlude the hardships that both immigrant and migrant workers face. They also obscure the cultural autonomy of various personal backgrounds that Bich in turn erroneously ignores.

The Homestead Act

Through her employment of memoir, Nguyen effectively redirects the process of the bildungsroman to shatter the accepted notions of civic duty and patriotism that she begins to see as remnants of a time past as well as threats of an uncertain future. Even in the age of postmodern pastiche and literary experimentation, the novel – and the bildungsroman in particular – remains potentially the "most salient genre for the literature of social outsiders, primarily women or minority groups" (Hirsch 1979, 300). Both Marianne Hirsch and Stephen Hong Sohn emphasize the empowering potential of the bildungsroman tradition for "outsiders," and most difficult for Bich is that she is drawn to the very stories that would somehow keep her on the periphery. Through somatically induced phenomena, Bich's image of herself as a perpetual outsider shifts and she explores alternate modes of consumption, and to Sohn's point, "self-representation," via both food and literary matter.

Bich's interpretation of the Little House series is initially overshadowed by feelings of jealousy and envy of pioneer life. Bich does not value her grandmother's wholesome meals, she is ashamed that her father tries to grow herbs in their yard instead of lawns of grass (as all of her American neighbors do), and she sees her stepmother's ban on brand-name junk food as a direct challenge to her attempts to become American. Yet in her reading practices, she wants nothing more than to connect with Laura's love of homesteading. Nguyen's main chapter on the Little House books is titled "Salt Pork," a nod to Bich's obsession with reading about Laura's consumption habits: "After I read the *Little House* books I began to pretend that bacon was salt pork and that I was Laura herself" (2007, 158). Bich understands certain parts of small-scale agrarian economies and how they function, and she is fixated on eating as homesteading and vice versa: "A pioneer in a covered wagon had to keep a careful eye on the provisions, gauge how much to eat and how much to save for the rutted path ahead. The goal of settling was farming, creating an independent cycle of crops, livestock, and vegetable gardens" (2007, 158). In many ways, Bich's romanticized version of American life was necessitated by the fact that to fit in somewhere, she needed to believe in a narrative of growth and belonging, but the narrative she found eventually required her to leave it.

Significantly, Bich makes direct connections between small-scale farming, domesticity, and being a good American. These three things are inextricably linked to notions of US citizenship and belonging. The Ingallses epitomize Americanness, and their success only further exposes Bich's family's failures to conform. In a sense, the Ingallses serve as the main litmus test by which Bich measures her chance of eventually becoming more like her white (and therefore successful) school friends. While Bich states that in the Little House series "the goal of settling was farming" (2007, 158), one could just as easily say that the goal of farming was settling. As capable farmers, the Ingallses are thus also model settlers, and as such, they represent the opposite of Bich's status as immigrant and foreigner. The motivating factor that Bich continually manages to ignore is the impetus for settling: the Homestead Act of 1862. The Homestead Act was created during the Civil War to ensure a more seamless narrative of America's past, present, and future. Open tracts of land that people were encouraged to settle through the Homestead Act were privatized and developed in the name of the nation. American identity and the expansion of empire received equal weight. By the beginning of the twentieth century, westward expansion connoted US nationalism.[4]

Over the course of the nineteenth century, the westward and southward expansion of the United States increased dramatically and became a defining factor in US history, and thus also in global history. The term "Manifest Destiny" originally appeared in 1845 and later came to invoke the divine sanction of the territorial and ideological expansion of the United States. The unnamed author of the article in which the term was first recorded was later identified as John O'Sullivan, the editor of *United States Magazine and Democratic Review*, who argued for the annexation of Texas and the Oregon Country. He made the case that opposition to this annexation should end so that the United States could quickly and profitably expand: "It is now time for the opposition to the

Annexation of Texas to cease, [with] all further agitation of the waters of bitterness and strife. ... [E]nough has now been given to party. It is time for the common duty of Patriotism to the Country to succeed—or if this claim will not be recognized, it is at least time for common sense to acquiesce with decent grace in the inevitable and the irrevocable" (1845, 5). According to O'Sullivan, following the precedent that England and France had set, patriotic duty is linked to economic fortitude and is coterminous with the acceptance of expansion. O'Sullivan states that to oppose the annexation is "limiting" the "greatness" of America's destiny and "checking" its potentiality (1845, 6). Americans are meant to meet "the fulfillment of our manifest destiny to overspread the continent allotted by Providence for the free development of our yearly multiplying millions. This we have seen done by England, our old rival and enemy . . . " (1845, 6). The idea of Manifest Destiny was used liberally by nationalists to push an agenda of aggressive expansion and territorial occupation.[5]

The Homestead Act was an effort to encourage immigrants to become US citizens and surrender their identities as foreigners. It was also a way for the free states to gain political influence during the US Civil War (1861–1865). Rapid expansion ensured that the seceded southern states would lose political clout. The anxiety that immigrants would not become good Americans informs much of the rhetoric around the Homestead Act, which encouraged settlement by offering 160-acre plots, privatizing what had been "public" land, and creating more than one million farms by 1900. The act encouraged individuals (both recent immigrants and people who were already US citizens) to move westward, and it offered plots at minimal cost to the new occupier. Put simply, to acquire a plot and become a citizen, one had to build a home, dig a functional well, and plow ten acres of land for agricultural use over a period of five years. Adult heads of family had to pay a nominal ten-dollar filing fee, work the land for at least five continuous years, and swear "that he has never borne arms against the Government of the United States or given aid and comfort to its enemies . . . " (Homestead Act of 1862 1862). Largely because of the Homestead Act, various ethnic groups moved westward together.

Bich first saw this as a sign of solidarity between the Joads and her own family (between pioneers and immigrants), because the Joads also had to abruptly say goodbye to their homes and communities. Bich notes that "As they search for new homesteads, they, too, experienced isolation and [had to] scramble for shelter, food, work, and a place to call home. ... the Ingallses say good-bye to their family in Wisconsin, and the finality is chilling" (Nguyen 2007, 159). Yet as Bich continues to read about the experience of homesteading, she notices the dark undertones of "the great anxiety of westward expansion" that runs deeper than leaving one's place of origin: "As the Ingallses travel in their wagon ... they meet settlers from Norway, Sweden, Germany. 'They're good neighbors,' Pa says. 'But I guess our kind of folks is pretty scarce.' Yet these European families would one day cease to be foreign and become 'our kind of folks'" (Nguyen 2007, 159). Bich quickly acknowledges that she cannot physically alter herself to appear European. She and her family, unlike these immigrants, would not "blend in, become American" and would not "eventually refer to their ancestry as something fond and distant" (Nguyen 2007, 159). Although as a child she refuses to dwell on these feelings of discomfort, in her adult years she sees them as traces of the incongruousness of her homesteading fantasies and the realities of being an immigrant in 1980s Michigan.

The vignettes of pioneer life ignore the fact that to have white European bodies tilling the soil, that soil had to be usurped from indigenous peoples. Pioneer life overtly perpetuated the systemic racism and classism from which Bich suffers. The Little House series barely mentions slavery and indigeneity, treating them as past events and not present realities. As Bich matures she is distressed by "Ma Ingalls's hatred of Indians, which persisted no matter what Pa said," and she is doubly upset by a song about "a little darky" and the blackface vaudeville show that Pa and his friends put on in *Little Town on the Prairie* (Nguyen 2007, 160). Bich is troubled when a neat story of assimilation and harmony is undermined by reminders of a messy past. She searches for a narrative frame within which to place her favorite books, which are either about England or the United States.

Images of homesteading and pioneer life were the bucolic fabric of Bich's comforting fantasies and of a US national mythos. Many of the Little House books took place in South Dakota, and their original covers shared the aesthetic

Figure 3.1 The 1895 iconic photograph of the 1862 Homestead Act: the John Bakken Sod House in Milton, North Dakota.

Source: Photograph by John McCarthy. North Dakota State University Libraries, Institute for Regional Studies, Fred Hultstrand History in Pictures Collection [ca. 1895]. Photo courtesy of North Dakota State University Archives.

of the previous image (Figure 3.1) – which, like the covers, idealizes homesteading. The photograph shows John Bakken, a first-generation Norwegian American; his wife, Marget, who was born in Norway, where John married her before bringing her to America; and two of their children. The Bakken sod house shown in the figure also appeared on two stamps: a 1975 Norwegian stamp commemorating Norwegian emigration to America, and a 1962 US stamp celebrating the hundredth anniversary of the Homestead Act's passage.

Bich's "strong reserve of denial" (Nguyen 2007, 160) allows her to ignore conflicting images like the one of Daniel Freeman (see Figure 3.3). Freeman is credited with being the first person to file a homestead claim, on January 1, 1863. Freeman purported to be a US soldier and a Secret Service agent, but according to a National Park Services post exploring the history of the Homestead Act ("Homestead National Monument: Its Establishment and Administration"), both claims were likely false. (2009). In a 1901 *Omaha World Herald* newspaper article Freeman was described as being busy "on the frontier furring [*sic*] the troubles with the Sioux Indians," and "while a loyal and steadfast friend he is also a steadfast enemy and right good hater" (Ashby 1901).

Nguyen grapples with these conflicting portraits of celebration and displacement. Her sense of inadequacy is plagued by unfulfilled desire. She wants to be like the Ingallses – to eat what they eat and to consume as they consume – but that would involve subsuming her distinct subjectivity in the spirit of, as she puts it, "manifest destiny and white entitlement" (2007, 160).

Figure 3.2 The official 1962 US postage stamp celebrating the hundredth anniversary of the Homestead Act's passage.

Source: North Dakota State University Libraries, Institute for Regional Studies, Fred Hultstrand History in Pictures Collection [1962]. Photo courtesy of North Dakota State University Archives.

Figure 3.3 Daniel Freeman standing, holding a gun, with a hatchet tucked in his belt.

Source: Photograph by J.A. Ball, Beatrice, Nebraska. Library of Congress [ca. 1904]. Photo courtesy of Library of Congress, Digital Collections.

Legible bodies

As narratives of colonialism and imperialism chafe against her own, Bich's reading practices become an attempt to work out incompatible ideas of nationalism and the bildungsroman. In his erudite work on literary form and international human rights policies, Joseph Slaughter echoes the idea that "truth" and "fiction" have long formed an unhealthy alliance in the spreading of colonial and imperial machinations: "Human rights law and the *Bildungsroman* are consubstantial and mutually reinforcing. . . . Both human rights and the novel have been part of the engine and freight of Western colonialism and (neo)imperialism" (2007, 5). Slaughter acknowledges that we often use the fictions of our national and cultural traditions to explore moral ambiguities. Further to Slaughter's point, Bich investigates the borders of her ethicality through fiction.

Bich's experiences with nature and her surrounding environment are almost exclusively through fiction. The stories of happiness that are tied to US expansionism and imperialism convince Bich that in order to be fully American she needs to consume as she imagines her contemporaries consume. She sees reading as the "one thing to call [her] own," and the Little House books are her favorite (Nguyen 2007, 150). In pursuit of the ghostly tracks of displaced indigenous peoples that are obscured by tales of fictional pioneer families, Bich tries to eat her way into existence and map herself onto the heartland of America: "I thought I could make myself over from the inside out" (247). By corporeally connecting to fictional protagonists and trying to absorb whiteness through osmosis and "sleep[ing] among the narratives," Bich hopes to transform herself into a symbol of all things American (151). The rare mentions of her father's herb garden and her outdoor excursions with her Brownie troop are riddled with feelings of anxiety and isolation. Bich's self-hatred is implicit in her description of "the other girls" in her troop, who were "straight-up Grand Rapidian – proper and Dutch, from good clean homes" (142). In the context of Asian American cultural criticism, Monica Chiu suggests that racialized domestic spaces often connote filth: "Economic differences" become rationalizations for untrue "judgments about health and welfare, equating low-income living to unsanitary domesticity" (2004, 99). Bich reveals her skewed understanding of whiteness as an indicator of "clean" living, however processed and unnatural that living is. The books she reads create and encourage Bich's desire for connections between small-scale food production and her own eating habits, but this desire appears to wane when Bich steps out of her imaginary world. For example, when Bich's Brownie troop goes to see the Gordon Food Services kitchen she finds that "the environment was both sterile and chaotic – part hospital, part factory." Yet she continues to harbor a deep sense of envy of her friends and their Betty Crocker cakes and Jiffy muffins (Nguyen 2007, 143).

Bich's sense of displacement is couched in culinary terms, but her focus on food cloaks her sadness over her mother's absence, something that is "the stuff of too much reality" (Nguyen 2007, 236). The sense of a loss of spatiotemporal fixity is common among immigrants and refugees, especially those who must unwillingly flee their countries and already have a destabilized sense of national identity. In this vein, Lisa Lowe comments: "Despite the usual assumption that Asians immigrate from stable, continuous, 'traditional' cultures, most of the post-1965 Asian immigrants come from societies already disrupted by colonialism and distorted by the upheavals of neocolonial capitalism and war" (1996, 16). Nguyen's family struggles to focus on a stable future especially because of its tumultuous past and because the uncertainty of Vietnam remains palpable. Lowe's insight further explains Bich's challenges in feeling safe since both her past and her present register as threats. While her father brought Bich, her sister, and her grandmother to the United States, her mother stayed in Saigon, and there is almost no mention of her until Bich is in fifth grade. It is only in chapter 15 – the second to last in Nguyen's book – that Bich's mother enters the memoir. Bich arrived in the United States when she was eight months old, so her childhood memories are American ones. After fleeing Saigon in 1975, Bich's family consists of her hard-working father; her grandmother, Noi (unrivaled in nurturing kindness); her three uncles (Chu Cuong, Chu Anh, and Chu Dai); and her older sister, Anh. The family is given three choices of where to settle: "my father brought back three options: sponsors in California, Wyoming, and Michigan. . . . California: warm but had the most lunatics. Wyoming: cowboys. Michigan was the blank unknown" (Nguyen 2007, 9). In the end it is Bich's grandmother (Noi) who because she had heard of the University of Michigan decides that Michigan holds the greatest promise of a good future for the family.

According to Nguyen, Grand Rapids, both welcoming by virtue of sponsorship and alienating because of widespread xenophobia, "brings to mind Gerald Ford, office furniture, and Amway" (2007, 10). On the last day of 1977 at a Vietnamese New Year's Eve party, Nguyen's father meets Rosa, a second-generation Mexican American woman with a young daughter of her own, Crissy. Nguyen's father and Rosa marry, and Rosa eventually gives birth to Vinh (who is Ahn and Bich's half-brother while Crissy is their stepsister). Rosa's hope for family unity is eclipsed by Bich's insatiable desire to become assimilated through her food choices: "I wanted to savor new food, different food, white food. I was convinced I was falling far behind on becoming American" (2007, 52). Bich's ambitious and misguided plan to eat white food and become white is yet another example of what Eileen Chia-Ching Fung has noted: that for subjects in ethnic minority groups, eating is "never simply about consumption" because the act of consuming reveals "a complex, at times, contradictory cultural economy that links identity politics to the production of labor" (2011, ii). Bich begins to lose herself in food without questioning the implications of her desires.

Food tropes have functioned as a major theme in US immigrant literatures, especially in Asian American fiction, memoir, and poetry.[6] Wenying Xu points to the legitimizing power of food: "Food, as the most significant medium of the traffic between the inside and outside of our bodies, organizes, signifies, and legitimates our sense of self in distinction from others" (2008, 2). In constructing one's critical subjectivity, culinary choices are moves against the machinery of unilateral assimilation to an American identity. The consumption of media and raw materials, including food, has been viewed as the end of the road in the travel of capital, or on the path of foodways. In particular where ethnic subjects are concerned, the idea of consumption as an endpoint of meaning is acutely troubling. Anita Mannur contends that there is an inherently cyclical nature to treating issues of consumption in Asian American literature: "Thinking about race, gender, and ethnicity begins with food, but thinking about food also ends with race, gender, and ethnicity" (2010, 221). Similarly, Arjun Appadurai rejects a teleological formula and proposes instead that "the consumption of the mass media throughout the world often provokes resistance, irony, selectivity, and, in general, *agency*" (1996, 7; emphasis in the original). The imagination as a social force is born, according to Appadurai, of the flesh and body of mass media and migration (1996, 4). He rightly notes that due to the rise of mass media and technology the body has "increasingly freed" itself from the work of consumption (1996, 83). By reinserting the body into the discourse of ethnic food studies, this chapter explains food's powerful symbolic agency as a form of cross-cultural communication.

US ethnic foodscapes are prime territory for the engagement of the imagination. Advancements in technology have allowed for humans to have a highly mediated relationship to foodways. I use the term "foodscapes" to indicate a deepening of the scope of food studies in mediated global exchanges.[7] Embodied attachments to food are disseminated across multiple platforms: cookbooks, food shows, and recipes on the Internet and in print. Entire websites and bookstores are dedicated to the pursuit of the perfect meal. In recognition of such shifts, an emerging field within food studies considers food in contemporary American ethnic literature – specifically, in the fiction and memoirs of Asian American writers.[8] Asian Americans, as Wenying Xu (2008, 8) and Jennifer Ho (2005, 11–13) point out, are associated with their various culinary traditions, and these associations are built on racial stereotypes that prohibit agency.[9]

The body and its connection to food seem elementary because consuming nutrients is a universal biological process. As Timothy Morton writes, "everyone eats: food is 'the great leveler'" (2004, 259). Morton posits that because eating is a basic human need and thus universal, it leads to an aesthetic crisis of taste: "Diet is particularly suited to this crisis" (2004, 259). But with food processing and advanced technology, the body has been incrementally divorced from food, and food culture has eclipsed food matter, although we might think food matter "levels" subjects into equality. For Asian American memoirists, the consumption of food – far from being a unifying force or a comforting practice – is riddled with anxiety, fear, alienation, and interpellation. Susan Kalčik writes that the rituals and performance of consumption are often more significant than the meals themselves: "foodways provide a whole area of performance in which statements of identity can be made – in preparing, eating, serving, forbidding, and talking about food" (1984, 54). Food has the ideological power both to subjugate as it seduces and to alienate as it pleases, and these are the oppositional forces that wage war for Nguyen's allegiance and consume her as she tries to consume.[10] While hoping to be seamlessly absorbed into mainstream America, immigrants to the United States often abandon their traditional cultural practices, especially their eating habits. Since food has become highly mediated, to characterize it as a one-way street of agency driven by the consumer is to elide the multiple registers of negation inherent in its consumption. The intense desires for "white" food by ethnic immigrant characters in literature could be read as their psychological hunger to "level" themselves into a monolithic regime of food culture. The bildungsroman tradition includes an expansion of the body, land (buying a home as one's nation prospers), and strong sense of self, but Bich's family does not register as following the trajectory of the fictional protagonists about whom she reads. In *Stealing Buddha's Dinner*, the individualistic model of maturation (the core definition of the bildungsroman) falters in the face of political and socioeconomic impossibilities.

Postcolonial disruption

In her gastronomic bildungsroman, Bich is drawn to stories of colonial prowess and conquest and the various people that Bich envies become powerful symbols of a historiography that would write her out of its past. Nguyen's chapter, "Salt Pork," presents Bich as she lists her favorite novels and explores how they contributed to her desire to shape herself according to hegemonic ideals of female American whiteness. Admitting that she was attempting to "read [her] way out of Grand Rapids," she names the books that made her "the whitest girl possible" (Nguyen 2007, 163). She recalls becoming obsessed with the Little House series and internalizing the underlying messages of US Eurocentric racism: "In a way, it makes sense that I would become enamored with a literature so symbolic of manifest destiny and white entitlement" (Nguyen 2007, 160). This statement affirms that as a young girl, Nguyen imaginatively aligned herself with texts that symbolically stood for the eradication of indigenous peoples in the United States. She admits that her cultural imaginary was swiftly colonized by archetypal figures of American expansionism: "For I had created, if somewhat unknowingly, a group portrait of protagonists – girls I wished I could be" (Nguyen 2007). Despite her fascination with the food habits of her protagonists, she does not query the connection between her insatiable hunger and the symbolic significance of her literary choices.

As the "epitome of American" (Nguyen 2007, 159), the Ingalls family filled young Bich's head with stereotypical ideas of what constituted a US citizen: farming, country food, and the Declaration of Independence. Bich notices that of all the protagonists of her beloved fiction, none consumed quite like Laura: "All of my fictional friends liked to eat, but perhaps no one did more than Laura Ingalls Wilder" (153). And even as she describes the dietary habits of the Ingallses in great detail – "ham or roast beef or chicken pie, mashed potatoes with gravy, baked beans" (155) – Nguyen stops short of connecting the expansionism and exploitation of white pioneers of the early and middle parts of the nineteenth century to the French colonization of Vietnam in the same period. Bich's gastronomic desires are awakened by imaginary chicken potpies, and this seemingly innocuous culinary seduction eclipses the troubling way in which she denies her own ethnicity and the colonial violence in Vietnam. Her father's problematic and reductive explanation of how easy it is to become American further exacerbates Bich's misguided thinking.

When the Nguyen family first arrived and was assigned to a refugee camp in Oklahoma, other refugees suggested that they were "*people without a country*," but Bich's father believed that by physically leaving the camp they would be transformed: "*Until we walk out of that gate. . . . And then we are American*" (Nguyen 2007, 10; emphasis in original). As Frederick Jackson Turner argued, "American history has been in a large degree the history of the colonization of the Great West" (1920, 1) – and what, we might ask, about the East? When westward expansion is no longer possible and industrialization is a fait accompli, how can a new national ethos be created? Turner's view of the frontier included ideas of rebirth of nationalism based on a commitment to advancement: "Thus American development has exhibited not merely advance along a single line, but a return to primitive conditions on a continually advancing frontier line, and a new development for that area. American social development has been continually beginning over again on the frontier. . . ." (1920, 2). The measuring stick for success at the beginning of the nineteenth century appeared to be an ability to expand quickly and nimbly across the continent. Turner's unique contribution to US historiography is his theory that in settling the frontier, the nation's newest members – from diverse religious and cultural backgrounds – would become American through a shared experience of rustic life. The twinned advancement along the frontier line consists both of migrants and immigrants becoming Americanized and of "virgin" and unconquered lands becoming American. This sense of industrious advancement, spurred by monetary incentives, creates a unique narrative of settlement and the dissemination of civilization.

The bucolic and agrarian way of life appears more egalitarian and democratic than its gritty realities suggest. Microfrontiers (individual and divergent pockets of the frontier that make up the "macro" line) become points of reference for an increasingly seamless story of American success and empire spreading westward. The frontier's mythology as a single advancing line makes it easy to forget that there was little uniformity and the story was not, in fact, one of unilateral progress. Yet as Turner states, "the frontier is the line of most rapid and effective Americanization. The wilderness masters the colonist" (1920, 4). The hardships of dealing with the elements, facing hunger, instigating violence and living under the constant threat of having that violence be redirected against you have been rewritten into a tale of triumph: "in the crucible of the frontier the immigrants were Americanized, liberated, and fused into a mixed race, English in neither nationality nor characteristics" (1920). The frontier is the superhighway to forced assimilation, and as Turner presents it, the wilderness dominates the colonist and encourages him or her to become more American.

Ethnic consumption

Nguyen's identification with this gut instinct to consume and conquer shows that one type of consumption hides inside another: colonialism erases identity through a series of expansionist narratives. When naturalized food matter and stories are together proven to be unnatural, Bich begins to imagine a multiplicity that confounds her and leads to an alternative understanding of what defines US citizenship. The chance to move to Michigan, the heartland of America, is dampened by Bich's fear of crossing its city lines. The first chapter of *Stealing Buddha's Dinner*, entitled "Pringles," is named in honor of Bich's earliest memories of living with her family as refugees in the basement of their sponsor, Mr. Heidenga. Bich vividly describes coveting the ready-made and brand-name junk food of the Heidenga children, a sign of economic ease and general comfort: "Anh and I were transfixed by the bright red cylinder and the mustachioed grin of Mr. Pringles's broad, pale face. The Heidenga girl pried off the top and crammed a handful of chips into her mouth. We watched the crumbs fall from her fingers to the floor" (Nguyen 2007, 3). Bich's exposure to brand-name junk food stokes the flames of her later fixation on food-based sections of books.

Chapter 1, "Pringles," is also the chapter in which Bich experiences the first markers of capitalism's reach as the colonization of space.

> I came of age in the 1980s, before diversity and multicultural awareness trickled into western Michigan. Before ethnic was cool. Before Thai restaurants became staples in every town. When I think of Grand Rapids I remember city signs covered in images of rippling flags, proclaiming 'An All-American City.' Throughout the eighties a giant billboard looming over the downtown freeway boasted the slogan to all who drove the three-lane S-curve. As a kid, I couldn't figure out what 'All-American' was supposed to mean. Was it a promise, a threat, a warning?
>
> (Nguyen 2007, 10)

The "promise," "threat," or "warning" seems innocuous enough, but for Bich the question of what happens if you do not fit in within the "All-American City" of Gerald Ford and Amway is urgent. She is quick to point out that Amway was headquartered just east of Grand Rapids, in Ada, a town her family later moved to – a town that is home to the DeVos and Van Andel families that "poured millions of dollars into Grand Rapids and the Republican Party" (Nguyen 2007, 10–11). The names of Amway's founders are "emblazoned on buildings" just as images of rippling flags cover city signs. The connection Bich makes between Amway's support of both Grand Rapids and the Republican Party is a connection that registers as a "threat" and not a "promise." The names of earlier settlers on the sides of buildings and at the heads of companies were "a reminder of what and whom the town represents, as if the sea of blond – so much so I could swear I was dreaming in wheat – could let a foreigner forget" (Nguyen 2007, 11). Bich continues to focus on the sight of blond heads that "glided" by her at school, no doubt adding to her sense of being haunted by a specter of something she assumes she can never attain.

Bich's racial ambivalence forcefully emerges when she relates: "That was the dilemma, the push and the pull. The voice saying, *Come on in. Now transform. And if you cannot, then disappear*" (Nguyen 2007, 11; emphasis in original). Once again we see Bich's interpretation of things as the shallow reading of a child who is unmoored. The city signs covered in the image of rippling flags are unwelcoming on multiple levels to a variety of gazes. The association Bich makes between the successful entrepreneurs who built Amway and the city signs with the American flag on them draws a parallel between capitalism and the American dream. Bich feels that she can never be a part of that dream, but ironically she could become part of the global US empire, at the cost of a kind of amnesia and dissociation from her four parental figures (her mother, father, stepmother, and grandmother) and the history of her arrival from Vietnam. This threat undergirds the words she imagines being spoken to her: "*Come on in. Now transform. And if you cannot, then disappear.*" If she buys into the American dream, she has purchased her own demise and the rejection of her multidimensional story with its nuances of refugee flight. Refusing to disappear, Bich begins to understand that her obsession with frontier food has little to do with physical hunger and everything to do with her physicality.

As alimentary images abound and the allegory of junk food becomes pervasive, the discerning reader begins to deconstruct Bich's appetite for chocolate-coated marshmallows as a coded desire for whiteness. For example, as Nguyen struggles to fit in and perfect her performance of whiteness, she moves away from using her hands, which she sees as indicative of "ethnic" eating; instead she practices with a fork and knife. Rosa, fluent in code switching and social hierarchies (based upon her Chicano background and work with GED and ESL students), knows that Nguyen is "enamored" of "all things British" and shows her a different way to hold her utensils: "'Americans don't know how to eat truly correctly, the way Europeans do.' She gave me a smile I couldn't interpret – part sad, part supercilious" (Nguyen 2007, 93). Rosa's knowledge foreshadows what Bich will later discover: that she is unknowingly perpetuating the very paradigms of power that continue to alienate her. Nguyen loves "Mary Poppins, Charles Dickens, names like Margaret and Elizabeth" (Nguyen 2007, 93), and her Anglophilia betrays her subconscious absorption of messages equating whiteness with a superior life and also mistakenly, with an American one.

Nguyen admits that although with time she became "increasingly uneasy" about her relationship to veiled narratives of colonial enterprise, she had the ability to ignore those nagging feelings in favor of her admiration for frontier narratives: "Though my relationship with the Ingalls family and other white characters grew complicated, I had a strong reserve of denial, an ability to push away the unpleasant parts" (2007, 160). The Ingalls family participates in consumptive regimes that advocate practicality and hard work (2007, 159). While aspects of their pioneer existence remind Bich of immigrant life, even as a child she recognizes that reading the stories leaves her feeling inadequate. The sense of female empowerment that Bich might gain from following the story of little Laura as a proto-feminist pioneer is muddied by the ethnoracial alienation she experiences. In his erudite reading of Bich's love of the Little House series, Martín-Lucas Belén writes that "it is the narrative of displacement and resettling in the Wilder books that captures Bich's emotional sympathy" (2011, 32), but this sympathy is later tempered by Bich's realization that "her identity can never be expressed in the singular" (34). As Belén suggests, it is the denial of multiplicity inherent in Laura Ingalls Wilder's books that finally alerts Bich to the fact that she and her favorite protagonist would not have been best friends. While there is certainly a reductive aspect to assuming that Wilder can refer to herself in the singular, the more important point is that Bich interprets that possibility as the expiration of hope.

Bich's inadequacy is plagued by unrequited desire because she expects in some way that her love affair with food and her passion for books about consumption will fulfill her. Her hopes to eat like – and therefore become – the Ingallses is an exercise in disappointment. You cannot actually become what you eat, and certainly, as Bich finds, participating in consumption practices that elide a long history of colonial domination will continue to void her sense of subjectivity. Morton suggests that in the "ideological gaze of imperialism" (as opposed to pure consumerism), what we eat signifies who we are: "We can 'eat Chinese.' In the ideological gaze of imperialism, that is pretty much (and increasingly so) that in which being Chinese consists" (2004, 259). Nguyen eats American in the hope of reversing but not subverting the ideological gaze. What she finds, ultimately, is that her rebellious desires for American food are fruitless – they do not fill her as she had hoped they would. In fact, as she matures and finds her voice, meets her mother, and makes peace with many of her childhood insecurities, the iconic signifiers of American popular – edible – culture seem spectral: "I mourn the false hope of all those vats of food. How slick they became, how glutinous the portions, cold on my plate. So much emptiness in so much possibility" (Nguyen 2007, 219–20). The semantic void that Bich wishes to fill through junk food remains a space of longing.

As Bich acculturates herself to US foodscapes, she becomes fluent in the language of cuisine. Part of the agency of food comes from its ability to connect the external and internal environments of our corpus: food speaks to and about the body with which it commingles. Perhaps the language of food is particularly interesting because of food's atypical role as a medium of exchange that shuttles between inner and outer, tangible and intangible. Morton firmly implicates food as the vessel that travels, albeit awkwardly, between the worlds of the material and immaterial: "Like other forms of aesthetic artifact, food holds a place between the material and the conceptual" (2004, 259).[11] The language of food, then, has imbricated registers of signification. The so-called everyday social practice of eating is something that Pierre Bourdieu might argue is the way that one becomes American.[12] But theorists of the everyday often overlook the complex feelings one has as one begins to learn the codes of a different habitus. There is a rupture inherent in the act of absorption that is romanticized as a successful story of assimilation. In the language of food, the translation of polyvocal foodways through normative cultural registers of American cuisine push immigrants toward homogenization. Thus Morton's claim echoes a problematic complicity with the flattening force of nationalistic agendas. Food ("American," brand-name, and white-signifying food) is not the great leveler for Asia – it is an antagonistic, interpolating force that consumes as much as it is consumed.[13]

Growth and maturity

The adult memoirist is able to identify the crippling sense of hunger in her younger persona as ultimately not related to actual hunger; rather, Nguyen recognizes that the driving force behind Bich's seemingly biological hunger for Pop-Tarts and Twinkies is a sociocultural desire to assimilate.[14] Nguyen becomes an astute reader and orchestrator of codified meanings and the concepts of "white" and "American" coalesce in Bich's mind as she categorically rejects Rosa's sopas and Noi's pho in favor of Hamburger Helper.[15] Bich's choices speak volumes about her wish to flee her Asian-Latino household and become absorbed in the mainstream through the consumption of instant, packaged, and standardized junk food. Nguyen is fascinated by how quickly she can consume and participate in American regimes of knowledge outside of the threshold of her home. While her fascination with temporality stems from her constant anxiety that she is falling far behind her friends in acquiring whiteness, it also betrays her sense of dislocation: she is searching for ways to efficiently establish herself within US borders.

Nguyen views her mixed family as a roadblock on her superhighway to Americanization. Nguyen's father is forced to leave his wife and homeland behind; the subtext of his traumatic passage and choice to flee from the North Vietnamese remains a key part of Nguyen's recollections of him. But Bich understands very little of this and is exasperated at having to grow up in the Midwest, "before ethnic was cool" (Nguyen 2007, 10). Her name, so easily mispronounced, is fodder for playground taunting and pushes her down a spiraling path of self-hatred. In the second grade, she befriends Loan (pronounced Lo-an), and the two of them face schoolyard prejudice. Nguyen navigates the waters of her memories, moving from childhood taunts to private desires, from the public playground to the domestic space of her family's kitchen:

> We went to the same school during first and second grade, and became the best of friends. Bitch and Loan, some of the kids said on the playground. *Hey, bitch, can you loan me some money?*
>
> At home, I kept opening the refrigerator and cupboards, wishing for American foods to magically appear. I wanted what the other kids had: Bundt cakes and casseroles, Cheetos and Doritos. . . . The more American foods I ate, the more my desires multiplied, outpacing any interest in Vietnamese food. I had memorized the menu at Dairy Cone . . . and every inch of the candy display at Gas City. . . . I knew Reese's peanut butter cups, Twix, Heath Crunch, Nestle Crunch, Baby Ruth, Bar None. . . . I dreamed of taking it all, plus the freezer full of popsicles and nutty, chocolate-coated ice cream drumsticks.
>
> (Nguyen 2007, 50)

The symbolic dimensions of foodscapes are crystallized in Nguyen's burning desire to consume, incorporate, and become one with iconic American brands; she unabashedly lists global icons of junk food at length ("Twix, Heath Crunch, Nestle Crunch, Baby Ruth, Bar Nonc") as she recalls that she "dreamed of taking it all." Most fascinating is her transition from racist verbal parody to corporeal desire. The verbal taunting indicates to Bich and Loan that they are not only poor, but that they are a betrayal to racist expectations that they should be good with money. Nguyen responds with fantasies of overconsumption; her capitalist desire to have "it all" is linked to what she understands American nationhood does. Nguyen wants to steal an American selfhood through food because she sees her Vietnamese identity becoming diluted through the food she is taught to want; she fetishizes American candy and fast food with an intensity equal to that of her desire to be assimilated – by absorbing she seeks to be absorbed.

While Nguyen's memoir revolves around food (as noted above, her chapters have titles such as "Pringles" and "Salt Pork"), her work is in many ways a typical coming-of-age story. Adolescent fears of abandonment, teenage angst, a desire to fit in – these are by no means solely the concerns of immigrants. In his review of *Stealing Buddha's Dinner*, Ben Fong-Torres is dismissive of memoirists whose extent of cultural analysis ends at "food parallels" (2007). He suggests that Nguyen's food-centered narrative offers depth: "her growing pains have less to do with what she eats than with how she copes with sibling envy, schoolmate rivalries, authoritarian figures, youthful insecurities and a nagging mystery that is another sort of 'missingness'" (2007). The "nagging mystery" to which Fong-Torres refers is Nguyen's mother's absence, which generates part of the void Nguyen tries to fill through food. While Fong-Torres rightly ascribes depth to Nguyen's book, I am more cautious than he is in departing from the meaning of food matter in and of itself.

Even if Nguyen were only to draw "food parallels," they are nonetheless significant. Bich's cravings for apple pie are more than a desire to be American. Her desires for classic American foods cannot be expressed without a corresponding negativity about her own identity. Nguyen's gastronomic bildungsroman does not reductively offer growth solely through food, but foodscapes are deeply rooted in her ethnic roots, her mother's absence, and her wish to fit in. According to Mannur, food registers on multiple levels that may be inextricably linked to the olfactory senses but are not limited to them: "The desire to remember home by fondly recreating culinary memories cannot be understood merely as reflectively nostalgic gestures" (2007, 13). Though Mannur's critical exploration appears in the context of Asian American studies, her approach is complicated by *Stealing Buddha's Dinner*, where the acts of craving foods and remembering them become recreations of experiences that Bich never had. Mannur states that stories anchored in ethnic food "must also be read as metracritiques of . . . one's relationship to seemingly intractable culinary practices which yoke national identity with culinary taste and practices" (2007, 13). Indeed, Nguyen questions the reasoning of Bich, who so badly wanted to depart from ethnic foodways and arrive at white American versions of consumption.

Nguyen's sense of autonomous subjectivity increases and expands as she becomes more familiar with the US media's portrayal of American citizenship as white and heteronormative. In *Modernity at Large*, Appadurai explains that with globalization the "weight" of the imagination has increased and that it has become a catalyst of the subject's ability to conceptualize agency: "In the past two decades, as the deterritorialization of persons, images, and ideas has taken on new force, this weight has imperceptibly shifted. More persons throughout the world see their lives through the prisms of the possible lives offered by mass media in all their forms" (1996, 53–54). Appadurai's approach can be applied to Nguyen's memoir, as Bich does see her life "through the prisms of the possible lives" offered on television, in magazines, and, of course, in books. The exponential expansion of Nguyen's subjectivity indeed stems from her ability to imagine herself through the hegemonic lens of American selfhood. Furthermore, she gains agency through the many denials of that imaginative space. When her access to American junk food is denied because of her family's differing cultural practices and financial constraints, Bich's cultural imaginary begins to redefine her Americanness. Bich feels that she does not have a real mother, and she turns to popular iconographic figures of motherhood disseminated by the media. The women who most closely approximate her notions of American motherhood are her white friends' mothers.

Bich is convinced that the ideal of white Americanness she sees can be achieved through consumption. In particular, she embraces television as a means by which she can define an improved identity for herself: "To me, life lived in commercials was real life. Commercials were instructions; they were news. They showed me what perfection could be . . . the layers of a cake would always be exactly the same size" (Nguyen 2007, 125). But it is also through commercials that Bich's mother's spectrality increases; they keep Bich from feeling normal as she processes information about what mothers or "perfection could be" because "commercials had a firm definition of motherhood, which almost all of my friends' mothers had no trouble filling" (Nguyen 2007, 125). Bich longs for different food and a different family than that offered by her fused Latino-Vietnamese household. To her, becoming American involves eating American, but Nguyen recalls that the more she ate, the less satiated she felt, and her "desires multiplied" for American food and by extension American selfhood (Nguyen 2007, 50). Her compulsion to consume her way into whiteness blinds her to the erasure of knowledge in which she is participating: the commercials, print advertisements, books, and other mediated indicators of whiteness fill her field of vision so completely that her friends' whiteness make their bodies a blankness to her. The "blank unknown" of Michigan that seemed foreign and inaccessible to her father as he chose a sponsor for his family is comparable to the blankness or whiteness that is the uncharted territory of two-dimensional families like those of her friends.

Bich's dissatisfaction comes from her slow awakening to the hollow substance of Twinkies and Kit Kats and her growing understanding that she has been given the "false hope" that she can find happiness through alimentary consumption (Nguyen 2007, 220). With every social interaction the language of food is refined and complicated. Homemade cookies are a turning point for Bich. They are loaded with significance and expose her faulty underlying assumptions that equate American food with white ethnicity.[16] When her next-door neighbors' all-American daughter, Jennifer Vander Wals, gives her a cookie, Bich is at first confused: "Nestlé's Toll House, she called it, and I thought, you name your cookies? . . . In our house, cookies came from Keebler, Nabisco, or more frequently, the generic company whose label shouted 'COOKIES' in stark black letters" (Nguyen 2007, 57–8). Nguyen is surprised to discover both that cookies can be homemade and that they can be branded by a global mogul like Nestlé's. The instant gratification promised through brand-name cookies comes at the price of distance from organic food matter.

Bich's obsession with American junk food stages a double instance of estrangement: the food she desires is a testament to the distance between raw food and global branding of junk food, and it simultaneously evokes her sentiments of foreignness to both Vietnamese and US cultures. Bich's assumption that if she consumes Nestlé's cookies she will become a part of America is destabilized by her exchange with Jennifer. Jennifer's food includes homemade cookies, but as Bich learns this she simultaneously realizes her distance from Jennifer's world – what is foreign to Bich is vernacular to others. Bich grasps that becoming American is not something that comes prefabricated or that can be instantly attained. In fact, Jennifer's cookies imply that the mixing and forming of one's identity happens in the kitchen and thus the home: "I had thought all American food came from a package and some mystical factory process" (Nguyen 2007, 58). Her "revelation" and then "desire" is to organically "create such a thing" herself (Nguyen 2007, 58).

Colonial food and melancholia

Late into her memoir, Bich's feelings of inadequacy and her conviction that she will always be an outsider eventually subside in the wake of her comprehension that she is in some ways more American than she realizes. Her Americanness is highlighted when Nguyen reflects on her scant recollections of her family's escape from Vietnam. Her father rarely speaks of the experience of becoming a refugee and does not share these memories with his daughters: "That I cannot imagine that moment, the panic and fear, the push to leave his country and aim for an unknown land, is perhaps his gift. It is my Americanness. . . . Our identities changed. We were Vietnamese, we were refugees, we were Americans" (Nguyen 2007, 251). His "gift" to Bich is that he shelters her from the horrors of war and full rupture from Vietnam, and she recognizes that what remains undeveloped is not her Americanness but her Vietnamese roots. The "gift" has indeed Americanized her because her identity relies not so much on what she has eaten, but on the absence of her experiences in Southeast Asia. She has been denied access to the memories of Vietnam, and as she matures, that absence rocks her sense of belonging more than childhood teasing ever could.

As a self-proclaimed "Vietnamese-born American girl," nothing underscores Bich's distance from Vietnam more than the two events of meeting her mother for the first time and traveling to Vietnam in 1991 with her grandmother, Noi (Nguyen 2007, 253). Her father's "gift" is a double-edged sword of lost memories and incommunicable grief. Nguyen recalls only two times when she dared ask her father how he had decided to leave Saigon without his wife. He gives different versions on those two occasions and refuses to elaborate. Her mother's version of the story, infinitely haunting and isolating, is a bricolage of memories ending in an empty house, abandonment, and a decimated country: "In the end, I left my questions unanswered. I couldn't comprehend the loss, the nearly twenty years' absence, the silence and unknowing" (Nguyen 2007, 237). Attempting to fill the space between them, Nguyen and her mother make small talk, "as though [they] were practicing language conversations out of a workbook" (235). Verbal communication fails Nguyen in Vietnam, where she and Noi are "guests" and she has "no way to keep up" with the fast exchanges in Vietnamese between Noi and her extended family (240). What separates *Stealing Buddha's Dinner* from other food odysseys is not Nguyen's introspectiveness but the manner in which she allows the food scenes to speak for and with her.

Bich's sense of emotional and geographical dislocation, a crucial facet of her memoir and the genre of the bildungsroman, is intensified by her sense of insecurity. The classic bildungsroman hero is orphaned or driven from his home at a young age; Bich loses her home in a different sense. Her home is "invaded" by outsiders (Rosa) and adopted siblings with whom she does not bond, it is later broken by the separation of her father and Rosa, and it becomes a space of guilt for her as she rejects her grandmother's traditions and advice. Much of the unrest in Nguyen's memoir stems from Bich's certainty that there is no respite from attack – she draws a connection between her body's vulnerability and that of the Indians in the Little House series. In reading about the American frontier, racked by violence and hatred of enemies and foreigners, Bich ultimately learns that for her, the bildungsroman project of rebirth is based on an illusion.

The repetitive nature of Bich's traumatic experiences recalls the second phase of the bildungsroman, in which the protagonist typically clashes with a hegemonic social structure. But here is where the logic of the bildungsroman does not apply to Nguyen's memoir, because the traditional protagonist moves from rebellion against hegemony to acceptance or even an endorsement of it. Franco Moretti suggests that the bildungsroman, more than any other genre, "has portrayed and promoted modern [Western] socialization" (1987, 10), and I contend that it also undergirded the push for global expansion (that is, empire) by its dissemination of a model of civilized society.[17]

One food scene that works to reveal the type of agency Bich slowly accrues occurs when she visits the Jiffy grain hotel and she questions the strong influence that brands like Jiffy once had on her. Bich idolizes her friend Holly Jansen, and is particularly envious of Mrs. Jansen's baking. When Holly gets a homework assignment to complete a "Report on a Natural Phenomenon," Holly bypasses more obvious choices and instead describes her mother's baking: "how she stirred the ingredients together; how she bent to put the loaf pan in the oven. Holly watched the bread rise and grow brown and delicious-smelling" (Nguyen 2007, 80). Bich finds out that "the bread, it turned out, came from a Jiffy mix. Her blueberry muffins, too" (Nguyen 2007). Bich pressures Rosa to buy her the same mix but judges her own muffins to be inferior: "They were missing the element no one in my family could supply" (Nguyen 2007, 81).

Yet the missing ingredient is so murky that even when Nguyen reflects back on that moment, she cannot identify it. As a college student, she drives to the Jiffy Corporation in Chelsea, Michigan, and she stands in front of the Jiffy grain hotel. She is distraught to find it a "monstrous" and eerie building: "the town was quiet and small, hushed but for the hum of electricity and this building, its sustaining presence. Something about the moment filled me with fear – as if the grain hotel would fall down, smother and erase me" (Nguyen 2007, 81). The fact that the hotel does not "erase" or "smother" her testifies to the agency she has fostered over the years. The "blank unknown" of Michigan ironically allows Bich to write herself onto it, so that the decidedly unnatural phenomenon of Jiffy-inspired cooking ceases to alienate her. Bich begins to consider the unsettling aspects of large-scale food production: the depletion of the earth's resources and the accompanying impact on laborers. Agribusiness will in fact "smother and erase" the type of lifestyle she values.

In the chapter titled "Down with Grapes," Bich faces a conflict between her insatiable desire to consume and her growing awareness of its ecological ramifications. After stating that "Rosa loved a good strike," Bich describes Rosa's boycotting policies in honor of César Chávez: "we were all boycotting lettuce, grapes, and everything made by Campbell's" (Nguyen 2007, 121). Bich begins to connect herself to a cycle of production and consumption and the role of "underpaid and exploited migrants" who were affected by her food choices (Nguyen 2007). Significantly, the figure of Chávez speaks to Bich's "sense of justice, stirred from reading *The Grapes of Wrath*" (Nguyen 2007, 122). John Steinbeck's novel ([1939] 1976) depicts the hardships of the Joad family as they migrate west alongside thousands of similarly displaced Dust Bowl farmers. Bich is not sure whom she is supposed to support in the novel, or what the significance of Steinbeck's writing on the laboring classes is for Chávez and her "sense of justice." Bich is especially impressed with scenes of consumption in *The Grapes of Wrath* and focuses on how Tom Joad "wolfed down his three hamburger patties" and the thick slices of pork that Ma Joad cooks (Nguyen 2007, 122). Bich is confused and troubled by the collision of fiction and fact, especially as they affect her own consumption. As I mentioned earlier, Eileen Chia-Ching Fung stated that for ethnic subjects the act of consumption reveals "a complex, at times, contradictory cultural economy that links identity politics to the production of labor" (2011, ii). Although Bich feels betrayed by Rosa because Bich wants to seem more normal and like the other kids, who were not missing the beginning of the school year, Rosa simply states, "no one in our house is going to cross the picket lines" (Nguyen 2007, 121). This viewpoint eventually gets through to Bich. Suddenly, she cannot ignore the overlapping politics involved in acts of consumption and means of production.

No longer able to read around passages about the politics of consumption or the environmental degradation and human rights violations inherent in large-scale food production, Bich "trie[s] to imagine Ma Joad" among a crowd of teachers on strike (Nguyen 2007, 123). Rosa keeps Bich and her siblings home from school for two weeks in a gesture of solidarity with the teachers, and Bich participates in the strike despite her ambivalence about it. But when she is told, "Your *mom*'s a Communist" (Nguyen 2007, 123; emphasis in the original), Bich begins to lose faith in Rosa's politics. Against the backdrop of the United Farm Workers strike, Rosa serves Mexican rice, and Bich stages her own hunger strike while demanding "better food" (Nguyen 2007, 127). Exasperated, Bich tells Rosa that she is not her "real mother," and after a few days during which the two do not speak to each other, Bich "never again wished for Rosa to be . . . a homemaker" (129). "Down with Grapes" begins with the words "the world is full of mothers," but Bich realizes that Rosa is a good mother to her and more real than the other mothers she imagines are perfect (117).

In Nguyen's version of the memoir-as-nonfictionalized bildungsroman, the protagonist becomes aware of the broken system that she desires to join, and she can no longer disseminate it as a model of citizenship. The social structures within which Bich operates are depleted and unstable. According to Moretti, in the last phase of the bildungsroman the protagonist establishes a stable social position with a formed idea of the self – what I referred to earlier as a mapped subjectivity. Moretti emphasizes that the path to formation is one that "gives rise to unexpected hopes, thereby generating an interiority not only fuller than before, but also . . . perennially dissatisfied and restless" (1987, 4). He describes youth as a condition of increased exchanges between a subject's conscious and subconscious, influenced by his or her social, political, and environmental surroundings. Though Bich first craved a fully developed imago that fit with those of Betty Crocker and Laura Ingalls Wilder, we later find her resisting the process of what Moretti depicts as the loading of the ego.

A postcolonial understanding of self and society seems bound to conflict with the bildungsroman tradition. In the bildung process, a subject builds the self; expands one's subjectivity, acquires jobs, partners, homes, and children; and aligns himself or herself with a set of societal coordinates, while notions of nationhood and empire bleed across the map. Bich does not reverse the bildungsroman process, but her consumption practices deconstruct the forms of selfhood she once valued. She understands that by leaving home, she is not leaving her past behind: isolation is not a way to escape from what Edward Said has called the "cultural integrity of empire" (1994, 106–10). How does Nguyen handle such fraught issues of self-representation within the confines of popular fiction? Nguyen deploys powerful anticolonial symbolism in palatable ways. What Bich must unlearn are the very things that, according to the bildungsroman model, she should be acquiring. Instead of accruing information that is heavily informed by the binary model of a violent and racialized borderland, instead of expanding her subjectivity, Bich tries to strip away the misguided modes of education and growth to which she once clung.

The intimate ties between ethnic identity and culinary practices in US immigrant literatures are a recurring motif that attests to the importance of the body. The effect of media marketing and the codifying of food practices have estranged food from the human body, which results in multiple estrangements for immigrants. Nguyen's memories of her obsession with American processed food and her alienation from homemade American food offer a rich geography of foodscapes and emphasize their importance in the immigrant experience. *Stealing Buddha's Dinner* ultimately suggests that in the contested territory of first-generation American subjectivity, one's conflicted desires wreak havoc on the body.

The most crushing moments in Nguyen's memoir are those filled with a catastrophic sense of loss and sadness. These moments are haunted by Nguyen's inability to reconcile her deep connection to narratives of US expansion with a past that feels spectral and unreal; stories about expansion westward that in effect went east, both in terms of food and American imperialism. In President Calvin Coolidge's 1925 speech to the Farm Bureau Federation, he favors the collective over the individual, the network over the node, and he makes clear his aims to recruit power from small farms and people from diverse backgrounds in order for America to demonstrate its prowess. According to Coolidge, a robust US economy, driven by agriculture, is consistent with the notion that individual farmers and small farms must subscribe to a new era of industrial agriculture. As a child, Nguyen could not possibly connect policy making in the 1920s to her feelings of dislocation; but the two are enmeshed in surprising ways. As further evidence of the deep repercussions that reading idealized versions of pioneer life had on Bich Mihn Nguyen, her next book after *Stealing Buddha's Dinner: A Memoir* (2007) is *Pioneer Girl: A Novel* (2014). Significantly, Nguyen moves away from food memoir to food fiction, so to speak, and both books center on food and narratives of westward expansion – *Pioneer Girl* more explicitly so.

The imbricated layers of nationalistic rhetoric housed in culinary discourse are complex and confusing, especially for refugees and immigrants whose country of origin has already been destabilized by imperialist regimes and political violence. In Nguyen's case, the intoxicating culinary and literary discourse she longs to be a part of as a little girl becomes a toxic landscape of alienation. Bich's corporeally anchored moments of interaction with food – both through fiction and outside of it – disrupt accepted notions of US citizenship and reveal the collision course she is on as a child who wants to become "the whitest girl possible" (2007, 163). She eventually usurps a power structure that will alienate and absorb her. Nguyen uses imaginative and subversive methodologies to bring our awareness back to a material corporeality.

Notes

1 Coolidge's speech anticipates a future filled with companies such as Monsanto that will produce food and chemical weapons in abundance. A great deal has been written about Monsanto and its practices of seed patenting, its usage of PCBs (polychlorinated

biphenyl) and DDT (dichlorodiphenyltrichloroethane), and its funding of nuclear weapons. The sources on which I most relied are Robin (2010) and Louv (2013).

2 To read Jefferson's own meditations on farming, see Jefferson (1774–1824). Two historians in particular helped me formulate my thoughts on how Jefferson's legacy has been manipulated through history to suit the needs of various politicos at different times (see Cogliano 2006, 2014; Peterson [1960] 1998).

3 The multiple meanings of consumption patterns are a central focus of Asian American diasporic and immigrant authors (see, for example, Kingston 1975; Lee 1990; Nieh 1988; Wong 1945). Culinary memoir is a particularly interesting medium because the body's function as a somatic memory bank is filtered by the memoirist's authorial decisions. Given his writing trajectory from food discourse to deep ecology and ecocriticism, Paul Outka's work (1997) on Kingston is especially relevant. For complex analyses of the particularities of Asian American food inside and outside of the United States, see Ku (2014); Mannur (2007, 2010).

4 Henry Nash Smith (1950) clearly outlines the importance of Frederick Jackson Turner's historicization of the frontier in US culture. Smith was criticized for his failure to recognize the violence involved in the ideas of Manifest Destiny and westward expansion and later reconsidered his own work. As a counterbalance to Smith's book, see Athearn (1986) and Slotkin (1973). Both Slotkin and Athearn condemn the ease with which Americans have thus far deployed the notion of a western frontier and mapped it onto blank territory. For more on the occlusion of Native American history and its relation to frontier myths, see Deloria (1998), Drinnon (1980), and Limerick (1987). Donald Worster is still regarded as having founded new Western history and seamlessly connecting ecological disturbance with westward expansion (1985, 1992).

5 The Indian Intercourse Act of 1834, backed by President Andrew Jackson, granted Native American tribes specific territories and a large amount of land. Yet from the 1840s onward, as partially demonstrated by the language used by O'Sullivan, Congress shifted direction and passed a series of territorial adjustments, overt efforts to claim for the railroads and thus for US industry land that had been granted to the tribes. To enforce these adjustments and displace Native Americans who were living on the land, the United States went to war with the Arapahoe, Sioux, and Cheyenne tribes. For more on US relations with Native Americans, the term "genocide," and the legalities of violence and displacement, see Jaimes (1992), Purcha (1962), and Rosen (2004).

6 Anita Mannur might term Nguyen's cravings as participation in "culinary citizenship" or "a form of affective citizenship which grants subjects the ability to claim and inhabit certain subject positions via their relationship to food" (2010, 20). For more on the negotiation of identity through foodways from the late eighteenth century on, see Gabaccia (1998). Linda Brown and Kay Mussell's introduction to their edited volume, *Ethnic and Regional Foodways in the United States* (1984), is a more regionally focused study; it presents a strong overview of performativity in foodways. For more on US ethnic foodways, symbolism, and performance in the same volume, see Kalčik (1984).

7 I am in part indebted to Appadurai's work for my terminology and, of course, to the many works on ethnic foodways. In addition to the photography of food landscapes, which are called "foodscapes," the term "foodscapes" is employed by a handful of other critics as a reference to engineered environments (Sobal and Wansink 2007) and as a visual argument for ethical consumption (Dolphijn 2004).

8 Scholars are paying increasing attention to the intersection of Asian American fiction, identity, and practices of consumption. For discussions of food and fiction, see Gardaphé and Xu (2007), Ku (2014), Wong (1993), and Xu (2008). For perspectives in US multiethnic culinary writing, see Avakian (1997).

9 I thank Stephen Hong Sohn for pointing out that food and cuisine is often the marker of ethnic authenticity and becomes a way for "minority" writers to make their identity stand out. In Bich's case it is her anti-identitarian claims that are troubling. She desires everything but Vietnamese food as a marker of her identity.

10 Sau-ling Cynthia Wong (1993) and Wenying Xu (2008) compellingly argue that food plays a central role in Asian American writing and often serves as a metaphoric and synecdochic symbol of alternately escaping and embracing one's ethnic ties.

11 Roland Barthes proposes a "widening of the very notion of food" from mere matter to a "system of communication" and "a body of images" ([1961] 2013, 24). Indeed, symbolic anthropologists have long studied the textual significance of gastronomic exchange. Symbolic anthropologists – including Mary Douglas, Clifford Geertz, Roland Barthes, and Claude Lévi-Strauss – laid much of the groundwork for later work in the field of food studies (Brown and Mussell 1984, 12).

12 Bourdieu argues that a subject enters into the discourse of a given social class via his or her everyday choices, and of course eating habits are chief among the ways in which the body is shaped by one's habitus. Habitus, or people's everyday social practices, is shaped by both external influences and predetermined categories such as class or family. According to Bourdieu, corporeal functions and appearance indicate social stratification: "the body is the most indisputable materialization of class taste" (1984, 190). Scholars note that one of Bourdieu's most significant contributions is his insistence on evaluating cultural influences on the production of societies: "for him food habits represent a naturalization of ideology" (Atkins and Bowler 2001, 6–7).

13 Shirley Geok-lin Lim recalls that when she experienced the physical and metaphorical cold and isolation of Massachusetts as an immigrant, she had an overwhelming "craving for sugar" and "tried bars of Mars, Mounds . . . Baby Ruth, Snickers, Bounty, and liked them all" (1996, 145). Yet Lim writes that she rejected American food and that "for the first year in the United States I was always hungry, a hunger that rebelled against American food" (148). Instead of buying groceries that seemed plastic and fake, she subsisted on candy from vending machines and used it as a bulwark against isolation and heartbreak (149). While Nguyen uses candy as an imaginative space of American identity, Lim employs it as a protective shield against full absorption into the hegemonic US culture. Both authors symbolically link American candy to American citizenship, something that for Lim does not happen until the birth of her son (194).

14 Bich's media-driven obsession with all things American may be explained by Susan Bordo's analysis of visual rhetoric in the 1980s. Bordo points out that the media's "claims of cultural diversity" were weakened by the representations of women that privileged "slenderness" and whiteness over different body types (1993, 35). Nguyen's own analysis of her younger self reiterates Bordo's research and is further testament to the ways in which Bich could not see herself represented in the popular media's narratives of American identity. Addressing the issue of technology and the gendered body in the late twentieth century, Anne Balsamo writes, "by the end of the 1980s the idea of the merger of the biological with the technological has infiltrated the imagination of Western culture" (1996, 5). Thus we have two different critics' views of the culture of the 1980s. Bordo posits that beauty standards were not only more visible but also more whitewashed, while Balsamo suggests that people were prompted to foresee a technologically enhanced body and better future.

15 A study looking at the role of "healthy" and "junk" foods in teen women's culture has shown that young women associate the consumption of junk food with independence from the home, while home-cooked meals connote family time and domesticity (Beagan and Chapman 1993, 108).

16 Claude Lévi-Strauss's (1975) formulation of the raw-cooked axis probes the power of food as language. The raw is what naturally occurs, while the cooked is human cultural productions. Lévi-Strauss saw food as atypical in its ability to cross the border between nature and culture. The study of myth (or stories) reveals where the raw ends and the cooked begins, or how the two function in relation to one another. The raw-cooked dichotomy is echoed in current scholarship.

17 Patricia P. Chu's (2000) illuminating research on Asian American literary tradition of the bildungsroman are greatly relevant to my readings of Nguyen; as a counterpoint, Alicia Otano's groundbreaking work (2004) examines Asian American bildungsroman as portrayed by US writing.

References

Appadurai, Arjun. 1996. *Modernity at Large: Cultural Dimensions of Globalization*. Minneapolis: University of Minnesota Press.

Ashby, W.H. 1901. n.d. "First Homesteader Can Prove His Title Clear." September 8. *Omaha World Herald*. Access provided by NewsBank/Readex, Database: America's Historical Newspapers, SQN: 111877E5267615A8.

Athearn, Robert G. 1986. *The Mythic West in Twentieth-Century America*. Lawrence: University Press of Kansas.

Atkins, Peter, and Ian Bowler. 2001. *Food in Society: Economy, Culture, Geography*. Oxford: Oxford University Press.

Avakian, Arlene Voski, ed. 1997. *Through the Kitchen Window: Women Writers Explore the Intimate Meanings of Food and Cooking*. Boston, MA: Beacon.

Balsamo, Anne. 1996. *Technologies of the Gendered Body: Reading Cyborg Women*. Durham, NC: Duke University Press.

Barthes, Roland. (1961) 2013. "Towards a Psychosociology of Contemporary Food Consumption." Reprinted in *Food and Culture: A Reader*, edited by Carole Counihan and Penny Van Esterik, 3rd ed., 23–30. New York: Routledge.

Beagan, Brenda L., and Gwen E. Chapman. 1993. "'Junk Food' and 'Healthy Food': Meanings of Foods in Adolescent Women's Culture." *Journal of Nutrition Education* 25 (3): 108–13.

Belén, Martín-Lucas. 2011. "Burning Down the Little House on the Prairie: Asian Pioneers in Contemporary North America." *Atlantis* 33 (2): 27–41.

Bentley, Amy. 1998. *Eating for Victory: Food Rationing and the Politics of Domesticity*. Chicago: University of Illinois Press.

Bordo, Susan. 1993. *Unbearable Weight: Feminism, Western Culture, and the Body*. Berkeley, CA: University of California Press.

Bourdieu, Pierre. 1984. *Distinction: A Social Critique of the Judgment of Taste*. Translated by Richard Nice. Cambridge, MA: Harvard University Press.

Brown, Linda Keller, and Kay Mussell. 1984. Introduction to *Ethnic and Regional Foodways in the United States: The Performance of Group Identity*, edited by Linda Keller Brown and Kay Mussell, 3–18. Knoxville: University of Tennessee Press.

Carruth, Allison. 2013. *Global Appetites: American Power and the Literature of Food*. New York: Cambridge University Press.

Chiu, Monica. 2004. *Filthy Fictions: Asian American Literature by Women*. Walnut Creek, CA: AltaMira Press.

Chu, Patricia P. 2000. *Assimilating Asians: Gendered Strategies of Authorship in Asian America*. Durham, NC: Duke University Press.

Cogliano, Francis D. 2006. *Thomas Jefferson: Reputation and Legacy*. New Haven, CT: Yale University Press.

———. 2014. *Emperor of Liberty: Thomas Jefferson's Foreign Policy*. Edinburgh: Edinburgh University Press.

Coolidge, Calvin. 1925. "Address before the Annual Convention of the American Farm Bureau Federation, Chicago, Ill., December 7, 1925." Library of Congress. http://memory.loc.gov/cgi-bin/query/h?ammem/coolbib:@field(NUMBER+@band(amrlm+ms09)).

Deloria, Phillip J. 1998. *Playing Indian*. New Haven, CT: Yale University Press.

Dolphijn, Rick. 2004. *Foodscapes: Towards a Deleuzian Ethics of Consumption*. Delft, the Netherlands: Eburon.

Douglas, Mary. 1972. "Deciphering a Meal." *Daedalus* 101: 61–81.

Drinnon, Richard. 1980. *Facing West: The Metaphysics of Indian-Hating and Empire-Building*. Minneapolis: University of Minnesota Press.

Fong-Torres, Ben. 2007. "Book Review: *Stealing Buddha's Dinner*." February 5. http://www.nytimes.com/2007/02/05/arts/05iht-bookmar.4474719.html.

Fung, Eileen Chia-Ching. 2011. Introduction to "Teaching Food and Foodways in Asian American Literature and Popular Culture." *Asian American Literature: Discourses and Pedagogies* 2: i–iii.

Gabaccia, Donna. 1998. *We Are What We Eat: Ethnic Food and the Making of Americans.* Cambridge, MA: Harvard University Press.

Gardaphé, Fred L., and Wenying Xu. 2007. "Introduction: Food in Multi-Ethnic Literatures." *MELUS* 32 (4): 5–10.

Hirsch, Marianne. 1979. "The Novel of Formation as Genre: Between Great Expectations and Lost Illusions." *Genre* 12 (3): 293–311.

Ho, Jennifer A. 2005. *Consumption and Identity in Asian American Coming-of-Age Novels.* New York: Routledge.

Homestead Act of 1862. 1862. Pub. L. No. 37–64. http://www.ourdocuments.gov/doc.php?flash=true&doc=31&page=transcript.

"Homestead National Monument: Its Establishment and Administration." 2009. National Park Service, November 2. http://www.nps.gov/parkhistory/online_books/home/history/sec1.htm.

Jaimes, M. Annette, ed. 1992. *The State of Native America: Genocide, Colonization, and Resistance.* Boston, MA: South End Press.

Jefferson, Thomas. 1774–1824. *Farm Book.* In the Thomas Jefferson Papers: An Electronic Archive. Original manuscript from the Coolidge Collection of Thomas Jefferson Manuscripts. Boston, MA: Massachusetts Historical Society. http://www.masshist.org/thomasjeffersonpapers/doc?id=farm_c2&mode=lgImg.

Kalčik, Susan. 1984. "Ethnic Foodways in America: Symbol and the Performance of Identity." In *Ethnic and Regional Foodways in the United States: The Performance of Group Identity*, edited by Linda Keller Brown and Kay Mussell, 37–66. Knoxville: University of Tennessee Press.

Kingston, Maxine Hong. 1975. *The Woman Warrior: Memoirs of a Girlhood Among Ghosts.* New York: Knopf.

Ku, Robert Ji-Song. 2014. *Dubious Gastronomy: The Cultural Politics of Eating Asian in the USA.* Honolulu: University of Hawaii Press.

Lee, Li-Young. 1990. "The Cleaving." In *The City in Which I Love You*, 77–87. Rochester, NY: BOA Editions Limited.

Lévi-Strauss, Claude. 1975. *The Raw and the Cooked.* New York: Harper and Row.

Lim, Shirley Geok-lin. 1996. *Among the White Moon Faces: An Asian-American Memoir of Homelands.* New York: Feminist Press.

Limerick, Patricia Nelson. 1987. *The Legacy of Conquest: The Unbroken Past of the American West.* New York: W.W. Norton.

Louv, Jason. 2013. *Monsanto vs. the World: The Monsanto Protection Act, GMOs and Our Genetically Modified Future.* London: Ultraculture Press.

Lowe, Lisa. 1996. *Immigrant Acts: On Asian American Cultural Politics.* Durham, NC: Duke University Press.

Mannur, Anita. 2007. "Culinary Nostalgia: Authenticity, Nationalism, and Diaspora." *MELUS* 32 (4): 11–31.

———. 2010. *Culinary Fictions: Food in South Asian Diasporic Culture*. Philadelphia: Temple University Press.

Moraga, Cherríe L. 1994. *Heroes and Saints.* In *Heroes and Saints and Other Plays*, 85–149. Albuquerque, NM: West End Press.

Moretti, Franco. 1987. *The Way of the World: The Bildungsroman in European Culture*. London: Verso.

Morton, Timothy. 2004. "Afterword: Let Them Eat Romanticism: Materialism, Ideology, and Diet Studies." In *Cultures of Taste, Theories of Appetite: Eating Romanticism*, edited by Timothy Morton, 257–75. New York: Palgrave Macmillan.

Nguyen, Bich Minh. 2007. *Stealing Buddha's Dinner: A Memoir.* New York: Viking.

———. 2009. *Short Girls: A Novel.* New York: Viking.

———. 2014. *Pioneer Girl: A Novel.* New York: Viking.

Nieh, Hualing. 1988. *Mulberry and Peach: Two Women of China*. Translated by Jane Parish Yang and Linda Lappin. Boston, MA: Beacon Press.

O'Sullivan, John L. 1845. "Annexation." *United States Magazine and Democratic Review* 17 (1): 5–10.

Otano, Alicia. 2004. *Speaking the Past: Child Perspective in the Asian American "Bildungsroman."*. Münster, Germany: LIT.

Outka, Paul. 1997. "Publish or Perish: Food, Hunger, and Self-Construction in Maxine Hong Kingston's *The Woman Warrior*." *Contemporary Literature* 38 (3): 447–82.

Ozeki, Ruth. 1998. *My Year of Meats.* New York: Penguin.

Peterson, Merrill D. (1960) 1998. *The Jefferson Image in the American Mind*. Reprint, Charlottesville: University of Virginia Press.

Purcha, Francis Paul. 1962. *America Indian Policy in the Formative Years: The Indian Trade and Intercourse Acts 1790–1834*. Lincoln: University of Nebraska Press.

Robin, Marie-Monique. 2010. *The World According to Monsanto: Pollution, Corruption, and the Control of Our Food Supply.* Translated by George Holoch. New York: New Press.

Rosen, Deborah A. 2004. "Colonization Through Law: The Judicial Defense of State Indian Legislation, 1790–1880." *American Journal of Legal History* 46 (1): 26–54.

Said, Edward W. 1994. *Culture and Imperialism*. New York: Vintage.

Slaughter, Joseph R. 2007. *Human Rights, Inc.: The World Novel, Narrative Form, and International Law.* New York: Fordham University Press.

Slotkin, Richard. 1973. *Regeneration Through Violence: The Mythology of the American Frontier, 1600–1860*. Norman: University of Oklahoma Press.

Smith, Henry Nash. 1950. *Virgin Land: The American West as a Symbol and Myth*. Cambridge, MA: Harvard University Press.

Sobal, Jeffery, and Brian Wansink. 2007. "Kitchenscapes, Tablescapes, Platescapes, and Foodscapes." *Environment and Behavior* 39 (1): 124–42.

Sohn, Stephen Hong. 2014. *Racial Asymmetries: Asian American Fictional Worlds.* New York: New York University Press.

Steinbeck, John. (1939) 1976. *The Grapes of Wrath*. Reprint, New York: Penguin.

Steinbeck, John, and Edward F. Ricketts. (1941) 2009. *Sea of Cortez: A Leisurely Journal of Travel and Research*. Reprint, New York: Penguin.

Turner, Frederick Jackson. 1920. *The Frontier in American History*. New York: Henry Holt and Company.

Wilder, Laura Ingalls. (1932) 2004. *Little House in the Big Woods.* Reprint, New York: HarperCollins.

———. (1933) 2004. *Farmer Boy.* Reprint, New York: HarperCollins Publishers.

———. (1935) 2004. *Little House on the Prairie.* Reprint, New York: HarperCollins.

———. (1937) 2004. *On the Banks of Plum Creek*. Reprint, New York: HarperCollins.

———. (1939) 2004. *By the Shores of Silver Lake.* Reprint, New York: HarperCollins.

———. (1940) 2003. *The Long Winter.* Reprint, New York: HarperCollins Publishers.

———. (1941) 1971. *Little Town on the Prairie.* Reprint, New York: HarperCollins.

———. (1943) 1971. *These Happy Golden Years.* Reprint, New York: HarperCollins.

———. (1971) 2004. *The First Four Years.* Reprint, New York: HarperCollins.

Wong, Jade Snow. 1945. *Fifth Chinese Daughter.* New York: Harper.

Wong, Sau-ling Cynthia. 1993. "Big Eaters, Treat Lovers, 'Food Prostitutes,' 'Food Pornographers,' and Doughnut Makers." In *Reading Asian American Literature: From Necessity to Extravagance*, 18–76. Princeton, NJ: Princeton University Press.

Worster, Donald. 1985. *Rivers of Empire: Water, Aridity, and the Growth of the American West.* New York: Random House.

———. 1992. *Under Western Skies: Nature and History in the American West.* Oxford: Oxford University Press.

Xu, Wenying. 2008. *Eating Identities: Reading Food in Asian American Literature.* Honolulu: University of Hawaii Press.

4 Toxic and illegible bodies

> San Francisco's Loron Hodge, 65-year-old executive director of the Kern County Farm Bureau, remembers growing up in Tulare County and helping his father in the alfalfa fields. "I never had any adverse reactions," he said. "Now, why would I have such a good life? I don't think you can explain it. There are people who adapt to this valley and people who do not."
>
> *SFGate*, 2004

In Loron Hodge's response to journalists about a 1992–2001 study that reported high infant mortality rates in Kern County, California, he employs a Darwinian approach to abnormal statistics. Some people adapt well, while others do not. The simplicity of his explanation takes a blunt edge to the underbelly of agricultural production and recasts it as a narrative of survival of the fittest. Hodge unwittingly naturalizes ecological and interpersonal violence. The 1992–2001 study focused on "Hispanic women" living in Kern County who inhabit "four of the 10 California ZIP codes with the highest rates of infant death" (Holding and McCormick 2004). Hodge's understanding of the survival of the fittest is in sync with a new moment in modernity – the turn of the twentieth century – where the reallocation of risk is commonplace and our own health becomes the litmus test for the state of the world around us. The haphazard nature of toxic exposure further underscores that where industrialization and its outliers are concerned, risk and disease do not follow a predictable pattern.

Hodge identifies the shifting ways in which we understand our participatory practices in risky behaviors to be individual and not communal. His reaction also reveals the easy deflection of responsibility and nostalgia for a time past of "alfalfa fields" (quoted in Holding and McCormick 2004). Interviewed in 2004 for an *SFGate* investigative series on infant death and health issues in Kern County, Hodge's words distill complex systems of production, processing, and global trade into the imago of a child in the fields helping his father. As executive director of the Kern County Farm Bureau, Hodge romanticizes a sprawling industrialized system by articulating what for most people remains an enduring pastoral fantasy of the Central Valley and the Midwest, the places that allow us to have food on our tables. The extreme dissonance between that fantasy and the reality is a gulf too large to bridge. According to the California Department of Food and Agriculture, in 2014 alone California's "76,400 farms and ranches received approximately $54 billion for their output" (2015). Milk and cattle production made up $13.1 billion, or 24 percent of total monetized output. Even excluding poultry, eggs, and other animal products, the statistics betray the complex food system undergirding California's economy. Together with field crops and fruits, California's total export value in 2014 was over $50 billion.[1] Overall, in 2014 US "agriculture-related industries contributed $835 billion to US gross domestic product" and of that US farms contributed $177.2 billion.[2] Following World War II, US agriculture expanded at blistering speed with animal production facilities and single-crop farms that allowed for a focalized intensity in production.

Both Cherríe Moraga's play *Heroes and Saints* (1994b) and Ruth Ozeki's novel *My Year of Meats* (1998), are works of fiction that express the effects of endocrine disruption as a direct result of the agricultural industry. They put down on the page (Ozeki) and on stage (Moraga) by-products of what environmental historian Linda Nash denotes as the Central Valley's history of "the relentless domination of space by capital and technology" (2007, 2). Moraga and Ozeki use the female body in particular to explore the intersection of environmental justice, gender, and the overlapping human and animal experiences of illness. This chapter attends to the voices of technologically poisoned female bodies across genres as well as documentary footage. I build on the writings of Pierre Bourdieu (1991), Linda Nash (2007), and Edward Soja (1989), and I contend that Moraga and Ozeki work to denaturalize what it means to "adapt," as Hodge phrases it, because to adapt in their narratives of industrial agriculture means that one's survival depends on the elided deaths of others.

Environmental justice and ecocritical approaches to literature often identify the field as being "vision deficient" because matters such as species extinction lack the dramatic impact and riveting optics that captivate the public's attention. Rob Nixon articulates this conundrum best and asks the question, "In an age when the media venerate the spectacular . . . how can we convert into image and narrative the disasters . . . that are anonymous and that star nobody . . . ?" (2011, 3). This chapter discusses two works that deal with the opposite issue: they are visually vibrant, the prose is supple and indulges in more detailed descriptions of dead bodies (that of animals and children), and yet we are continually refocused on the long shot and not the close-up. In transferring of our attention between micro and macro, Ozeki and Moraga enact a denial of full access to their audiences. Sociologist Pierre Bourdieu states that in order to enable people to fundamentally shift their thinking, they must be "astonished and disconcerted" and that is "why you sometimes have to begin with the most difficult things in order to understand the easier things properly" (1991, 207). I see Bourdieu's theory manifest in the shock-and-awe narrative techniques of Moraga and Ozeki, who present the reader and viewer with hyperbolic and surreal moments of violence and quickly contrast them with the banal. Their tactical approach alters the audience's experience of time and space.

California's Central Valley has already appeared in *Environmental Justice in Contemporary US Narratives* as a site of extremes. John Steinbeck's *The Grapes of Wrath* ([1939] 1976) depicts the challenges of Dust Bowl migrants in California's San Joaquin Valley. While it is now widely accepted as a literary classic, it was polarizing at the time of its publication and was banned in Kern County, California. Another work specifically about the Central Valley and abusive labor practices is *Heroes and Saints* (1994b).[3] *Heroes and Saints*, by the author and dramaturge Cherríe Moraga, is lesser known even within her own oeuvre.[4] Steinbeck identified state-driven industrialization as the evil that caused the Dust Bowl, but he did not have the scientific tools to make sense of apparently unrelated outliers: human mental instability, animal illness, and a general sense of malaise among workers. Steinbeck had difficulty defining the causal relationship between human intervention in nature and human disease. Nonetheless, he sensed that California's Central Valley would suffer at the hands of agribusiness and become a hotbed of toxicity and disease. Like Moraga and Ozeki, he directly questioned the divides between the synthetic and the man-made, in particular how the latter claims to create and control the former.

The body as a material nexus for ecological and sociocultural ills in disease-based narratives is of paramount importance, especially as related to food systems and environmental justice. According to the National Institute of Environmental Health Sciences (NIEHS), there is a "range of substances, both natural and man-made . . . thought to cause endocrine disruption" (2016). The NIEHS warns that endocrine disruption "may pose the greatest risk during prenatal and early postnatal development when organ and neural systems are forming" (2016). Both Moraga and Ozeki usurp accepted ideas of how sickness manifests and progresses and how women's bodies are particularly at risk.[5] They endow agricultural products (grapes and beef, respectively) with meaning and agency in ways that reanimate the discourse of what Carol J. Adams (1990) describes as the sexual politics of meat, the idea that the meat industry objectifies and then fragments a subject (the animal) in order to render it palatable to the consumer. She identifies a dual erasure of both female and animal bodies in the production of dairy and meat. Alongside a revitalization of inanimate objects (beef, grapes), comes the question of origin. Adams underlines the correlation between patriarchy and the oppression of animals, charting a system wherein the animal as a biological being and whole body is obliterated when presented as a piece of meat, and likewise how women's bodies suffer the same fate when sexualized and displayed as separate parts. This chapter builds on ecofeminist readings of the connections between women's bodies and the environment.[6] Moraga and Ozeki identify the ills of a food system gone awry, and they do so not only by pointing to the empty referents implicit in a single grape or slice of beef (that is, the absented human and animal bodies), but also by allowing their audiences to imagine the vast, monetized networks through which such products travel. If audiences begin to imagine not only the capital behind such circulation but their facilitation of it, then the renderings of absented human and animal bodies suggests our involvement in that circulation as part of an infrastructure that we are helping to sustain.

Moraga and Ozeki communicate in highly tactile and visual language, and they are influenced by film as a medium of communication. Drawing on visual rhetoric in addition to the written word, they encourage a type of distracted reading and viewing that necessitates a perpetual questioning of medium and apparatus. They tell stories in ways that are jarring and disorienting at times, cultivating a relationship with the reader and viewer whereby in order to reorient yourself, you must engage more fully with the work. The play and the novel partially reveal their staged natures and therefore also present opportunities for critique. Commenting on the contrasting narrative perspectives within Ozeki's novel, Allison Carruth identifies "a conflict between these two registers – the interpersonal and the systemic" (2013, 118). Carruth rightly notes the constant scale jumping between the planetary and the microscopic, the personal and the public, and in these two texts in particular, the close-up versus the long shot. Indeed, in both *Heroes and Saints* and *My Year of Meats* the transnational trade of goods and the local impact of that trade on human bodies is repeatedly portrayed in visceral and disturbing ways.

DES and DDT

Like Moraga's *Heroes and Saints*, Ozeki's *My Year of Meats* is a fictional account in part about the nonfictional poisoning of women. It is also about the deployment of pesticides and hormones that the agricultural industry used during the same time period – and spilling over into the present – that have similarly lethal effects. The synthetic hormone diethylstilbestrol (DES, the main toxin discussed in *My Year of Meats*) and dichlorodiphenyltrichloroethane (DDT, not directly referred to in *Heroes and Saints* but the predecessor of the chemicals Moraga writes about) are known endocrine disruptors that cause birth defects, cancer, and a long list of lesser side effects. While in Moraga's play women suffer in part due to the involuntary absorption of poisonous pesticides, in Ozeki's novel they are most affected by the voluntary ingestion of DES.

A plant-based synthetic estrogen, DES was widely used from 1938 to 1971 in women and livestock to generate what were thought to be robust pregnancies and offspring. DDT was banned from agricultural use in the United States in 1972 and has a more public legacy than that of DES, in part because to discuss DES would entail exposing the gendered nature of its administration to humans and the continued problems of its ties to the meat and dairy industries in the United States. The Pesticide Action Network, North America (Kegley et al. 2014) lists methyl bromide, dinoseb, parathion, and phosdrin as "suspected" endocrine disruptors.[7] Alarmingly, these are four of the five pesticides that the United Farm Workers of America (UFW) worked to eliminate under the leadership of César Chávez. According to the NIEHS, "From animal studies, researchers have learned much about the mechanisms through which endocrine disruptors influence the endocrine system and alter hormonal functions. . . . Chemicals that are known endocrine disruptors include diethylstilbestrol (the synthetic estrogen DES), dioxin and dioxin-like compounds, polychlorinated biphenyls (PCBs), DDT, and some other pesticides." (2016). The animal studies part is vital because there is little chance that science will move beyond this. Even the minimal studies done prove a causal link between PCB exposure and later manifestations of cancer and reproductive-related illnesses.[8] Thus, to change regulations, the burden of proof is on the consumer to demonstrate the substances' harmful effects. While research on the impact of PCB exposure in women is increasing, the lack of studies and the dearth of information available on the effects on women's bodies and reproductive health is disturbing. In the feedback loop of corporate negligence, human and environmental degradation, and public misinformation, the consumer takes on risk without knowledge or warning.

Both *Heroes and Saints* and *My Year of Meats* are exercises in storytelling: they narrativize unfathomable data and facts. Telling stories of greed that disregard the value of human and other forms of life is made all the more challenging by having to address the fact that certain human bodies are seen as disposable and part of the expected loss of a profit-and-loss formula. Telling stories with a common thread of often-undetectable and lethal chemicals that most people have never heard of is doubly challenging. Endocrine disruptors like DES and derivatives of DDT defy predictability. As Nancy Langston writes in her groundbreaking work on DES, "instead of being dose dependent, with a threshold below which the chemical is safe," endocrine disruptors behave unpredictably in four important ways: dose, threshold level of toxicity, timing (how long after exposure the effects last), and age of the people they affect (2010, 5–6).

Ozeki's novel and Moraga's play tackle similar issues of pollution, globalized and industrialized agribusiness, and the largely migrant workers who suffer most as a result. Moraga uses a fixed locale and clearly outlined community to add urgency to her presentation of issues that might otherwise be difficult to imagine. Ozeki, on the other hand, drives home the impact of the global consumption of meat and dairy by locating her two protagonists in the United States and Japan. *Heroes and Saints* and *My Year of Meats* delineate both the challenges and the urgency of seeking environmental justice. In Moraga's play, *Cerezita*, the child protagonist who has visible signs of pesticide poisoning adamantly tells the community priest, Father Juan, "Nobody's dying should be invisible, Juan. Nobody's" (1994b, 139). Yet clearly there is a hierarchy of death in the world, based on wealth, race, gender, and class – and species. In direct challenge to Cerezita's claim that "nobody's dying should be invisible" are the disregarded deaths of migrant workers and animals, and the illnesses in later generations caused by the ingestion of harmful substances.

Valleys and vistas

California's Central Valley is known more for its dramatic landscapes and beauty than for the astonishing quantity of meat, dairy, and nuts that leaves the valley for destinations around the world. Delano, Visalia, and McFarland are at the epicenter of agricultural production. In 2004, Tom Frantz, a teacher and environmental activist in Kern County, California (a two-hour drive inland from Los Angeles), showed journalists around the county to give them a sense of the scope of the risk posed by agricultural pollutants. After Frantz drove them through the county, they reported their disbelief at the artificiality behind Kern County's biggest industry: "Here, the pesticides change with the seasons. In April, farmers spray herbicides to clear their fields for planting. In May, hormones are applied to make the grapevines bloom. In June, agricultural crews use a chemical fungicide to prevent fruit from rotting. In August, they add sulfur to get rid of mildew" (Holding and McCormick 2004). Frantz paints a portrait of seasonal change driven not by nature, but coaxed by and dependent on synthetic substances. In fact, the pesticides do not "change with the seasons"; instead, hormones produce spring by making grapevines bloom.

The bodies of mothers in McFarland contain the poisonous residue of negligent greed and toxic man-made chemicals. Herbicides, synthetic hormones, fungicide, and sulfur by no means constitute a comprehensive list of pollutants absorbed by the fetus, the part of an expectant mother that is most vulnerable to chemical exposure.[9] In fact, doctors and biologists agree that most of the chemicals circulated in McFarland and in the valley at large were likely not disclosed by the companies that used them for fear of being held legally accountable for the medical expenses of the people who worked or lived near production centers. The stillborn babies and deformed and cancer-ridden children delivered by McFarland mothers in the 1980s manifested what their families knew to be true: fetuses were ingesting significant amounts of toxins before birth because their mothers were being exposed to dangerous levels of lethal chemicals. Most shocking to subsequent investigators of the McFarland children diagnosed with cancer between 1978 and 1988 was that nine different types of cancer were identified. Beverly Paigen, a biochemist and geneticist formerly at Children's Hospital in Oakland, explained that what might account for the different cancers is a process called somatic recombination (see Newman 1989; Sexton and Linder 2010; Siegrist, Cvetkovich, and Gutscher 2001). Somatic recombination is triggered by toxic agents and results in the change of genetic arrangement. In other words, when a toxic agent alters a single gene, many different types of cancer can develop. This process metonymically links the "purely" biological process that caused an explosion of illness to the environmental justice movement that ensued. The inextricable ties between humans and between things and humans are exposed when something mutates or falls out of balance.

The valley of McLaughlin in Moraga's *Heroes and Saints* (a fictional name referring to McFarland, California), just like the valley in Steinbeck's *Grapes of Wrath*, is bountiful yet dangerous: "But we, we live in a land of plenty. The fruits that pass through your fingers are too many to count – luscious red in their strawberry wonder. . . . And yet, you suffer at the same hands" (Moraga 1994b, 148). To "suffer at the same hands" could be read as referring both to the violation of human rights in terms of overworking field laborers and to the toxic effects of coming into contact with poisonous chemicals in the fields. The Natural Resources Defense Council describes a defining impetus of environmental justice activism as instances when "communities of color, which are often poor, are routinely targeted to host facilities that have negative environmental impacts – say, a landfill, dirty industrial plant or truck depot" (Skelton and Miller 2006). The cancer cluster of McFarland is a microcosm that is used to question corporate ethics and government ambivalence about human suffering. People's anger over the denial of the cancer cluster, coupled with the lack of acknowledgment of its own complicity by the US government, exacerbated issues unique to racialized and stratified toxic dumping.

In the works of Ozeki and Moraga, human bodies are at first silenced by the power of the state, but they slowly begin to speak and insert themselves into a discourse that challenges the very fabric of the nation-state. Ozeki and Moraga enter the dialogue of biopolitics by mapping human bodies onto a landscape of public and private risk and asking their audiences to consider the violence involved in complacency. Their entangled critique of US agricultural industry practices and the nation-state is sharpened through their focus on human bodies that exhibit signs of illness and disfigurement. If one follows the evolution from the "regulatory" government practices that subsidize agribusiness to the resulting toxic exposure and absented bodies of workers, it renders visible the way the body is both regulated and appropriated.

Heroes and Saints: documenting the undocumented

Heroes and Saints (hereafter *HS*) dramatizes the human and environmental cost of agribusiness and toxic dumping. The play is set in the San Joaquin Valley, and the Chicanos working the valley's fields are harmed both by the pesticides to which they are exposed and by the polluted water and land on which they depend. The people, called "El Pueblo," discover that their housing tract, built entirely with federal subsidies, is also a toxic waste burial site. Corporate greed, government bureaucracy, and institutionalized US racism all contribute to the widespread illnesses and deaths of the people of McLaughlin. The protagonist, Cerezita Valle, is a member of this cancer cluster. She exists as a head alone, pushed around on a rolling, "tablelike platform" referred to as "her ride," or "raite," in the play (*HS*, 90). Cerezita's reliance on technology to move and the way it is made part of her character depict her as a type of cyborg.

Written in what Jorge Huerta, an expert on Chicano drama, calls a "cinematic, episodic 'montage' of scenes, monologues and dramatic images" (2000, 68), *Heroes and Saints* is a play in two acts, the first having sixteen scenes and the second thirteen. The second act becomes increasingly jarring and uses what one might call a "jump-cut" technique. *Heroes and Saints* reads, in many ways, like a translation of documentary film onto the page and stage. Two documentaries in particular proved pivotal to Moraga's activist, experimental playwriting and to the UFW's struggle to fight for access to health care, better pay, safety standards,

Figure 4.1 Hector Correa and Jaime Lujan in *Heroes and Saints*, 1992.

Source: Photograph by David M. Allen. Photo courtesy of David M. Allen.

and the right to unionize: *The Wrath of Grapes* (Parlee and Bourin 1986) and *Fighting for Our Lives* (Pearcy 1975). Because the subject matter of the play is complicated and Moraga's myth making can be disorienting, it is crucial to start with the historical event that galvanized the UFW and Moraga into action.

In her author's notes, Moraga describes the real events that inspired the creation of her central character, Cerezita.[10] The events were the discovery of the cancer cluster in McFarland in the period 1978–1988, the brutal beating of Dolores Huerta by San Francisco policemen, and President George Bush's "refusal to honor the boycott" of grapes led by Chávez (*HS*, 89). At the time of her beating, Dolores Huerta was vice president of the UFW. She suffered fractured ribs and a ruptured spleen. The force used against her was notable also because it was at a public demonstration and the video footage proves that she was cooperating with officers. The final impetus was the UFW's documentary *The Wrath of Grapes* (Parlee and Bourin 1986), with its image of a "child with no arms or legs, born of a farm worker mother," who became Cerezita (*HS*, 89).

The main characters of the play are the Valle family, composed of Cerezita, the young girl without a body; her sister, Yolanda; her gay and HIV-positive brother, Mario; and her passive and frightened mother, Dolores. Other important characters include Dona Amparo, the activist; Ana Pérez, the Latina news anchor represented as a betrayal to her fellow Chicanos; and El Pueblo, the people of McLaughlin. In Moraga's description of the play's characters, she writes: "El Pueblo, the children and mothers of McLaughlin; THE PEOPLE / PROTESTORS / AUDIENCE participating in the struggle (ideally, EL PUEBLO should be made up of an ensemble of people from the local Latino community)" (*HS*, 90). Dona Amparo is depicted positively and described as "the comadre and activista" (*HS*, 90). Amparo he closely resembles Dolores Huerta, the UFW activist. The character of Ana Pérez, a news anchor with a grating personality, has an important role in the play. *Heroes and Saints* and *My Year of Meats* both portray well-meaning journalists wondering if they themselves are in fact exploiting tragedy in their reportage. Lastly, audiences watching *Heroes and Saints* see projected archival images of the UFW's strikes and activities and Chávez's 1968 hunger strike.

The relationship between the outside world as dirt and foreign matter that infects the interiority of the home and human body is a recurring theme in both Ozeki and Moraga. In her consideration of society's discrimination between the clean and the dirty, the toxic and the natural (among others), Mary Douglas has offered the analysis of dirt as "matter out of place" that "must not be included if a pattern is to be maintained" ([1966] 2002, 50). As I argued in chapter 2, the domestic space in Steinbeck's *The Grapes of Wrath* is not only invaded by agricultural industrialization (symbolized by dust seeping into homes), it is permanently transformed by them. The same is true in *Heroes and Saints*. The public space of work and its hazards becomes the private space of domesticity, and the risks thus increase because one does not think of having to guard oneself against one's own home. Lisa Thompson comments that Moraga has spent her career "documenting the undocumented" and, more recently, demonstrating how "progress that fails to empower citizens alienates them instead" (2004, 524). The hazards in the domestic space result from that "progress," which in *Heroes and Saints* not only "alienates" but also causes corporeal harm to its inhabitants. Progress marketed as a more efficient and controlled process of agricultural production creates a kind of "anti-place" that violates spatiotemporal norms and accommodates the human rights violations against which the UFW protests.

The major inspiration for Moraga's play, *The Wrath of Grapes*, documents the struggle by Chávez and the UFW to eliminate dangerous pesticides that plague the lives of workers and consumers. Five pesticides are listed against the background of a red bottle with a skull and crossbones that reads "POISON: Captan, Dinoseb, Methyl Bromide, Parathion, Phosdrin." This quick listing of pesticides is accompanied by a voice-over stating the grievances of the UFW: "To wage this war César Chávez and the United Farm Workers of America have once again called for a boycott of California table grapes. Chávez wants growers to stop using five very dangerous pesticides that kill and injure farm workers and threaten consumers with toxic residues" (Parlee and Bourin 1986). Following the logic of the narration, the documentary seems to present a conflict between the farm workers (repeatedly represented as Latino males) and the growers who spray the pesticides (repeatedly represented as Caucasian good old boys wearing cowboy hats).

Regardless of the narration, which might lead one to believe that it is consumers and adult Latino males who will suffer from pesticides, the visual cues tell a different story, one of suffering writ large on the bodies of children and women who will no longer be silenced. The image of the pesticides' names and the poison label follows a quick view of a young boy's face, and it in turn is followed by a still of a woman' shouting behind the wide-brimmed hat of what looks like a sheriff's deputy. While the man's face is obscured, the woman looks directly into the camera, as does the young boy. *The Wrath of Grapes* effectively demonstrates the acute corporeal cost – particularly to women and children – of rampant greed and industrial agribusiness. Moraga distills such moments from the documentary and presents to her audience a text saturated with them. *Heroes and Saints* is a multimedia production that raises questions about the role of audience members, the role of the reader, and the power of the media and society's viewing and reading practices.

While *The Wrath of Grapes* outlines the issues in a direct manner, a related documentary, *Fighting for Our Lives* (Pearcy 1975), illustrates why aural and tactile experiences are emphasized in the play. One clip in particular from *Fighting for Our Lives* provides the necessary context to understand key issues addressed by *Heroes and Saints*. Produced and directed by Gary Pearcy, *Fighting for Our Lives* is based on the 1973 series of activities and strikes by the UFW and was nominated for an Academy Award for Best Documentary Feature. The clip begins by showing a vocal but peaceful demonstration organized by the UFW on the 107th day of their strike in hopes of winning a labor contract. The UFW had been organizing workers in a pacifist manner against the International Brotherhood of Teamsters, a labor union that worked in the interest of growers. The viewer begins to hear the sound of a helicopter above a camera crew. The clip highlights two facets of the play: the importance of sound and the importance of bodies. As the clip continues, viewers witness a brutal confrontation between members of the Kern County Sheriff's Department and UFW demonstrators. The people in the helicopter coordinate their activities with the Sheriff's Department representatives to silence and overpower protesters and bystanders. It protectively hovers above members of the media (there are two cameramen underneath it) while sending wind and dust into the eyes of unofficial reporters, including the person holding the camera through which we see the scene. The beating of a young Latino male by law enforcement officials begins, the protesters are outraged, and in response the police begin to use pepper spray.

The brief excerpt from *Fighting for Our Lives* demonstrates that the erasure of disempowered bodies by those in power is far from a distortion of an overactive imagination. Rather, it is a reality of the history of the US labor movement and the agricultural industry in California's Central Valley. In the documentary, a Kern County police officer freely uses pepper spray until the moment when he realizes the camera is focusing on him – at which point he abruptly stops. The camera's gaze and, by extension, the audience's, hold the police officer accountable for his actions and viewers are made to feel participatory in the cessation of an infringement on civil liberties. The officer's fleeting look into the camera, his averted eyes, and his furtive glance back at the camera speak volumes about his sense of shame or at least his fear of being identified: he realizes that if his actions are viewed by a wider audience he could be held accountable outside of Kern County. This is a revealing glimpse into the historical background of Moraga's fiction. Notably, the style of both documentaries is translated onto the page as Moraga and Ozeki employ a similar narrative style that asks readers and viewers to piece together the context of a given moment.

Anatomy of an opening

Scene One in the first act of *Heroes and Saints* demonstrates how the play hinges on the performance of erasure and the mutilation of the body. The documentary footage briefly mentioned above shows how bodies – especially nonwhite ones – lack the legibility they deserve. As explained earlier, Moraga's protagonist, Cerezita Valle, is a girl with no body who is pushed around on a cart: she is considered a heroine and a saint by her community. In contrast to usual expectations of religious behavior, Cerezita is highly tactile, sexual, and voraciously alive. Although *Heroes and Saints* addresses racialized and violent confrontations between bodies, it contains eerily silent and haunting images of the grotesque. The opening scene is one of silence. There is no dialogue – only the image of a crucifix with a small child on it, "silhouetted" against the "dawn's light" (*HS*, 92). As the scene unfolds, a group of small children "wearing calavera masks" go into the grape vineyard and erect the "child-sized" cross (*HS*, 92). Cerezita's boisterous personality and sexual vitality stand in opposition to the silenced women of her community and the children. Moraga conceptualizes a character that points to the direct and symbolic actions available to those who search to disrupt broken systems; systems (in the play) that involve orchestrated brutality against a community, targeted beatings, slow poisoning of land and people, and overtly racist and gendered violence. Cerezita's unapologetic sexuality and intellect serve as the lens that brings into focus the community as something that should register. The contrasting qualities of Cerezita's character are many: her absent body highlights the possibility of other absented bodies, and her recursive speech makes one wonder about other narratives in the community. It also, in the end, ties the body's legibility to agential forms of speech, ultimately tethering material and immaterial, visible and invisible.

Moraga's choice to dress the child activists in calavera masks – traditional Mexican skull masks associated in part with civil disobedience – gestures toward masquerade and performativity and mobilizes silent dead bodies into a complex cosmology of protest.

These are acts of defiance: the otherwise silenced bodies speak out, suggesting that Moraga sees them as mobilizing forces for change. Sharon Patricia Holland articulates an aesthetics of resistance in the activation or reanimation of dead bodies through speech or presence (2000). Additionally, in her cogent

Figure 4.2 José Guadalupe Posada's original "La Calavera Garbancera" and later known as "La Calavera Catrina," ca. 1910. Dapper Skeleton (aka The Fancy Lady) was meant as political and social satire. In this etching Posada is calling attention to the corruption of aristocracy and to Mexicans who wanted to appear more European.

Source: Image from the portfolio entitled "1880–1980: 100 Years of Popular Art in the Morelos Labradores 91 Neighborhood," 1983. Relief etching restrike from vintage plate, N.N. Photo courtesy of National Museum of Mexican Art Permanent Collection.

essay on the politics of death in Moraga's play, Linda Greenberg (2009) posits that the state's insistence on silent, segregated death is laid bare by the display of dead bodies. The lifeless bodies of small children lend themselves to two different readings, suggesting either passive victimization or active sacrifice. One cannot deny that Cerezita's final act of moving into gunfire and toward her own death unites her with the dead children. Regardless of one's interpretation of her in that final act as victim or martyr, in the first scene there is little possibility for empowerment.

The politics of sight and the tension between speech and silence, and visibility and invisibility, drive the narrative in both the documentary footage and the play. The play opens with the audience's attention focused on the sacrificial and arranged body of a dead child. Once the children have erected the cross, the only sounds the audience hears are the "mechanical hum" of Cerezita's electric cart and then the sound of a "low-flying helicopter" (*HS*, 92). Moraga's stage directions describe the scene of protest as the dead of night gives way to morning, and Cerezita and the "crucifi[ed]" child are starkly illuminated by the light of dawn (*HS*, 92). Moraga is not only foreshadowing Cerezita's eventual sacrifice but also highlighting the shared vulnerability of the child and Cerezita, as well as the existence of their embodied harm (*HS*, 92). The public display of death is viewed by the activist leader in the play, Dona Amparo, as an affirmation that "they are not [her] enemy" and that "they [are] always dead first" and should be displayed for the public to see, because "if you put the children in the ground, the world forgets about them" (*HS*, 168). The repeated public display of the poisoned body as sacrifice suggests that victimhood is not in the vocabulary of the community and that burial equals a final silence only if history erases or rewrites the event.

Desiring bodies

In a play that violates the usual discourse about invisible and deformed bodies, Cerezita's imaginary body and the body of her brother, Mario, become subversive forces of agitation. Cerezita is fully present to tactility and to her sexuality, and especially so in her exchanges with Father Juan. Yvonne Yarbro-Bejarano argues that Moraga's earlier plays – *Giving Up the Ghost* (1994a), *Heroes and Saints* (1994b), and *Shadow of a Man* (1994c) – are revolutionary in that they first presented the US drama scene with portraits of "Chicanas as desiring subjects" (Yarbro-Bejarano 2001, 25). Indeed, Cerezita is a desiring subject, and in the process of constructing her as such Moraga makes it difficult for audiences to infantilize her and even more challenging to reify her. In one of the more perplexing scenes of the play, Father Juan and Cerezita have sex. Although Moraga writes that Juan "comes to an orgasm," she leaves much of the encounter vague. Juan first strokes Cerezita's hair and cheek, he rubs his pelvis against her raite, and then against her face. Copulation seems impossible, but Cerezita and Juan have some form of sex (*HS*, 140). After their intimacy he flees, then returns, and Cerezita chides him for what she considers to be cowardly behavior:

JUAN: I'm a priest, Cere. I'm not free. My body's not my own.

CEREZITA: It wasn't your body I wanted. It was mine. All I wanted was for you to make me feel like I had a body because, the fact is, I don't. I was denied one. But for a few minutes, a few minutes before you started *thinking*, I felt myself full of fine flesh filled to the bones in my toes. . . . I miss myself. Is that so hard to understand?

JUAN: No.

CEREZITA: And I'm sick of all this goddamn dying. If I had your arms and legs, if I had your dick for chrissake, you know what I'd do? I'd burn this motherless town down and all the poisoned fields around it. . . . You're a waste of a body.

(*HS*, 144; emphasis in the original)

Cerezita attempts to use Juan's body to awaken her sexual desires, to live in her body; by the same token, she claims that she was "denied one." Her gendered understanding of agency rests on Juan's delinquent masculinity. Juan is "a waste of a body" because even with the power inherent in his position he cannot take action against "this motherless town."

Cerezita reveals her own gendered assumptions about the world, linking men with industrial agriculture and toxic dumping and women with nature and a prophetic connection to the land. Her associations are troubling because they simplify the complex gender relations of her community. While *Heroes and Saints* contains powerful female figures, they enact a range of responses to the illnesses and deaths plaguing their families. Cerezita's mother, Dolores, discourages Cerezita's thirst for carnal knowledge (whether through books or sense of touch), and she is irked to find Cerezita reading one of Mario's old anatomy books:

CEREZITA: God, Mom, it's just the body.

DOLORES: So, what biznis you got with the body? This jus' puts thoughts in your head. (*She flips through the book.*) ¿Qué tiene que ver una señorita [What does a young lady have to do] with this kind of pictures? (*Slams it shut.*) I should call in the father.

CEREZITA: Father Juan?

DOLORES: Jus' cuz you don' got a body doesn' mean you can't sin. The biggest sins are in the mind.

(*HS*, 112–13; emphasis in the original)[11]

Dolores's statement proves to be tragically true. The biggest "sins" in the play are those coordinated first by the mind – whether it is the abandonment of an entire community by those in power, the negligence of a single father, or the government's refusal to take responsibility for its role in subsidizing the lethal dumping of chemicals buried underneath Cerezita's housing community.

Dolores identifies oppressive societal scaffolding as more insidious than the sight of a broken body, much less images of human anatomy.

In Moraga's efforts to demonstrate how racialized bodies are persecuted and marginalized in invisible ways, she continually points to machismo as a common problem in Chicano culture. Father Juan and Mario's plotlines end in tragedy. They are the only two male characters in the play who are physically present, yet that presence and their sexual desires are undermined by guilt and suffering. Mario's homosexuality is not accepted by Dolores, who pressures him from a young age to "be a man" and asks him why he is effeminate: "Why you wannu make yourself como una mujer [like a woman]? Why you wannu do this to the peepo who love you?" (*HS*, 123). Dolores continues to reject her son when she refuses to give Mario her blessing to live his life freely ("no puedo"; literally, "I cannot") (124). She claims that he will contract the "sickness" (HIV) because it is a form of punishment for the gay community from God (124). Mario attempts to fill the void in his life caused in part by the lack of his mother's approval with material gifts he gets from the "sleazy-looking gringo" and by taking drugs and engaging in reckless sex (105). The recurring image of a white man in a car reads as predatory This man in an abusive position of power is united by virtue of his anonymity with all the other men, or "the man," who Moraga implies are at fault for the deaths in McLaughlin. Moraga continually reinforces the embedded nature of machismo in Chicano culture.

Moraga's linkage of men in power (white and nonwhite) troubles easy dismissals of "a Chicano" culture that monolithically reads people as either one way or another. In repeatedly challenging audience members to question echelons of power she destabilizes a number of accepted norms. The two central male characters, a gay man and a priest (both of whom die), reveal that productive alliances must traverse gender, race, and religion, but they must also begin by first looking within communities to overturn harmful stereotypes that force people into cyclical violence. It is also, it seems, the place of art and criticality to evaluate from the periphery and create space for just systems of power. Institutions have failed to protect Juan and Mario and are in fact the reason for their deaths. Mario's queerness challenges the macho Chicano culture he grew up in, and his isolation contributes to his demise. His father abandons him, and his mother rejects him. Mario's statement that "lung cancer's the least of [his] worries" (141) can be read not only as an implicit acknowledgment that he knows he has contracted HIV but also as a blanket statement about the institutionalized racism and homophobia he experiences. Mario is all too aware of the hatred of his community and the socioeconomic divide between himself and somebody like his "sleazy-looking gringo" (105). No amount of assurance by Juan can convince him otherwise, and he leaves McLaughlin.

In *Heroes and Saints* addiction, HIV, and exposure to hazardous substances have different degrees of institutional complicity, and this is where Juan's and Mario's situations intersect. After Mario runs away from home, Father Juan comes across Mario sleeping on a bench in McLaughlin. Mario explains that he has been trying to leave his hometown for years, but he feels trapped by McLaughlin. As they sit together on the bench, Mario coughs with illness and describes the eerie sensation of the valley: "Just one hundred yards off that highway, and you're already right smack back into the heart of the Valley" (*HS*, 141). The highway should represent progress and the urban realization of rural dreams, but according to Mario "The city's no different. Raza's dying everywhere. Doesn't matter if it's crack or . . . pesticides, AIDS, it's all the same shit" (*HS*, 141). Father Juan's and Mario's narrative strands reflect Moraga's heavy-handed depiction of the culture wars of the 1980s. Yet they also reveal how the domination of the valley by agribusiness pulls from a disempowered labor force and feeds back into the city its most disenfranchised members.

At the conclusion of *Heroes and Saints*, Moraga implies that the solidarity of the community holds the possibility to trump the systemic violence of the agricultural industry, but the ending involves El Pueblo's death and does not offer resolution. The abrupt and unexplained reappearance of Mario in the final scene of the play marks an important reconciliation between him and both his mother and the community at large. He leaves in Scene Seven and reappears in Scene Eleven. The stage directions simply state: "MARIO *appears upstage. He goes to* DOLORES. *They embrace*" (*HS*, 149; emphasis in the original). Mario is silent as he watches Dolores bless Cerezita, then watches Juan and Cerezita go into the vineyards. Dolores's symbolic acceptance of Mario at the end of the play is a gesture of hope that helps him find the strength to protest the violations of the environment and laborers surrounding him. Juan and Cerezita lead the charge into the vineyard and presumably are killed by machine guns.

Cyborg and saint

The deaths of characters for whom the audience has formed affection comes as a shock and further derails a sense of resolution. Just as the deaths of Cerezita and others point to a parasitic and dichotomous relationship between the residents and the town, so too does the tension between technology and nature indicate Moraga's interest in exploring artificially constructed boundaries. As Jorge Marcone notes, Cherríe Moraga and Gloria Anzaldúa "expose the complicity of the human/non-human binary opposition with politics of oppression and colonialism" (2011, 196). The domination of the Central Valley by "capital and technology" (Nash 2007, 2) is broached by Moraga through Cerezita's cyborg existence. Always accompanied by the whirring sound of her raite, Cerezita represents the yoking together of the discourses of the human and nonhuman, monster and saint, deformity and "normality." Although she exists as only a head, Cerezita repeatedly reminds those who doubt her humanity that she has plenty of "imagination" and "a tongue" (*HS*, 107). Moraga's notes on Cerezita describe her as a "head of human dimension, but one who possesses such dignity of bearing and classical Indian beauty she can, at times, assume nearly religious proportions. (The huge head figures of the pre-Columbina Olmecas are an apt comparison)" (*HS*, 90). She carefully opposes two descriptions of Cerezita, presenting her as an indigenous goddess of the land and

Mexican people, which is to be "contrasted with the very real 'humanness' she exhibits on a daily functioning level" (*HS*, 90).

Cerezita's "humanness" is the contested territory in question, and Moraga constructs a subtext that plays with people's notion of the human. In her notes, Moraga elaborates on how Cerezita should be presented to the audience: "For most of the play, CEREZITA is positioned on a rolling, tablelike platform, which will be referred to as her 'raite' (ride). It is automated by a button she operates with her chin. The low hum of its motor always anticipates her entrance" (*HS*, 90). The sound that accompanies Cerezita's entrance serves as a reminder of the double-edged sword of technological advances (she is simultaneously disabled because of industrial-grade pollutants and able to move because of technological developments). Echoing the hum of the raite's motor is the menacing sound of helicopters, the other prevalent sound in the play.

Sonic and ocular experiences are vital to Moraga's discourse of the power dynamics of the Central Valley. In the stage notes for the first scene of the play, Moraga first describes the infected children and Cerezita, but the sonic presence of agribusiness and corporations dominate the hum of Cerezita's raite: "the sound of a low-flying helicopter invades the silence. Its shadow passes over the field. Black out" (*HS*, 92). Moraga forges a connection between the humming raite and the louder helicopter, both in terms of sound and technology. Even Dolores reveals her underlying belief that her daughter is not fully human: "What sins could a girl like her have, Padre? She was born this way. Es una Santa [she is a saint]" (*HS*, 101). She negates Cerezita's agency and fails to acknowledge that Cerezita is far from being a disembodied subject. Jorge Huerta sees Cerezita's lack of a body as allowing her to represent the plight of "Everywoman" (2000, 69), and Linda Greenberg similarly positions the spectrality of Cerezita's body as a unifying force with the McLaughlin community, "allow[ing] her to claim the valley and its community, uniting them through the absent boundaries of her flesh" (2009, 172). Indeed, her elided flesh signifies a genealogy of racialized and gendered violence, and it also ironically maps her onto the poisonous landfill. Her lack of traditionally recognizable corporeality solidifies her reputation as one of the most obviously affected "bodies" in the cancer cluster. As Dona Amparo shows Dolores, Yolanda, and Cerezita a chart of multicolored dots representing houses (red), tumors (blue), birth defects (green), miscarriages (yellow), and less severe issues of digestion and rashes (orange), Cerezita finds herself in the green dot, and her sister Yolanda jokes that Cerezita increases their status: "You put us on the map, Cere" (*HS*, 129). Their exchange unveils that aberrance contains potential for agency:

AMPARO: Hice un mapa [it's a map] (*She unrolls the chart onto the table.*) A chart of all the houses in la vecindad que tiene la gente con [in the area that have people with] the health problems.

YOLANDA: What are all these orange dots?

AMPARO: Bueno [well], smaller problems como problemas del estómago, las ronchas, cosas así [like stomach problems, hives, these kinds of things].

YOLANDA: Cheezus, it's the whole damn neighborhood.
CEREZITA: Where's our house?
AMPARO: Aquí donde están [Here where there is] the orange dot and the green dot.
CEREZITA: That's me, the green dot.
YOLANDA (*lightly*): You put us on the map, Cere.

(*HS*, 129)

In fact, as a victim of toxic poisoning Cerezita literally maps her stucco home onto the grid and draws attention to the hazardous waste beneath it. This alternative cartographic signification reconfigures the national imaginary: Amparo's dots cannot be erased and articulate what some people might describe as a disarticulated movement against corporate agribusiness – a movement driven by immigrants and migrant workers.

Moraga makes sure that the vague accusations of El Pueblo against institutionalized violence and racism are clarified in the play. Amparo finds an "old, thick rubber hose" while digging "vigorously" in her yard and declares to Dolores, "You don' believe me, but they bury all their poison under our houses. Wha' chu think that crack comes from? . . . The house is sinking" (*HS*, 102). Amparo reminds the audience that the poisoned fields are one piece of a larger puzzle pointing to the lethal actions of the growers (backed by the government). She suspects that the practice of burying toxic waste is responsible for the soft and cracked earth on which the residents' federally subsidized houses are built. And amid a crowd of demonstrators with signs such as "Sin Agua No Tenemos Vida" [Without Water We Don't Have Life"], Ana Pérez looks at the camera and gives the following report on the protest of the McLaughlin mothers:

> Local residents are outraged by the school board's decision to refuse Arrowhead's offer of free drinking water for the schoolchildren. They believe local tap water, contaminated by pesticides, to be the chief cause of the high incidence of cancer among children in the area. They claim that the extensive spraying, especially aerial spraying, causes the toxic chemicals to seep into the public water system. The majority of residents are from a nearby housing tract of federally subsidized housing. It has been alleged that the housing was built on what was once a dump site for pesticides with the full knowledge of contractors. What we have here, Jack, appears to be a kind of 1980s Hispanic Love Canal.
>
> (*HS*, 110)

Later in the play Pérez questions her participatory actions in capitalizing on tragedy, her personality softens, and she claims that the "mothers' demands are quite concrete" (*HS*, 132). The demands include new housing, an environmentally safe community, and a free health clinic.[12] What later became known as the cancer cluster of McFarland is just one real example of environmental racism, whereby predominantly poor nonwhite people are forced to suffer the worst consequences of pollution – becoming the literal and metaphorical dumping site of unregulated business and lenient government policies. Cerezita's flesh, a startling and visible fusion of human and technology, outlines how underprivileged communities are often forced to absorb the toxic by-products that others can afford to avoid.

Cerezita's bodily configuration is the opposite of an acephalous operation: she has an astounding intelligence and is a head without a body. The workers' rights and environmental justice movement that forms around her becomes united with her in the series of events leading to her death. Refusing to disappear into the invisible network of disabled and disappeared bodies, she uses her imagination, tactility, and speech to reinsert herself into the discourse of humanity while simultaneously subverting expectations of what it means to be human.

The media's glare

Ana Pérez, the newscaster for "Hispanic America" whose behavior in the face of the cancer cluster is initially offensive, is a caricature of "the American media" machine and is portrayed as parasitic in her manipulation of her own heritage. She serves as a cultural interpreter and translator, but her form of cultural translation is to dismiss the significance of McLaughlin and the struggle of its inhabitants. Nonetheless, she is shocked to see how the migrant community is treated, and the audience hopes (even fleetingly) that this experience might change her future reporting. Moraga begins and ends her play with appearances by Ana Pérez. At the end of the play, Moraga's stage directions underscore this hope as the community joins Mario when he unites people and together they storm the vineyards: "EL PUEBLO *(rising with him]):* ¡Enciendan los files! [Burn the fields!] (*They all, including* ANA PEREZ, *rush out to the vineyards, shouting as they exit.*) ¡Asesinos! ¡Asesinos! ¡Asesinos! [Assassins! Assassins! Assassins!]" (*HS*, 149). Initially spared by the attack that follows Cerezita's speech, Mario marches into death. As a last sign of solidarity and a break with mainstream media, Pérez joins in protest. Carl Gutiérrez-Jones (1995) and Ramón Saldívar (1990) both allude to the power of Chicano narratives to challenge "hegemonic modes of thought which are subtly embedded in formal conventions" (Gutiérrez-Jones 1995, 49).

I described the opening scene of the play, in which the crucified body of the child "glows" together with Cerezita's head in the light of dawn and a low-flying helicopter "invades the silence" (*HS*, 92). Moraga's choice to follow the helicopter with Pérez's reporting in the form of a special on "Hispanic America" places the responsibility on audience members to consider their own nonchalance and to think about activism in an oppositional way: if you are not actively organizing and protesting against injustice, you might be supporting it. The character of Ana Pérez functions to expose the detrimental impacts of passive voyeurism.

Moraga begins the second scene by purposefully contrasting the appearance and socioeconomic class of Pérez and Amparo. Pérez fusses over her hair and makeup although Moraga describes her as "perfectly made up," while Amparo is simply described as "a stocky woman in her fifties" who "is digging holes in the yard" and "wears heavy-duty rubber gloves" (*HS*, 92). Pérez's name and linguistic capabilities identify her as a part of "Hispanic America," but she resides somewhere outside it and stumbles when trying to "translate" Amparo's speech for the camera (*HS*, 94). Her gentrified Spanish differs from that of the laboring class, and when Amparo implies that it is not a crime to hang the children, but rather to bury and forget them, Pérez assures the cameraman that they will "edit her out later" (*HS*, 94). Pérez's promise to "edit out" Dona Amparo draws attention to the very thing that the audience is being asked to splice into their montage of ethics. In the staging of the play the actress playing Pérez looks somewhere off to the side and speaks "to the camera" (*HS*, 94). Thus, as Pérez makes derogatory comments about the people of McLaughlin and believes she is speaking to her audience, Moraga is working to alienate the real audience members (and readers) from Pérez's discourse. In other words, Moraga teaches the viewer and reader of the play how and what to read.

Pérez treats the Day of the Dead as cultural kitsch, but as she alienates Moraga's audience, alternative readings of the importance of the Day of the Dead and the calavera masks emerge. Pérez resurfaces at the end of the play to report on the tenth cancer-related death of a child in McLaughlin, a "miracle" in the Valle family, and the procession leading to Evalina Valle's crucifixion. Cerezita's transformation into the likeness of the Virgin of Guadalupe elevates her struggle from the realm of the political to that of the religious. Politics and religion overlap: "DOLORES pushes the raite with la virgen [the virgin] out the door" (*HS*, 147). Pérez is the first character to speak, and she directly benefits from the dramatization of tragedy. Poignantly, by the end of the play her position shifts:

ANA PÉREZ: Why would someone be so cruel, to hang a child up like that? To steal him from his deathbed?

AMPARO: No, he was dead already. Already dead from the poison.

ANA PÉREZ: A publicity stunt? But who's –

AMPARO: Señorita, I don' know who. But I know they are not my enemy. (*Beat.*) *Con su permiso* [*with your permission*] (AMPARO *walks away.*)

ANA PÉREZ (*with false bravado*): That concludes our Hispanic hour for the week, but watch for next week's show where we will take a five-hour drive north to the heart of San Francisco's Latino Mission District, for an insider's observation of the Day of the Dead, the Mexican Halloween. (*She holds a television smile for three full seconds. To the "cameraman":*) Cut! We'll edit her out later.

BONNIE *and a group of small* CHILDREN *enter wearing calavera masks. They startle her.*

(*HS*, 94)

While Pérez promises viewers an "insider's observation of the Day of the Dead," she is undermined by Moraga's visual juxtaposition of the calavera masks and Dona Amparo. In other words, Pérez is shown to be an outsider to "Hispanic" America (Chicano culture) – or perhaps Moraga wants audience members to feel that if she remains an insider, they don't want to be a part of "Hispanic America." Moraga demands that audience members become more deeply engaged in their reading practices and coaxes them to develop a new sense of civil disobedience.

The absence of human agents highlights the issue of disembodied but articulated power. Moraga perpetually contrasts silent corporate and state power with the loud presence of the media. The corporations in the play are notably absent, only signified by impalpable poisons and the sounds of the helicopters and machine guns,[13] "The men in the helicopters, they're hired by the growers. Anybody out en los files [in the fields] tonight, they'll shoot them. They don' wan' no more publeesty about the crucifixions" (*HS*, 137). Anonymous corporate power is menacingly organized, but its body remains invisible, while Cerezita's embodied and seemingly disarticulated activism is fully exposed. Although Dona Amparo warns others of the people inside the helicopters, the audience never sees them. While urging Father Juan not to let Cerezita outside, she explains that the men in the helicopters are hired goons (by the growers) and will shoot anybody in the fields because the crucifixions are bad for business. Whiteness is powerfully disembodied while embodied Chicanismo suffers at its hands.

Moraga's decision to effectively have Cerezita murdered by disembodied power represented only by the sounds of machines (machine guns and helicopters) demonstrates that she recognizes that the public's attention, the media's spotlight, and the reader's critical gaze come at the price of yet another death. This death, however, is spectacular and dramatic, attempting to recruit the myriad other deaths that have gone unnoticed. *Heroes and Saints* ends in the sacrificial gesture by Cerezita and Father Juan, as they walk into the vineyards as a sign of solidarity and protest. The stage directions simply read: "CEREZITA and JUAN proceed offstage into the vineyards. Moments later, the shadow and sound of a helicopter pass overhead. EL PUEBLO watch the sky. Then there is a sudden sound of machine gun fire" (*HS*, 149). The people fall to the ground and shield themselves in terror from the helicopters and gunfire as Mario yells out, "Burn the fields!" (*HS*, 149). El Pueblo burn not only the fields but the housing development as well, as the fire "spreads over the vineyard and the Valle home" (*HS*, 149). The implication that the homes are as dangerous as the pesticide-laden fields further troubles the paradigm of contained risk and controllable industry.

From cyborg to cyborg

Ozeki and Moraga locate visibility in the least visible and legally cognizable bodies, which are normally occluded from society's vision. This move parallels the authors' larger projects: to frame disease-based narratives and represent corporeal interaction with man-made toxins. This is most clear in chapter 1, in which I discussed Susanne Antonetta's *Body Toxic* (2001). In this chapter I trace the strategies of two works that articulate the material, corporeal, and personal impact of global risks undertaken by corporate powers at the expense of human and animal bodies.

Ozeki's *My Year of Meats* (1998; hereafter *MYM*) illuminates the global collusion between US capitalist ventures in food production and the media. *My Year of Meats* takes place in America and Japan, following the two main narrative strands of Jane and Akiko, two women of Japanese descent whose lives intersect in unexpected ways. Jane is an out-of-work documentary film director who is offered a job producing a new television program called *My American Wife!*, a Japanese cooking show designed to get Japanese housewives to buy and cook American beef.

The show's sponsorship by BEEF-EX – the Beef Export and Trade Syndicate, a Texas-based meat lobbying organization – increases the pressure on Jane to equate beef consumption with the American dream. Akiko's husband, Joichi (John), is the Tokyo public relations representative of BEEF-EX. He calls himself "John Wayno," an Americanized version of his real surname, Ueno. Joichi is obsessed with Texas; he compares big-breasted strippers from Texas to big-boned cattle. Joichi's skewed view of what he believes to be authentically American is rivaled only by his perverted understanding of male-female relations and his megalomaniacal drive to have children. During Jane's travels in search of American wives who fit the producers' model of a perfect housewife – that cook wholesome beef-based meals like "Coca-Cola Roast" (*MYM*, 25) – she meets and dates Sloan, a jet-setting saxophonist. Through both Jane's aversion to peddling antibiotic-laden meat and Jane's and Akiko's trouble conceiving children, the story of DES poisoning emerges. Jane's and Akiko's trajectory toward one another involves uncovering layer after layer of truth about DES poisoning and their commonalities because of it.

My Year of Meats connects human reproduction to consumption of animal products and testing through the prism of DES. Paul Hermann Müller, a Swiss chemist, first synthesized and used DDT for agricultural purposes in 1939, and Charles Dodds, a British researcher, invented DES in 1938. Separated by just a year, the inventions of these two synthetic endocrine disruptors would change history. DES was used to produce healthy pregnancies and offspring in both humans and livestock. By "healthy," physicians meant bigger babies and fewer miscarriages. DES was marketed and patented abroad before being widely distributed in the United States to pregnant women. The US Centers for Disease Control and Prevention (n.d.) estimates that during the period from 1938–1971 between five and ten million people (including mothers and their male and female offspring) were exposed to DES. In 1971 it was proven to cause a host of problems in women who used DES and subsequent generations, including cancer, infertility, and cysts in male offspring. DES was the first hormonal modifier of note, and farmers administered it to animals to fatten them up, ensure healthy births, and chemically castrate male steers.

DES was hailed as a miracle drug that put estrogen treatment at the forefront of cutting-edge medical treatments that made women and animals into "improved" versions of themselves; technologically aided reproduction with machine-like efficiency seemed ideal. Significantly, although DES has since been banned from being administered to women, it is widely believed that it continues to be used with livestock.[14]

In an interview about her novel, Ozeki observes that she is "suspicious of binary oppositions," and in *My Year of Meats* she interrogates what seem like fortified walls between borders of animal and human, health and disease (to name just two binaries). Ozeki states: "I see our lives as being a part of an enormous web of interconnected spheres, where the workings of the larger social, political, and corporate machinery impact something as private and intimate as the descent of an egg through a woman's fallopian tube" (Ozeki 1998, 9). These intersecting private and public sites create opportunities for resistance and conversation. American studies scholar and environmental justice advocate Julie Sze's research on DES, Ozeki, and Donna Haraway bring into focus what Sze writes of as a complex set of issues that require an intersectional approach (2006, 809). Haraway's foundational work in the field of technology and the body has sparked debates about the man-made borders between nature and technology, human and machine, and humans and nonhumans. Her vision of these debates as inherently violent articulations of contact zones between organism and machine is clear: they are a "border war" (1991, 150). The "stakes" of this war, she continues, "have been the territories of production, reproduction, and imagination" (1991, 150). Haraway crystallizes how the female body has long been a space onto which agendas are mapped and discourses formed. Ecofeminist approaches to both Ozeki and Moraga recognize the "border wars" taking place about and within women's bodies, especially as related to the involuntary ingestion of toxins.

DES and "pharmacooticals"

As Jane begins to explore the business behind agribusiness she realizes that she, like the cattle she films, may be the involuntary recipient of hormone poisoning. Jane's mother and Akiko are the foil to Jane's false "hybrid vigor." Joichi accuses Akiko of being frail, insubstantial, and asexual. When Joichi tours strip clubs in Austin, Texas, Jane discovers that he has a weakness for large-breasted American women (*MYM*, 42). During one of his alcohol-propelled emotional breakdowns, he crumbles at the sight of Dawn, a stripper in an Austin club: "'Japanese girl not like this,' he cried out mournfully. 'Scrawny, you know? Not happy-go-lucky'" (43). Jane's Japanese American genetic mixture should mean that she is "happy-go-lucky" and bountiful, ample in her sexuality and girth, the opposite of Akiko in Joichi's eyes. As Dawn lap-dances for Joichi he commends Jane on what he considers to be her superior genetic makeup:

> "You, Takagi, are good example of hybrid vigor, you know?" . . . "Yes." John Wayno surveyed me critically. . . . "We Japanese get weak genes through

> many centuries' process of straight breeding. Like old-fashioned cows. Make weak stock. But you are good and strong and modern girl from crossbreeding. You have hybrid vigor."
>
> (*MYM*, 43)

Jane's parents' "crossbreeding" may have resulted in hybrid vigor, but it is the intervention of modern medicine at the ethnocentric hands of a Norwegian doctor that leads her down the path of DES-instigated disease.

Ozeki's own self-proclaimed muckraking journalism is mirrored by her fictional alter ego's discoveries and both journeys move at breakneck speed.[15] Ozeki (like Moraga) depends on the structure of knowledge accumulation by the reader through her protagonist. Ozeki observes: "I started doing research on the [meat] industry, and I was pretty appalled at what I found out. I fed this information to Jane, who acted upon it, and this is how the plot of the novel developed. With each bit of research, the plot took another twist or turn, building in speed and intensity. . . . Jane's process of discovery mirrors mine, the reader's process mirrors Jane's" (1998, 7). Thus, like Ozeki, Jane begins to find out about herself through her assignments and her research for them. This approach to what Ozeki describes as the primary theme of the novel – "that we live in a world where culture is commerce and where global miscommunication is mediated by commercial television" (1998, 6) – applies to Jane's slow awakening and discovery of the larger and more disturbing narrative surrounding her mother's transition to US culture. But even more important for my purposes is that in both *My Year of Meats* and *Heroes and Saints* the reader and audience member is barraged by a sense of speed, subjugated, in a way, by the same technocratic apparatus that dominates the meat and dairy industries.

In *My Year of Meats*, racial and genetic hybridity is seen sometimes as a promise of a more diverse future and sometimes as a haunting trauma of the past. Jane's "hybrid vigor" is actually a façade behind which hide man-made cancer and disease. Jane does not initially question her mother's cross-cultural marriage and move to Minnesota or the doctor's underlying racist views that motivated his prescription of the synthetic estrogen, DES, to Jane's mother. But as the novel progresses, Jane's version of her mother's immigrant experiences evolves. While she tells Sloan that her mother made a difficult transition to Minnesota because her Great-Granny Little was an incurable racist who referred to Jane as a "little Jap," who could not possibly be a "Little baby," Jane does not connect her grandmother's attitudes to the doctor's prescription (*MYM*, 235). The seemingly innocuous attitude of Doc Ingvortsen – he finds Jane's Ma "*so* delicate," compared to, as Jane puts it, "large-bodied Swedes and sturdy Danes" – is rooted in culturally driven beliefs about what health and beauty look like and perhaps also post-World War II racist views of Japanese people (156; emphasis in the original). Jane's mother admits that when she was pregnant things were "crazy," because she had a "very bad time" with a baby that was "much too big" for her body (155).

Literal and metaphoric immigration and hybridity permeate *My Year of Meats* and encourage both a celebratory and a cautionary approach to the meeting of technology and the global food trade. The brief digression or "interlude" that Jane plans to use in her filming of Vern and Grace of Askew, Louisiana, and their twelve adopted children (*MYM*, 72–73), concerns kudzu, a plant introduced from Japan into the American South as an answer to drought and inhospitable soil. But kudzu "grew rampant, and was soon out of control," as it took over "indigenous vegetation" and "smothered" it (76). Kudzu, adds Jane, is largely used metaphorically to connote the "inroads of Japanese industry into the nonunionized South" (77). Ozeki plants this information in the documentary interlude. This unassuming explanation of the history of kudzu in the United States mirrors the type of textual violence that Jane experiences when reading Frye's *Grammar School Geography*.

The leitmotif of Frye's book appears multiple times in Jane's narrative, and it resurfaces at pivotal points in the plot when Jane is trying to pull apart official from unofficial forms of history. As Jane begins to synthesize her childhood memories in Quam, Minnesota; the excerpts from Frye's *Geography* that haunted her into adulthood; and her mother's patchy recollections of the medicines she took while pregnant (including DES), a number of conflicting feelings arise that eventually lead her to make a documentary. The book is first mentioned just after Jane thinks about her experiences of puberty. She admits that while her friends were chasing after boys who fit white, heteronormative constructions of idealized masculinity, she was just becoming conscious of her racial difference and thinking ahead to procreating and making "a baby who could one day be the King of the World" (*MYM*, 149). Jane's childhood "breeding project," to "mate" with a person who is racially mixed, or at least nonwhite, seems to be achievable when she meets Emil at Kyoto University. Originally from Zaire by way of Paris, Emil is "tall, coal black, utterly different" from the people in Japan, and something about his obvious difference attracts Jane and revives the intentions of her forgotten breeding project (151). Their difficulty in conceiving destroys their marriage. When DES poisoning is later revealed to be the cause of Jane's infertility, the complex relationships among race, gender, and technology are underscored.[16]

In a conversation with Sloan, Jane explains her process of choosing "real-life" American housewives for *My American Wife*: "The BEEF-EX people are very strict. They don't want their meat to have a synergistic association with deformities. Like race. Or poverty. Or clubfeet. At the same time, the Network is always complaining that the shows aren't 'authentic' enough" (*MYM*, 57). Jane assures Sloan that if she were in charge, she would present the world with "some real Americans," not the bland snapshots of American life that she is being pressured to sell. In fact, Jane takes a stab at getting a story past network executives when she shoots a little boy (Bobby) and his pet playing in front of a white farmhouse: "Bobby smiled at the camera. A little Mexican boy shyly offering his American Supper to the nation of Japan" (61).

Jane's tongue-in-cheek description of Bobby offering Texas-style Beefy Burritos denies her instrumental role in the depiction of Bobby as American. Ecocritic Lawrence Buell writes that the idealization of a "poisoned child" is equivalent to imagining an "eco-sensitive indigene" (2005, 24) and Robert T. Hayashi (2007) has warned of the dangers of multiethnic literature becoming monolithically associated with environmental justice literature. Jane knows that Bobby is the son of Mexican immigrants, Alberto and Catalina – or Bert and Cathy, as they ask to be called. Bert "lost his left hand to a hay baler in Abilene seven years earlier, a few months after he and Catalina (Cathy) emigrated from Mexico, just in time for Bobby to be born an American citizen. That had been Cathy's dream, to have an American son, and Bert had paid for her dream with his hand" (*MYM*, 58). Here, the cost of US citizenship is overtly measured in body parts and stands in stark contrast to the immeasurable and invisible ways in which women like Jane's mother also "paid" for their difference with corporeal taxation.

The strongest and most surprising of the many parallels drawn between American women and cattle, women's reproductive health and misguided ideas about animal reproduction, appear in Jane's experiences with Bunny Dunn. Bunny is larger than life. A former exotic dancer who marries an older man and is despised by his son (Gale), she defies easy categorization. Many of Ozeki's characters are exaggerated in some way, and Bunny Dunn is no exception. Jane describes her as "amplitude personified, replete with meats, our ideal American Wife" (*MYM*, 252). Ironically, the very things that make Bunny the perfect on-camera American wife make it most difficult to film her: "The problem with Bunny Dunn was one of framing" (*MYM*, 252). Her expansive bosom, huge hair, and garish outfits (all strategically coordinated by Bunny to create a proportionate frame out of disproportionate parts), lead to a crisis of representation (253). A study in opposites, Jane (an ethnically marked lean woman who is six feet tall) tries to edit and work around Bunny. However, the issue of "framing" Bunny accrues added significance because Bunny breaks the mold of gold-digging former stripper and is instrumental in releasing Jane's documentary to the media.

The section of the novel that involves the Dunn family is the same section in which the eeriest parallels are drawn between government tampering with nature on a global scale and the agricultural industry's disregard for human health on a microscopic one. Before arriving at the Dunn feedlot Jane comes across the Hanford site of the US Department of Energy, where the atomic bomb that was dropped on Nagasaki was produced. Amid barbed-wire fencing she sees the warning: "Department of Energy – Keep Out" (*MYM*, 246). Jane describes the vistas of Colorado as she and her crew (escorted by Dave, their driver) drive to the Dunn feedlot, and the border that separates the US government's Hanford site from those vistas metaphorically disappears as the novel develops. Before meeting the Dunn family and confirming her suspicions about her own DES poisoning, Jane "read all about" Colorado and narrates an ecohistorical perspective on Colorado after World War II (245). She constructs a series of connections showing that big business and government are in cahoots with one another, at the expense of human health. Jane begins the section by calling Colorado "one of the most beautiful states in the country" and anthropomorphizing its topography to give the reader the sense that something special happens in Colorado (245). But it soon becomes obvious that the natural landscape is inflected with unnatural – human-induced – phenomena. Eric Schlosser's (1998) *Rolling Stone* article offers one of the most haunting descriptions of Cheyenne Mountain as a "hollowed out" epicenter of military operations and fast-food orders. The North American Air Defense Command established an air base inside Cheyenne Mountain in 1966, and in 1989, after multiple contaminations and leaks, the Rocky Flats plutonium plant outside of Denver was shut down (245–6).

During Jane's filming of the Dunn feedlot she is horrified to uncover the pollution of animal – and thus human – flesh that stems from the feedlot. Gale Dunn, John Dunn's son and Bunny's stepson, takes Jane on a tour. Although there is something off-kilter about Gale, "a pale, flaccid man with a chin that simply receded into the swollen flesh of his neck," Jane is impressed by the way he commands the camera and the pride he takes in his work and his land (*MYM*, 256). Gale's father, John, represents an older generation of ranchers, and Ozeki carefully contrasts him and his son. Jane imagines how the scene will appear in the film: "Bunny and John would look on approvingly as the knowledge and traditions of the American West were passed on to the next generation" (261). Bunny's daughter, Rose, will help mix the medications with the feed, and she and her half brother, Gale, will be part of the next generation of US agribusiness: wholesome, tied to tradition but technologically savvy, and ready to dominate transpacific meat brokering. John Dunn disapproves of his son's farming methods: "'Crazy, that's what it is,' John growled. 'Used to be you waited till an animal was sick or needed it before you pumped 'em full of drugs. It's all a scam, son. You're just throwin' your money at these big pharmacooticals. . . . Them scientists of yers, they git their paychecks from the pharmacooticals, and they're all in cahoots with the gov'ment'" (263). The collusion of the government, the media, and pharmaceutical companies manifests itself in — and takes its toll most urgently on — the human body.

The porous boundary between nature and technology dissolves for Jane when she realizes that cattle are being fed a host of disturbing substances ranging from plastic-infused fecal matter to hormones. "You feed animals *plastic*?" Jane exclaims as she begins to uncover the web of violations happening at Dunn & Son, Custom Cattle Feeders (*MYM*, 259; emphasis in the original). Gale takes it upon himself to brag to Jane, and as it turns out, plastic is just one of a number of disturbing substances being fed to the cattle:

> There's scientific developments in feed technology happening all over America, all the time. Some guy down at Kansas State I read about has come up with plastic hay. It's these plastic pellets you can feed cattle instead of regular hay. Hay's a bitch, but this plastic stuff – it's clean, it's easy to

> deliver though an automated feed system. . . . And the best thing is they can get back about twenty pounds of it – right out of the cow's rumen at the slaughterhouse. Make new pellets. Talk about recycling!
>
> (*MYM*, 259)

Gale's ironic distortion and use of the word "recycling" flies in the face of the vernacular of twentieth-century green movements. Gale's perverse discourse of how plasticized feed made in the likeness of hay is superior to real hay further estranges the Dunn feedlot from what readers might imagine as spaces that operate according to the "laws of nature."

Meat and machines

My Year of Meats reveals the way that in the business of agribusiness, time and space become warped categories whose manipulation sanitizes the unsavory. Eric Schlosser notes that working in the meatpacking industry is still "the most dangerous job in the United States," adding that "despite" technological advances within the industry the majority of the work is "performed by hand" (2001, 172). It might be, however, that the root of the problem is that precisely because of technological changes in slaughterhouses and meatpacking plants, labor conditions have worsened. Schlosser's chilling account of the impacts of industrialization uncovers that technological "advances" have radically altered not only how meat is produced but also "the towns that produce it" (2001, 149). The cyclical and destructive nature of the drugs and violence in slaughterhouses can be attributed in part to the increased speed of the machinery, which desensitizes the act of killing and thus makes workers more likely to engage in dehumanizing behavior. The competing paradigms of power and the warped reality fostered by technology and blurred images of carcasses and blood lead Schlosser to conclude that although "sex, drugs, and slaughterhouses may seem an unlikely combination," they are in fact linked (2001, 176). He notes that "some supervisors become meatpacking Casanovas, engaging in multiple affairs" (2001, 176).

In Schlosser's book, human, machine, and animal entities are unified on the slaughterhouse floor: "crime, poverty, drug abuse, and homelessness have taken root in towns" (2001, 149). Towns have deteriorated because of the importation of slaughterhouses and meatpacking plants, but what Schlosser tirelessly works to prove is that, in the end, agribusiness is responsible (2001, 149). The web of life does not include only humans. One worker has the job of slitting the carotid artery of each steer as the suspended cattle whir around him: "for eight and a half hours, a worker called a 'sticker' does nothing but stand in a river of blood, being drenched in blood" (2001, 171). This image recalls Haraway's suggestion that the mechanical is becoming all the more alive as we physically degenerate and increasingly depend on technology: "Our machines are disturbingly lively, and we ourselves frighteningly inert" (Haraway 1991, 153). While critics like Haraway are more concerned with intelligent machines, the parallels to the use of machinery in the meat industry are uncanny.

The task of cleaning up a meatpacking plant is left to the invisible labor force of the United States: "some of the most dangerous jobs in meatpacking today are performed by the late-night cleaning crews. A large proportion of these workers are illegal immigrants. They are considered 'independent contractors,' employed not by the meatpacking firms but by sanitation companies" (Schlosser 2001, 176). Because of the hot cleaning fluids that the workers spray around the plant, the temperature rises, and "the crew members can't see or hear each other when the machinery's running" (Schlosser 2001, 177). This inability to hear or see each other metaphorically links the working conditions of the cleaning crew to the inhumane treatment of the cattle and workers alike. Yet even as Schlosser depicts what is supposed to appear as if it is humane killing versus inhumane working conditions, readers understandably question the distinctions. Jonathan Safran Foer acknowledges that "language is never trustworthy, but when it comes to eating animals, words are as often used to misdirect and camouflage as they are to communicate" (2009, 45). In the same section of his work, where he tries to define the word "animal," Foer writes, "nothing could seem more 'natural' than the boundary between humans and animals" (2009, 45). Foer astutely pinpoints the ways that language is deployed to naturalize and normalize states of being that we might otherwise challenge.

The boundaries between machines, animals, and humans are blurred, and each alternately subsumes and consumes the other. Schlosser's chapters indicate a cyclical relationship among the three: man-made intelligent machines force faster slaughtering of animals; humans slaughter animals; and animal blood spills in rivulets on the slaughterhouse floor, where both humans and animals are drained of life as the machine marches on. But the machine, in turn, responds to and is run by humans. The three seemingly separate entities are unified by a wearing down of their borders. As Haraway states in her seminal work on the posthuman, "by the late twentieth century in United States scientific culture, the boundary between human and animal is thoroughly breached" (1991, 151). Ozeki's ecofeminist project treats embodiment as being intrinsically human. Katherine Hayles explores the idea of disembodied information as a fallacy of a constructed posthuman subjectivity. The question of "how information lost its body," as she puts it, suggests how and why in the late twentieth and early twenty-first centuries we have tried (unsuccessfully) to sever the mind from the body (Hayles 1999, 5).[17] Through different approaches, Schlosser and Haraway demonstrate the importance of registering the corporeal in exchanges that effort to absent them.

Ozeki and Moraga reconsidered

I began this chapter by discussing the different ways that Steinbeck, Ozeki, and Moraga engage with the resulting risks of industrialization and its outliers, which do not follow a logical and predictable pattern. Strikingly, both *Heroes and Saints* and *My Year of Meats* center on the historical effects of overexposure to endocrine-disrupting chemicals. Equally striking is the fact that the accepted notion that dose makes the poison has not only been proven inaccurate but has also been detrimental to environmental movements hoping for change. A quick perusal of resources on toxicology demonstrates that the accepted truth is that the amount of the toxin matters most: the larger the dose, the greater the toxicity. In Ozeki's novel environmental degradation becomes a background to human suffering caused by the ingestion of medications and meat; in Moraga's play the sinister and scientifically unknowable nature of chemical poisoning is underlined. Yet in these works people who would seem to have the least risk of exposure appear to have the highest rate of illness. As Langston so powerfully writes of endocrine disruptors, they "violate every aspect of this definition of risk" (2010, 5). In both *Heroes and Saints* and *My Year of Meats*, the body serves as a receptacle for toxic by-products of transnational trade and suffers from unequal exposure to risk; it is the female body, however, that is most damaged. Field tests demonstrate that women are more susceptible than men to dioxin, PCBs, and various other chemicals that are stored in the body's fatty tissue (Verchick 2004). Real cases of environmental and human disease in McFarland become the fictional stories of Moraga, just as the real legacy of DES becomes Jane's documentary in Ozeki's novel. Moraga and Ozeki strive to expose the dangers of large-scale agriculture as a machine that destroys more than it produces and one that places the onus of risk on the consumer.

Food safety and risk assessment are indelibly intertwined, to the point of being inseparable. Renowned food scholar Marion Nestle writes, "food safety is a highly political issue" (2003, 1). Nestle identifies two differing approaches, that of the US Food and Drug Administration, with its principle of generally regarded as safe (GRAS), and that of the European Union, with its precautionary principle (2003, 22–5). The contrast between the two approaches speaks volumes about how Americans, as a society, value the right to remain informed and safe consumers. Food and social historian Amy Bentley notes that during and after World War II, eating meat was seen as patriotic, and prescribed portions were increased and marketed as a national must: "beef, long a symbol of status and wealth, increased in symbolic value in the war partially because of wartime government and private industry propaganda" (1998, 92–3). Moraga and Ozeki both ask their audiences to think about the symbolic power of food in the United States and how, as Bentley suggests, it has become inherently political. Indeed, in *Heroes and Saints* and *My Year of Meats*, food choices directly impact women's reproductive rights and health.

Food safety becomes a platform for thinking about environmental safety. In the case of the Central Valley it outlines a clear parallel between a reactive versus proactive approach both to food safety and cancer clusters. Speaking to Kurt Rivera, a reporter for *Bakersfield Now*, Joseph L. Wiemels, a childhood leukemia specialist at the University of California, San Francisco, comments on the lack of knowledge about what causes cancer clusters: "I think we continue to have a situation where there's a lot more frustration than answers to cancer clusters and that's, that's true for McFarland as well" (Rivera 2012). Wiemels underlines an important facet of childhood cancer cluster investigations: researchers are "always looking back." In other words, the manner in which we tackle cancer clusters and instances of high cancer rates is retrospective and reactive, not proactive. In Ozeki's and Moraga's work, the past continually haunts; looking back is not a choice, but a necessity for survival. They force dead bodies into the consciousness of the audience and the protagonists to prove that the past is never the past.

The tie that binds the works considered in this chapter (Moraga's play, Ozeki's novel, and the UFW documentaries) is an attempt to explain and represent the inexplicable, and to translate the knowledge of the body into quantifiable, communicable terms. They also anticipate future modes of representation and documentation. As Moraga's character Dolores puts it, "I don' need a chart to tell me que tengo problemas [that I have problems]" (*HS*, 129). Dolores and other characters in the play and novel do not need data to tell them what, psychosomatically, they know to be true: their environment, after being tampered with by humans, is making them ill. Importantly, the question of how to mobilize the public repeatedly comes up in all of these works.

The valley as an anti-place

In Ozeki's book, as in Moraga's play, renderings of toxic laboring bodies not only force the national body politic to grapple with the ripple effects of its consumption practices, but they also articulate an emerging politics of disruption. Through both the form and content of their works they create narrative threads and depict human bodies that mimic the workings of the very endocrine disruptors they vilify. In other words, the authors present us with stories and bodies that do not behave in predictable ways and that are profoundly unsettling. In *Global Appetites*, Allison Carruth captures a key component of Ozeki's fiction, "to make the contemporary novel a living-breathing instrument of knowledge transfer" (2013, 151).[18] Akin to Carruth, I too see Ozeki (and Moraga) working toward the transfer of knowledge, but it is of a related if different ilk: corporeal knowledge. Accessing readers' imaginations becomes paramount for ecocritical authors who are attempting to concretize and describe olfactory and sensory experiences, especially as these are often the first sounding of the alarm of risk and toxicity.[19]

The focus on materiality in these two works, on the way that the matter of the body matters and suffers, is a purposeful choice by Moraga and Ozeki that harnesses the illogical and often obscure risks caused by the agricultural industry through the biosphere of the body. Timothy Pachirat wrote *Every Twelve Seconds: Industrialized Slaughter and the Politics of Sight* in hopes to "provoke reflection on how distance and concealment operate as mechanisms of power in modern society" (2011, 3). His poignant prose, based on his first-hand experience of working on the kill floor, describes how "the contemporary slaughterhouse is 'a place that is no-place'" (2011, 3). As I wrote in my first chapter, Arjun Appadurai makes a convincing case that American bodies and the "known power of the American state" (2006, 120) are often blurred boundaries. US bodies become an extension of US-branded neoliberal capitalism. Taken together, Pachirat and Appadurai's work crystallizes the notion that only in an "anti-place," a space where normal rules and regulations do not apply, are people able to breach boundaries of violence they might otherwise not traverse. Just as the discourse surrounding climate change works to help people conceptualize the scale of destruction and alteration to the earth, so too *My Year of Meats* and *Heroes and Saints* ask readers and viewers to stretch their imaginations to think of the enmeshed ways that the transnational food trade causes transdermal shifts in both biological and abiological matter. Pachirat and Appadurai together articulate something that authors of works about animals and industrial agriculture continue to struggle with: how to effectively shuttle between the most intimate spaces and the most industrial and global ones.

Images and descriptions of interrupted and dismembered bodies haunt *My Year of Meats* and are staged front-and-center in *Heroes and Saints*. These two works of fiction about the circulation of flesh across borders underline the sense of loss that accompanies a global bartering system of labor and goods. That loss is – ironically – brought into focus through the ways in which these artists handle the protagonists' and the audiences' relation to space. In her book on ethical ramifications of viewing practices, Susan Sontag offers a critique of the nature of photography as narrative: "Nonstop imagery (television, streaming video, movies) is our surround, but when it comes to remembering, the photograph has the deeper bite. . . . The photograph is like a quotation, or a maxim or proverb" (2003, 22). Sontag continues and states that images are meant to "arrest attention, startle, surprise" (2003, 23). According to Sontag, the photograph, in its stillness, is more impactful than moving images. Moraga and Ozeki certainly seem to assault the reader with information overload and with the speed and movement of plot, but when they pull back it is akin to Sontag's description of arrested movement. The medium of these works, a play and a novel, and the strategic approaches of Ozeki and Moraga, inhabit symbolic forms of violence and risk that test the audience's ability to look away (from the page or stage).

In 1989, political geographer Edward Soja wrote that in our postmodern era, a new "critical human geography is taking shape, brashly reasserting the interpretive significance of space in the historically privileged confines of contemporary critical thought" (11). In the creations of Moraga and Ozeki the importance of space and corporeality converge with twinned attention to temporality and spatial politics. This chapter began with a quote by Loron Hodge, former head of the Kern County Farm Bureau, who told reporters that he'd "never had any adverse reactions" to Kern County's high concentration of contaminated land and air (quoted in Holding and McCormick 2004). Hodge's refusal to engage the possibility that industrial agribusiness (resulting in methane emissions), pesticides, antibiotics, and waste might have something to do with the poor quality of the air and water in Kern County seems astounding: "My opinion is that we are seeing more pollution in the valley because we have more people coming, bringing their automobiles" (Holding and McCormick 2004). For Hodge, as for countless others, living in the Central Valley means generating and absorbing risk. Hodge wishes that farmers would stop getting a "bad" reputation: "the frustration we (farmers) have is that we get this broad brushstroke that says agriculture is doing bad things, when all we want to do is provide food and fiber to the people we serve" (Holding and McCormick 2004). The "broad brushstroke" allows for the quiet reallocation of risk accompanied by an orchestrated and politicized push to divide societal sectors from one another: producer against consumer, as we see in the example with Hodge. Such divisions are translated onto the bodies of characters like Cerezita, Jane, and Akiko, bodies that render palpable the geography of risk.

Notes

1 Depending on your sources, the number can fluctuate slightly but I used the "California Share of U.S. Agricultural Exports by Category and Commodity, 2013 and 2014" report generated by the CDFA, California Department of Food and Agriculture.

2 These statistics come from the United States Department of Agriculture's site, which also states that food makes up 12.6 percent of the average US household's expenditures.

3 *Heroes and Saints* was commissioned by José Luis Valenzuela's Latino Theatre Lab of the Los Angeles Theatre Center, and it was performed as a reading in 1989. The play was presented again as a staged reading under Moraga's direction in San Francisco in 1991 (the world premiere was on April 4, 1992, at El Teatro Misión in San Francisco) and it was published in Moraga's *Heroes and Saints and Other Plays* (1994b).

4 Moraga's more popular writing includes *Giving Up the Ghost*, 1994a; *The Hungry Woman*, 2001; and her coedited collection with Gloria Anzaldúa, *This Bridge Called My Back: Writings by Radical Women of Color*, 1981.

5 Jane Bennett breaks down the divide between humans and food, arguing that the latter is not a series of inanimate objects without agency. She suggests that the slow food movement urges people to "recognize the agency of food . . . to incorporate a greater sense of the active vitality" of food matter (2010, 51).

6 In her article on Ozeki and ecofeminism, Shameem Black defines cosmofeminism as "enabling responses to the dilemmas created by globalization" (2004, 229). For ecofeminism in general, see Greta Gaard (1993, 1998, 2001). For transnational approaches that include a treatment of gender politics in Ozeki see Monica Chiu (2001), Cheryl J. Fish (2009), and Julie Sze (2006).

7 For general information on pesticides and the most recent issues related to pesticide exposure and legislation, see Pesticide Action Network (2014). For information about the suspected endocrine disruptors (methyl bromide, dinoseb, parathion, and phosdrin), search "PAN Pesticides Database."

8 One of the most gripping reads on PCBs, Monsanto, and the collusion between industry and government is a book by investigative journalist Ted Dracos, *Biocidal: Confronting the Poisonous Legacy of PCBs* (2010).

9 In its "National Report on Human Exposure to Environmental Chemicals" the US Centers for Disease Control and Prevention (CDC) states that the average person absorbs toxicity in "low levels through foods or by breathing in air that contains the chemical" (2012). A study published in *Environmental Health Perspectives* (Harley et al. 2010) found that not only are the number of dangerous chemicals increasing, but exposure is beginning in utero – not only after birth. Traditionally, breast milk has been considered the major carrier of toxins (in addition to air, water, and dust); significantly, studies are increasingly linking in utero exposure to endocrine disruptors as the cause of a host of health issues both for the mother and for the child.

10 Moraga's author's notes are part of the play *Heroes and Saints* (1994b, 89).

11 In Moraga's play she does not translate the mixture of Spanish and English into standardized English. I am not entirely comfortable translating the text because hers is a political statement, and after having spent some time with her at a conference I thought long and hard about the translations. In the end I chose to translate the text, but I am cognizant of the issues at stake.

12 Kenneth Chay and Michael Greenstone (2003) found links between economic depression, toxic dumping, and infant mortality. They explain the health benefits of cleaner air in economic terms: the benefits are one result of economic privilege.

13 I wish to thank Allison Carruth for first introducing me to the play itself and later bringing my attention to the sound of the helicopters as a presence. In turn, she credited a former Stanford graduate student as raising the issue in a seminar.

14 Cause for further unrest is that bisphenol A (BPA) – found in hard, clear polycarbonate plastics – has a chemical structure that closely resembles that of DES. BPA produces effects like those of estrogen and has proven to be toxic in both negligible and large doses. Julia Barrett reports that two studies on BPA have definitively proven that dose is not a surefire predictor of risk (2006). The possibility of human exposure through water bottles, baby bottles, and toys caused widespread panic in 2008–9 in the United States.

15 For a fuller consideration of *My Year of Meats* and muckraking journalism, see Allison Carruth (2013, 132–6).

16 Jane's frequent glossing over of the impacts of global meat corporations on US immigrant populations, and of BEEF-EX's attitude toward anything considered not part of the American dream, resembles her relationship to her mother's past. The Little family of Minnesota consisted of dairy farmers who went bankrupt because of "agribusiness and turbocows," although Jane claims not to remember the details (*MYM*, 235). The ironic undercurrent of *My Year of Meats* crescendos when Jane reveals that her paternal ancestors were dairy farmers and her mother was a botanist of sorts herself.

17 Hayles is most interested in the shifting grounds according to which we define subjectivity: "I view the present moment as a critical juncture when interventions might be made to keep disembodiment from being rewritten, once again, into prevailing concepts of subjectivity. I see the deconstruction of the liberal humanist subject as an opportunity to put back into the picture the flesh that continues to be erased in contemporary discussions about cybernetic subjects. Hence my focus on how information lost its body" (1999, 5).

18 Carruth (2013) employs the work of Anthony Giddens (1990) and examines Ozeki's *My Year of Meats* (1998) and *All Over Creation* (2003).

19 Three texts that are particularly useful for thinking through representations of somaticism and anthropocentricism across platforms are Laura U. Marks, *The Skin of the Film* (2000); Anat Pick, *Creaturely Poetics* (2011); and the coedited collection *Screening Nature: Cinema beyond the Human* (Pick and Narraway 2013).

References

Adams, Carol J. 1990. *The Sexual Politics of Meat: A Feminist-Vegetarian Critical Theory.* New York: Continuum.

Antonetta, Susanne. 2001. *Body Toxic: An Environmental Memoir.* New York: Counterpoint.

Appadurai, Arjun. 2006. *Fear of Small Numbers: An Essay on the Geography of Anger.* Durham, NC: Duke University Press.

Barrett, Julia R. 2006. "Endocrine Disruptors: Bisphenol A and the Brain." *Environmental Health Perspectives* 114 (4): A217.

Bennett, Jane. 2010. *Vibrant Matter: A Political Ecology of Things.* Durham, NC: Duke University Press.

Bentley, Amy. 1998. *Eating for Victory: Food Rationing and the Politics of Domesticity.* Champaign: University of Illinois Press.

Black, Shameem. 2004. "Fertile Cosmofeminism: Ruth L. Ozeki and Transnational Reproduction." *Meridians: Feminism, Race, Transnationalism* 5 (1): 226–56.

Bourdieu, Pierre. 1991. *Language and Symbolic Power.* Edited by John B. Thompson. Translated by Gino Raymond and Matthew Adamson. Cambridge: Polity Press.

Buell, Lawrence. 2005. *The Future of Environmental Criticism: Environmental Crisis and Literary Imagination.* Malden, MA: Blackwell.

California Department of Food and Agriculture. 2014. "California Share of U.S. Agricultural Exports by Category and Commodity, 2013 and 2014." https://www.cdfa.ca.gov/statistics/PDFs/AgExports2014–2015.pdf.

———. 2015. "California Agricultural Production Statistics." https://www.cdfa.ca.gov/statistics/.

Carruth, Allison. 2013. *Global Appetites: American Power and the Literature of Food.* New York: Cambridge University Press.

Centers for Disease Control and Prevention. 2012. "National Report on Human Exposure to Environmental Chemicals." http://www.cdc.gov/exposurereport/faq.html.

———. n.d. "About DES." http://www.cdc.gov/DES/CONSUMERS/about/.

Chay, Kenneth Y., and Michael Greenstone. 2003. "The Impact of Air Pollution on Infant Mortality: Evidence from Geographic Variation in Pollution Shocks Induced by a Recession." *Quarterly Journal of Economics* 118 (3): 1121–67.

Chiu, Monica. 2001. "Postnational Globalization and (En)Gendered Meat Production in Ruth L. Ozeki's *My Year of Meats.*" *LIT: Literature Interpretation Theory* 12 (1): 99–128.

Douglas, Mary. (1966) 2002. *Purity and Danger: An Analysis of Concepts of Pollution and Taboo.* New York: Routledge.

Dracos, Ted. 2010. *Biocidal: Confronting the Poisonous Legacy of PCBs.* Boston, MA: Beacon Press.

Fish, Cheryl J. 2009. "The Toxic Body Politic: Ethnicity, Gender, and Corrective Eco-Justice in Ruth Ozeki's *My Year of Meats* and Judith Helfand and Daniel Gold's *Blue Vinyl.*" *Multiethnic Literatures of the United States* 34 (2): 43–62.

Foer, Jonathan Safran. 2009. *Eating Animals.* New York: Little, Brown and Company.

Gaard, Greta, ed. 1993. *Ecofeminism: Women, Animals, Nature.* Philadelphia: Temple University Press.

———. 2001. "Women, Water, Energy: An Ecofeminist Approach," *Organization and the Environment* 14 (2): 157–72.

Gaard, Greta, and Patrick D. Murphy, eds. 1998. *Ecofeminist Literary Criticism: Theory, Interpretation, Pedagogy.* Urbana and Chicago: University of Illinois Press.

Giddens, Anthony. 1990. *The Consequences of Modernity.* Stanford, CA: Stanford University Press.

Greenberg, Linda M. 2009. "Learning from the Dead: Wounds, Women, and Activism in Cherríe Moraga's *Heroes and Saints.*" *MELUS* 34 (1): 163–84.

Gutiérrez-Jones, Carl. 1995. *Rethinking the Borderlands: Between Chicano Culture and Legal Discourse.* Berkeley, CA: University of California Press.

Haraway, Donna. 1991. *Simians, Cyborgs, and Women: The Reinvention of Nature.* New York: Routledge.

Harley, Kim G., Amy R. Marks, Jonathan Chevrier, Asa Bradman, Andreas Sjödin, and Brenda Eskenazi. 2010. "PBDE Concentrations in Women's Serum and Fecundability." *Environmental Health Perspectives* 118 (5): 699–704. doi:10.1289.

Hayashi, Robert T. 2007. "Beyond *Walden Pond*: Asian American Literature and the Limits of Ecocriticism." In *Coming into Contact: Exploration in Ecocritical Theory and Practice*, edited by

Annie Merrill Ingram, Ian Marshall, Daniel J. Philippon, and Adam W. Sweeting, 58–75. Athens: University of Georgia Press.

Hayles, N. Katherine. 1999. *How We Became Posthuman: Virtual Bodies in Cybernetics, Literature, and Informatics.* Chicago: University of Chicago Press.

Holding, Reynolds, and Erin McCormick. 2004. "Too Young to Die/Part Two: Toxic Legacy." *SFGate,* October 4. http://www.sfgate.com/green/article/TOO-YOUNG-TO-DIE-PART-TWO-TOXIC-LEGACY-2720160.php.

Holland, Sharon Patricia. 2000. *Raising the Dead: Readings of Death and (Black) Subjectivity.* Durham, NC: Duke University Press.

Huerta, Jorge A. 2000. *Chicano Drama: Performance, Society and Myth.* Cambridge, MA: Harvard University Press.

Kegley, S.E., B.R. Hill, S. Orme, and A.H. Choi. 2014. "PAN Pesticides Database." Pesticide Action Network, North America. http://www.pesticideinfo.org/Search_Chemicals.jsp#ChemSearch.

Langston, Nancy. 2010. *Toxic Bodies: Hormone Disruptors and the Legacy of DES.* New Haven, CT: Yale University Press.

Marcone, Jorge. 2011. "A Painful Pastoral: Migration and Ecology in Chicana/o Literature." *Pacific Coast Philology* 46 (2): 194–209.

Marks, Laura U. 2000. *The Skin of the Film: Intercultural Cinema, Embodiment, and the Senses.* Durham, NC: Duke University Press.

Moraga, Cherríe. 1994a. *Giving Up the Ghost.* In *Heroes and Saints and Other Plays*, edited by Cherríe L. Moraga, 1–35. Albuquerque, NM: West End.

———. 1994b. *Heroes and Saints.* In *Heroes and Saints and Other Plays*, edited by Cherríe L. Moraga, 85–149. Albuquerque, NM: West End.

———. 1994c. *Shadow of a Man.* In *Heroes and Saints and Other Plays*, edited by Cherríe L. Moraga, 37–84. Albuquerque, NM: West End.

———. 2001. *The Hungry Woman: A Mexican Medea.* Albuquerque, NM: West End.

Moraga, Cherríe, and Gloria Anzaldúa. 1981. *This Bridge Called My Back: Writings by Radical Women of Color.* Watertown, MA: Persephone Press.

Nash, Linda. 2007. *Inescapable Ecologies: A History of Environment, Disease, and Knowledge.* Berkeley, CA: University of California Press.

National Institute of Environmental Health Sciences. 2016. "Endocrine Disruptors." http://www.niehs.nih.gov/health/topics/agents/endocrine/.

Nestle, Marion. 2003. *Safe Food: Bacteria, Biotechnology, and Bioterrorism.* Berkeley, CA: University of California Press.

Newman, Penny. 1989. "Cancer Clusters among Children: The Implications of McFarland." *Journal of Pesticide Reform* 9 (3): 10–13.

Nixon, Rob. 2011. *Slow Violence and the Environmentalism of the Poor.* Cambridge, MA: Harvard University Press.

Ozeki, Ruth. 1998. *My Year of Meats.* New York: Penguin.

———. 2003. *All Over Creation.* New York: Penguin.

Pachirat, Timothy. 2011. *Every Twelve Seconds: Industrialized Slaughter and the Politics of Sight.* New Haven, CT: Yale University Press.

Parlee, Lorena, and Lenny Bourin, producers. 1986. *The Wrath of Grapes.* Keene, CA: United Farm Workers of America and AFL-CIO. VHS.

Pearcy, Gary, dir. 1975. "Fighting for Our Lives." http://www.youtube.com/watch?v=Zq0SO3R9HeI.

Pesticide Action Network, North America. 2014. "Home Page." http://www.panna.org.

Pick, Anat. 2011. *Creaturely Poetics: Animality and Vulnerability in Literature and Film*. New York: Columbia University Press.

Pick, Anat, and Guinevere Narraway, eds. 2013. *Screening Nature: Cinema Beyond the Human*. New York: Berghahn Books.

Rivera, Kurt. 2012. "Theory Sheds New Light on McFarland Cancer Cluster." *Bakersfield Now*, May 11. http://bakersfieldnow.com/news/local/theory-sheds-new-light-on-mcfarland-cancer-cluster.

Saldívar, Ramón. 1990. *Chicano Narrative: The Dialectics of Difference*. Madison: University of Wisconsin Press.

Schlosser, Eric. 1998. "Fast-Food Nation Part One: The True Cost of America's Diet." *Rolling Stone Magazine* 794, September 3. http://www.rollingstone.com/culture/news/fast-food-nation-part-one-the-true-cost-of-americas-diet-19980903.

———. 2001. *Fast Food Nation: The Dark Side of the All-American Meal*. New York: Houghton Mifflin.

Sexton, Ken, and Steven H. Linder. 2010. "The Role of Cumulative Risk Assessment in Decisions about Environmental Justice." *International Journal of Environmental Research and Public Health* 7 (11): 4037–49.

Siegrist, Michael, George T. Cvetkovich, and Heinz Gutscher. 2001. "Shared Values, Social Trust, and the Perception of Geographic Cancer Clusters." *Risk Analysis* 21 (6): 1047–54.

Skelton, Renee, and Vernice Miller. 2006. "The Environmental Justice Movement." Natural Resources Defense Council. https://www.nrdc.org/stories/environmental-justice-movement.

Soja, Edward W. 1989. *Postmodern Geographies: Reassertion of Space in Critical Social Theory*. New York: Verso.

Sontag, Susan. 2003. *Regarding the Pain of Others*. New York: Picador.

Steinbeck, John. (1939) 1976. *The Grapes of Wrath*. Reprint, New York: Penguin.

Sze, Julie. 2006. "Boundaries and Border Wars: DES, Technology, and Environmental Justice." *American Quarterly* 58 (3): 791–814.

Thompson, Lisa B. 2004. "Watsonville/Circles in the Dirt (review)." *Theatre Journal* 56 (3): 523–5.

Verchick, Robert R. M. 2004. "Feminist Theory and Environmental Justice." In *New Perspectives on Environmental Justice*, edited by Rachel Stein, 63–77. New Brunswick, NJ: Rutgers University Press.

Yarbro-Bejarano, Yvonne. 2001. *The Wounded Heart: Writing on Cherríe Moraga*. Austin: University of Texas Press.

5 Bodies on the border

Previous chapters have mapped patterns of consumption in unique ways: Moraga's protagonist put her family "on the map" while Steinbeck charted his anxieties about impending war and industrialized agriculture onto the seascape and intertidal zones.[1] This chapter offers a different type of mapping and grid and more directly tackles the connection between race and environmental injustice. Alex Rivera's science fiction film, *Sleep Dealer* (2008a), and Karen Tei Yamashita's novel, *Tropic of Orange* (1997), not only investigate what environmental justice might look like, but they also indicate a sea change in their commitment to magical realism and science fiction as tools to help us reimagine nature and its relationship to culture.[2]

Histories of colonialism, imperialism, gendered violence, and racialized toxicity pump through the veins of the protagonists of these works, unequivocally demonstrating the authors' commitment to connecting body and place. *Sleep Dealer* and *Tropic of Orange* are purposely disorienting texts that play with the space-time continuum and illustrate the manner in which issues of environmental justice have been ignored in traditional ecocriticism. Donald Worster's foundational *Nature's Economy* ([1977] 1985) helped establish the field of environmental history and made careful study of the scientific discipline of ecology. William Cronon's "The Trouble with Wilderness" (1995) challenged accepted environmentalist notions by asserting that our focus on wilderness preservation has led to a neglect of our everyday built environments. Yamashita's and Rivera's texts follow this shift from romanticized representations of colonized space to futuristic imaginings of decolonized and synthetic spaces.

In this chapter, natural elements (air and water in particular) reveal the faulty and vexed manner in which nations have constructed borders that fail to address the realities of our uncontainable lives. The texts discussed here not only challenge ideas of naturalized boundaries but also clearly indicate the ways in which spatiotemporal markers require recalibration. In an age when we seem to be trying desperately to comprehend the modern condition, works like *Sleep Dealer* and *Tropic of Orange* clarify that we have caused immeasurable harm through our efforts to advance civilization while ignoring important signs of things going awry.[3]

The US–Mexico divide

> All 2,000 miles of the frontier
> stretched across from Tijuana on the Pacific,
> . . .
> to the end of its tail
> on the Gulf of México.
> It waited with seismic sensors and thermal imaging,
> with la pinche migra,
> . . .
> with coyotes, pateros, cholos,
> steel structures, barbed wire, infrared binoculars,
> INS detention centers, border patrols, rape,
> . . .
> the deportation of 400,000 Mexican
> citizens in 1932,
> coaxing back of 2.2 million
> braceros in 1942
> only to exile the same 2.2 million
> wetbacks in 1953.
>
> Karen Tei Yamashita, *Tropic of Orange* (pp. 197–98)

In the above excerpt, the narrator dramatizes the past and present tension between the United States and Mexico, illustrating the threat of barbed wire and thermal imaging being used at the border to detain and violate illegal immigrants. The two thousand miles of that border are a combination of dirt, water, and air, yet the narrator focuses on the steel and wire that have now become synonymous with media images of the border region. Multinational corporations in search of cheap labor have long looked to Tijuana, Mexico, as a source of profit and a location for unregulated business practices.[4] In the overlapping themes between *Tropic of Orange* and *Sleep Dealer* there is a shift in concern over how environmental degradation and corporate greed manifest themselves along the border.

Both *Tropic of Orange* (hereafter *TO*) and *Sleep Dealer* engage with such issues as the North American Free Trade Agreement (NAFTA) and the Department of Homeland Security's ongoing project to build a wall between the United States and Mexico. Founded in 2002, the Department of Homeland Security was established as a response to 9/11, and one of the stated purposes of Operation Gatekeeper is to enhance the militarization and materiality of the border. The valuable and monetizable natural resources that are located in contested territory further complicate any attempt to cordon off such spaces and claim them as "US" or "Mexican."[5] Although Operation Gatekeeper was founded by the Immigration and Naturalization Service (INS) in 1994, during the administration of President Bill Clinton, the Department of Homeland Security's stated reasons for continuing the operation is to protect American citizens from illegal "aliens" and anti-American "terrorists" (Bush 2002). In *Sleep Dealer*'s post-9/11 future, the imbalance of power in transnational exchanges is symbolized by a dam, and the battle over water rights is waged in the name of US national security and anti-immigration policy.

Environmental justice activists have long criticized the absurdity of national boundaries. Nations both lay claim to resources that they exploit and refuse responsibility for the resulting human rights violations and toxic offloading. Yamashita's narrator describes how Arcangel – the pseudomythological five-hundred-year-old figure fighting past and present oppressions south of the border – hooks to his back a broken-down bus and with it the Tropic of Cancer. He connects cables from the bus into his battered flesh, he bleeds into the earth, and he slowly pulls the bus along like "the burden of gigantic wings, too heavy to fly" (*TO*, 197). The narrator states that this "superhuman" feat, as sensational as it is, can be understood only by those present: "The virtually real could not accommodate the magical. Digital memory failed to translate imaginary memory . . . it could not be recognized on a tube, no matter how big or how highly defined. In other words, to see it, you had to be there yourself" (*TO*, 197). The self-anointed messiah of the oppressed, Arcangel's thoughts may very well be those expressed in the free verse that interrupts the prose (excerpted on the previous page), but Yamashita's narrative strategy leaves unclear whether these are collective or singular musings.

According to the narrator, the "New World Border" (a play on the New World Order) and Arcangel's superhuman strength cannot be recorded by anything but human memory; it requires that you be physically present to bear witness. If you indeed have to "be there yourself" (*TO*, 197) to comprehend a surreal version of reality that "no tube" can accurately represent, it seems that fiction *is* the closest approximation to the real. Yamashita's splicing of digitally inspired prose and poetry and the manner in which she organizes the grid of her novel contribute to the reader's experience of disorientation and the blurring of fiction and fact, but they are also offered as the only alternative to experiencing "the magical" in person. "In other words," to quote Yamashita, you (the reader) are there, experiencing the catastrophic effects of free trade and globalization and trying to keep track of "the frontier," the "end of its tail," the "deportation" of human flesh in 1932 (after Depression-era anti-immigration raids), the "coaxing back" in 1942 (the Bracero Program), and the "exile" of the "same 2.2 million / wetbacks in 1953" (the INS's Operation Wetback) (*TO*, 197–8). The militarization of the US–Mexico border region and the accompanying egregious labor conditions for those working in factories near the border are a topic of frequent debate (Calavita 1994; Massey, Durand, and Malone 2002). Moral ambiguities abound as the reader is coaxed back and forth between the familiar and the bizarre, the real and the surreal.

Yamashita creates a discursive space in which one can begin to see the ethical complexities of border control. The "frontier" snakes back and forth like a terrible animal composed of biometric tools and violence; the undercurrent of multiplicity continues as the author presents her characters in such diverse ways that it becomes impossible to define them as one thing or another. Through both form and content she pushes the reader to reimagine his or her ideas of citizenship and human rights. Both *Sleep Dealer* and *Tropic of Orange* effectively challenge Yamashita's narrator's statement that experiential knowledge is the only effective mode of knowledge acquisition. In fact, the virtually real scopic regime of *Sleep Dealer* and the textual pastiche of *Tropic of Orange* deftly confront issues of biopolitical violence and environmental injustices on the US–Mexico border. Rivera's post-9/11 discourse on US security reveals the "steel structures, barbed wire, [and] infrared binoculars" in Yamashita to be the tools of corporate greed as it divides up natural resources in contested territory.

The capitalist-driven and nationally inflected war over the natural resources of water (in *Sleep Dealer*), fruit, and human organs (in *Tropic of Orange*) causes environmental devastation. Corporeal violence traverses borders as a result of rapid economic growth. *Sleep Dealer* and *Tropic of Orange* foreground the biopolitical violence that accompanies contemporary restrictions of global capital – not only its appropriation of natural resources, but also the expropriation of bodies, organs, blood, and tissue. Environmental justice activists would argue, as Vandana Shiva does, that the "enclosure of the commons" benefits the rich and harms the poor (2005, 53). The "commons" are those things that should belong to all people equally, or the earth's resources. Ecocriticism is increasingly overlapping with the field of environmental justice. Spurred by the civil rights movement and Rachel Carson's foundational *Silent Spring* (1962), environmental justice activists draw attention to the often concurrent exploitation of nature and humans and to the accompanying intersections of race, class, and gender.[6] As I wrote about at length in the first chapter, ecocriticism is increasingly seen as having multiple overlapping interests with environmental justice and transnational American studies, so much so that Lawrence Buell has deemed environmental justice a part of the "second wave" of ecocritical thought (2005, 22–3). In part responding to international activism and grassroots movements like those led by Vandana Shiva and Ken Saro-Wiwa (Comfort 2002), second-wave ecocriticism has expanded and further explored, as Buell notes, the "organicist models" of the environment (Buell 2005, 21).[7] Ecocritics are evermore acknowledging the narrowing gap between environmental justice, ecocriticism, and community-driven movements for social justice and equal access to safe and clean natural resources (Adamson and Slovic 2009; Buell 2005; Deming and Savoy 2002; Gaard 2001; Glotfelty 1996). Although the importance of nature and place to the construction of multiethnic identity is fundamental, the green movement in the United States has by and large been perceived as virtually white; but Scott Slovic and Joni Adamson refer to a "third wave" of ecocriticism that exposes a renewed acknowledgment of the inherently transnational and global dimensions of the natural world (2009, 6). That acknowledgment existed in Buell's first wave, it certainly was present in the second, and critics are now using the relationship between literature and the environment to narrativize and clarify much of what is currently taking place in the United States. In both *Sleep Dealer* and *Tropic of Orange* natural elements of the borderlands and land formations function as metaphors for issues of globalization and environmental justice and their attendant gendered implications. The border is portrayed as a US-run entity that absorbs what it needs and rejects what it does not want.

Fictional representations of the border region and its resources focus on the unsustainable model of bartering with nature and the violence involved in the purchase and sale of natural resources (water, oranges, bodies, and so on). The sale of nature is directly and inextricably linked to the rape and death of the most disenfranchised, and particularly to the fate of women; it is also inarguably racialized. Julie Sze suggests that *Tropic of Orange* serves as a "case study of how to 'read' environmental justice perspectives" because the "novel's insights about globalization, immigration, and labor highlight how contemporary struggles are linked to the historical exploitation of nature and people of color" (2002, 163). Sze further underscores Yamashita's linkage of past and present exploitation of natural and human resources by proposing that the abrupt and frequent temporal shifts in *Tropic of Orange* function as a reminder that present-day "corporate domination cannot be separated from historical colonialism" (2002, 171). In Yamashita's postindustrial Los Angeles the perils of globalization directly refer to a history of colonial violence and exploitation. Both *Tropic of Orange* and *Sleep Dealer* create ontological dissonance, especially when comparing bodies (those of humans, animals, machines, and the earth itself) and the ways in which they are scarred. Colonial history is shown as in some way altering these various bodies, and the authors do not let their audiences ignore the real matter of the material body.

Los Angeles, Tijuana, and Empire

The events in *Tropic of Orange* take place over a period of seven days, and the novel revolves around the lives of seven characters. At the book's beginning Yamashita provides a grid called "HyperContexts" that maps the characters and events onto chapters and days, mirroring the grid of traffic and the flow of products in and out of Los Angeles. Yamashita's choice to title her grid "HyperContexts" points to the central role that new forms of media play in creating global order. It simultaneously reorders the table of contents that directly precedes it and offers a different vantage point. In the novel's first few pages, Yamashita asks the reader to be open to alternative forms of truth and to reordering facts. When reading the novel it is helpful to refer back to the grid, not the table of contents, which makes this diverse spatiotemporal rubric more relevant. The reader is forced to not only interact differently with the book (physically flipping pages) but also with the philosophy of narrative as having a beginning, a middle, and a resolution. While here such a narratological thread is distorted, it also offers the creative freedom of thinking differently about things.

The characters include Gabriel, a Chicano newspaper reporter in pursuit of the Pulitzer Prize who is dating Emi, an Asian American news executive. Emi continually pushes Gabriel toward new media and also goes beyond his comfort zone with her outlandish comments on sex, race, and the modern condition. Emi's Japanese grandfather (Manzanar Murakami) is homeless and becomes a leading figure as he conducts a symphony of sound amid the pandemonium of Los Angeles. A former surgeon and second-generation Japanese American who has by all accounts disgraced the Japanese American community of Los Angeles, Manzanar's role in the story initially seems minute. Gabriel and Emi are both involved in the news and in chasing the next big scoop, usually a story of disaster. They are ultimately united by a disaster of apocalyptic proportions on the Harbor Freeway when fires, gridlock, and violence erupt. Emi dies while trying to get a message out to Gabriel: "Just cuz you get to the end doesn't mean you know what happened" (*TO*, 252). Emi's poignant commentary at the end of the novel acts in a similar fashion to Yamashita's manipulation of story order and the chapter grid. Yamashita keeps her readers off-balance and questions not only their wish for resolution but also their expectations of how plotlines should unfold and be intertwined.

Gabriel buys a home in Mexico in an effort to reconnect to his roots and escape from the fast pace of Los Angeles; when he finds it difficult to care for the home, he lets Rafaela move in with her young son, Sol. Rafaela's estranged Chinese Singaporean husband, Bobby Ngu, continues to work in Los Angeles. Yamashita's vignettes of Bobby are fascinating and highly entertaining: her prose moves as quickly as the story she creates for him. The two remaining characters are Buzzworm, an African American grassroots activist, and Arcangel, the symbolic archangel of the people. Buzzworm's enigmatic character is hard to understand because of the way he speaks. Yamashita gives him a style of speech that is both rich and frenetic, jumping from subject to subject with varying cadence and rhythms. Buzzworm is first introduced by the narrator in chapter 4, "Station ID—Jefferson & Normandy," as somebody who questions the difference between reality and fantasy. As the narrator puts it, Buzzworm "tapped your worst phobias" because he makes you question what you know to be true: "Buzzworm figured that some representations of reality were presented for your visual and aural gratification so as to tap what you *thought* you understood. It was a starting place but not an ending. . . . Just about everybody thought they knew the truth" (*TO*, 25; emphasis in the original).

Throughout *Tropic of Orange*, Yamashita continually notes that endings are not beginnings, and beginnings are not endings. Moreover, she splices things together so that the whole spectrum of temporality is destabilized. Buzzworm's focus on time and how much of it people have is not only a nod to the fact that time is running out for characters like Emi, but it also serves as a reminder that time does not function linearly. The repetition of history's ugliest truths is a key part of the argument that human history is haunted by a circling back to violence, even as it is punctured by moments of divine beauty. Whatever the moment in which the reader finds the characters, it becomes clear that the characters are not going to develop in an orderly and resolute fashion. Arcangel is the ultimate embodiment and fusion of past, present, and future; he serves as a reminder that history cannot be ignored and dismissed. Time marches on, but Arcangel demonstrates that history does not stay fixed in the past. The characters that Yamashita presents to the reader are full of contradictions and wild parallels that in part explain the mixed reception of her text. *Tropic of Orange* is – or at least seems – like a frantic ride for the reader because the characters are searching for truth and reality while being thrown off the scent left and right.

Tropic of Orange begins with a scene that challenges dichotomies of the natural and the synthetic. Rafaela sweeps Gabriel's home in Mexico, trying to cleanse it of the plant and animal life that invades it daily: "Rafaela Cortes spent the morning barefoot, sweeping both dead and living things from over and under beds, from behind doors and shutters, through archways, along the veranda – sweeping them all across the deep shadows and luminous sunlight carpeting the cool tile floors" (*TO*, 3). Her efforts prove fruitless because animals and dirt keep violating the borders of the home. The narrator's description of Rafaela sweeping "both dead and living things" is striking in that it begins the novel with the idea that the two are not mutually exclusive. Living (biological) and dead (abiological) matter are fused, which calls into question the many boundaries that humans construct for these categories, and, on a smaller scale, the boundaries between the inside and outside of Gabriel's home. The border between natural and unnatural is continually breached and seems to be suspended in time: "every morning it was the same" (*TO*, 3). Time does not march forward in a recognizable way, and the appearance of invasive species is cyclical: "each somehow made its way back into the house" (*TO*, 3), although the narrator notes that sometimes they are dead and sometimes alive. According to the narrator, Rafaela feels the intertwining of inner and outer ecologies: "On some days, it seemed to twirl before her broom communicating a kind of dance that seemed to send a visceral message up the broom to her fingertips. There was no explanation for any of it" (*TO*, 3). The "visceral" message that Rafaela receives – signals from the natural world to her body – is confusing and works against the order of things that she hopes to keep in Gabriel's home. Cleanliness and organization trump disorder, which is equated with an organic state of life.

The natural world is out of place in the urban landscape of Los Angeles, but it is an unstoppable force in Mexico. Gabriel's house is situated on the Tropic of Cancer, the northernmost latitudinal point reached by the overhead sun. While the Tropic of Cancer is a line that people have understood as separating the global North from the South, Yamashita toys with notions of hemispheric divides. Picked from Gabriel's backyard in Mexico, a single orange contains the loose end of the Tropic of Cancer. As the orange travels north through Mazatlán, it pulls the line with it, and North and South no longer apply as descriptive terms for Mexico and North America.

Arriving in Los Angeles, the orange and the Tropic of Cancer together bring the warmth, the sun, and the very basics of the hemispheric South. In Molly Wallace's trenchant analysis of how the rhetoric of NAFTA promises eventual economic union between the United States and Mexico, she points to the use of the weather as a rhetorical device to "naturalize capitalism" (2001, 145). Wallace cites Yamashita as somebody who is not only engaging with the politics of globalization and free trade but also looking at the "politics of the discourses" surrounding such phenomena (2001, 148). Yamashita's portrayal of Gabriel as a do-gooder is complicated by his relationship to Mexico. As a member of the media, Gabriel tries to separate truth from fiction, and he becomes aware of his role in disseminating half-truths (to himself and others) about the state of affairs in Los Angeles and the relationship of California to Mexico.

The irony of Gabriel's colonialist attitude toward Mexico is only underscored by the suggestion of his family and friends that he buy a house in his real homeland, "East L.A." (*TO*, 224). Describing Gabriel's impulsive desire to buy a house on the Tropic of Cancer in Mexico, the narrator states: "It had begun one summer when Gabriel felt a spontaneous, sudden passion for the acquisition of land, the sensation of a timeless vacation, the erotic tastes of chili pepper and salty breezes, and for Mexico" (5). Although Gabriel is aware that his notions of Mexico are "romantic" and that the "old-fashioned" (6) design he wants for the house is similarly unsettling, it is not until the end of Yamashita's novel that he begins to synthesize the series of events that have occurred and his own responsibility for them. When Rafaela barely survives a severe beating and sexual assault, Gabriel returns to Mexico to find her in tatters: "I thought she might fall in love with me but she was only fixing up my house, and I was part of a net of favors and subtle harassments that unconsciously set her up. And she had taken this beating for me. It was my story" (225). Gabriel grows conscious of the net of the world, the manner in which one's actions affect and change the course of events. The power of natural elements is what ultimately awakens Gabriel's understanding of his global responsibility, which reaches across national borders.[8]

Although the violence against Rafaela's body is the most gruesome in the novel, migrant and immigrant bodies in *Tropic of Orange* all exhibit the wounds of imperialism. Bobby's body receives special attention in the novel; it is constantly in motion, and he is presented as a cyborgian entity. The description of his flesh is of a machine-like amalgamation of movement, ceaselessly toiling to make ends meet: "Ever since he's been here, never stopped working. Always working. Washing dishes. Chopping vegetables. Cleaning floors. Cooking hamburgers. Painting walls. . . . Recycling aluminum. Recycling cans and glass. Drilling asphalt. Pouring cement. Building up. Tearing down. Fixing up. Cleaning up. Keeping up" (*TO*, 79). The country that offers him political asylum simultaneously enslaves him in a drone-like existence. In chapter 34, "Visa Card – Final Destination," Bobby goes to rescue Xiayue, a little girl who some criminals claim is his niece or distant relative. When Bobby meets her in Mexico, he buys two fake passports and tells her to act like his daughter. To smuggle her into the United States, he changes her look: "Get rid of the Chinagirl look. ... Now get her a T-shirt and some jeans and some tennis shoes. Jeans say Levi's. Shoes say Nike. T-shirt says Malibu. That's it" (203). Treating her like a blank slate, Bobby encodes her as a little American girl; the "Chinagirl look" signifies the production of labor, while the American girl look connotes the mindless purchase and consumption of that labor. Bobby and Xiayue "drag themselves through the slits jus' like any Americanos. Just like Visa cards" (204).

Bobby and Xiayue's racialized bodies act as US passports, and American citizenship is attained through buying power – at the expense of Bobby's humanity. Symbolically completing his transformation from flesh to a worker drone, Bobby becomes the plastic Visa card (or visa) and is waived through the border by INS officers. Conspicuous consumption and labels elide race with American national identity through the literal and figurative branding of the body. Scars on the body, markers of hard labor such as callouses, and the ingestion of dangerous cleaning aids are all ways in which human and animals bodies are sutured into something proprietary. The repackaging of the outer body is the erasure of ethnicity with nationality.

Tropic of Orange concerns the global trade of people, bodies, and products as goods and underscores the resulting harmful by-products of the trade in nature and biology when people are treated as goods – especially as they travel into the United States. The commodification of immigrants as laboring bodies, of women as factory workers and sex slaves, and of peripheral characters as wasted members of traditional groups of American citizens naturally leads to critiques like that of Sze, who argues that Yamashita's work is a commentary on neoliberalism and free trade: "women of color, along with transportation networks, embody how production and consumption work" (2000, 30). Indeed, the infrastructure of production and consumption in Yamashita's novel reveal large quantities of risk to those involved but not directly benefiting.[9] Yamashita pits neoliberalism against the kind of ethos furthered by Arcangel, Buzzworm, and Manzanar: a politics for the people by the people.

Democracy per se does not seem to be Yamashita's (or Rivera's) solution; in both the film and the novel, democracy serves as a cover for unseemly actions and the destruction of lives. Naomi Klein suggests that a "fundamentalist version of capitalism" grows at an exponential rate only when preceded by, in her words, "some kind of shock" (quoted in Rooney 2007). The shock is accompanied by a swift manipulation of the area's crippled state for economic and capitalistic gain. Capitalism is wedded to the ideology of democracy, and the two are portrayed as inseparable, yet in Yamashita's and Rivera's works there is a sharp criticism of the marriage between them. Both *Tropic of Orange* and *Sleep Dealer* attempt to show that neoliberalism gains traction by claiming to be the only solution to threats of violence and destabilization. In *Tropic of Orange*, and even more so in *Sleep Dealer*, it is the constant threat of disaster that keeps people operating within the status quo. The societies depicted in these works appear to be shaped by fear-mongering politicians who use fiduciary gain as a justification for keeping populations at bay – especially underserved and poor populations. The vicious cycle of mining Mexico's resources for foreign gain, which contributes to unprecedented levels of pollution in Mexico (as well as states south of it and elsewhere in the world), and then brutally repressing voices of discontent or requests for retribution is the cycle that Yamashita's characters are attempting to disrupt. In *Tropic of Orange*, valuable resources from Mexico and Central and South America cross the US border in the form of fruit, water, human tissue and organs, drugs, and labor, and they are symbolized by a single orange. In addition to the flow of goods, in the following sections of this chapter I examine the moments of disjuncture when free trade is symbolically or actually blocked – that is, when capital aggrandizes resources. The visual and literary representations of these moments reveal a subversive voice that denies corporate and national entities the ownership of nature.

Bartering with bodies

The bendable borders in Yamashita's text propose the idea that even in a new reality, old habits of ethnoracial biases and violence die hard. Arcangel's self-proclaimed "manifest destiny" is to "go North," to be a "Conquistador of the North" (*TO*, 132 and 198). Fighting for the third world, Arcangel uses the stage name "El Gran Mojado" while his enemy symbolizes the first world and is called "SUPERNAFTA" (*TO*, 256–7).[10] The two symbols of the global North and South, or the first and third worlds, face off in a large arena in Los Angeles replete with all the vestiges of a World Wrestling Entertainment match. Arcangel announces the match to the stadium: "Ladies and Gentlemen! Welcome to the Pacific Rim Auditorium here at the very Borders. (And you thought it was a giant bookstore. Ha!)" (*TO*, 256). The "very Borders" to which Arcangel refers are the borderlands between the United States and Mexico and the liquid borders extending out to the Pacific Rim. His conceptualization of borders implicates capitalism as an enemy of the planet (Lee 2007). Or, following Ruth Hsu's argument that SUPERNAFTA symbolizes whiteness, Arcangel represents all that works against subjugation and injustice (2006, 78). Although Arcangel is certain of his destiny to conquer the North and rectify centuries of injustices, he is stopped at the US–Mexico border by officers of the INS. As the borders of economic trade come down, US immigration laws become increasingly stringent, thus highlighting the dichotomy between American attitudes toward products and those toward people.

"Free trade" acquires new meaning when the borders are warped across space and time, as Arcangel pulls the thread of hemispheric divides with him. Yamashita's portrayal of trade is troubling because of what we see traded: little girls, human organs, human labor, and drugs. The sale of human organs becomes a major plot twist and combines the various narratives. Rafaela mistakenly trusts her neighbor, Doña Maria (a busybody who checks on her frequently), and gets mixed up in an organ-smuggling operation spanning South, Central, and North America run by Doña Maria's son, Hernando (*TO*, 151).

Certain that Hernando is after her son's kidneys, Rafaela flees to the border, but she is eventually confronted by Hernando, and an epic battle ensues. Unfolding in a scene of transmutation and sexual violence, Rafaela's body becomes a symbol of ethnically marked and gendered bodies globally:

> Two tremendous beasts wailed and groaned, momentarily stunned by their transformations, yet poised for war. Battles passed as memories: massacred men and women, their bloated and twisted bodies black with blood, stacked in ruined buildings and floating in canals; one million more decaying with smallpox. . . . But that was only the human massacre; what of the ravaged thousands of birds once cultivated to garnish the tress of a plumed potentate, the bleeding silver treasure of Cerro Rico de Potosí, the exhausted gold of Ouro Preto, the scorched land that followed the sweet stuff called white gold and the crude stuff called black gold, and the coffee, cacao and bananas, and the human slavery that dug and slashed and pushed and jammed it all out and away, forever.
>
> (*TO*, 220–1)

As the "tremendous beasts" battle, Rafaela's body channels the long history of mythical, imperial, and colonial violence against women, or what Sze terms the "environmental cost of colonialism" (2000, 39). Mixing fantasy and reality, violence and love – the two were "copulating in rage, destroying and creating at once . . . blood and semen commingling" (*TO*, 221) – Yamashita suggests how difficult it is to separate fact from fiction, especially when the acknowledgment of truth brings personal responsibility. She extends this violence to nonhuman victims. The human "massacre" is also the rape of the land, of the "birds" and precious metals ("bleeding silver" and "black gold"), and fruit and vegetable products cultivated by forced "human slavery." Yamashita draws a parallel between the violent attack on Rafaela and the forgotten and repeated rape and pillaging of whole peoples and species. When Rafaela at last consumes her enemy, relief comes in the form of celestial birds that pull away the blanket of night: "Suddenly the sky was a chorus of heavenly chanting, a terrible blessing, and a great fluttering of millions of wings withdrawing nightfall away" (*TO*, 222). The battle symbolizes a crisis in representing and defining categories such as human and animal, male and female. The break with reality intermixed with "true" history usurps the reader's comfort with conventional stories of world order.

Laboring bodies are generally those of immigrants in Yamashita's novel, but she presents women's bodies as especially susceptible to the perils of globalization. Rafaela's experience as a young mother moving between Mexico and the United States raises a variety of issues facing immigrant and low-wage workers, particularly women in migrant and immigrant communities. The bodies of Yamashita's two lead female characters (Emi and Rafaela) endure life-threatening gruesome violence, and the laboring bodies and hands of women are a major theme in the text. With increased free trade comes decreased corporeal safety from violence, toxins, malnourishment, and poverty. The chaos and destruction in Los Angeles can be traced to the organ-smuggling trade from South to North, the drug trade, and the trafficking of women and "goods" in which one space is forcefully mined for the economic prosperity of another. When the thread that is the Tropic of Cancer shifts, the harm done to another place also shifts. Because there are no national borders in a natural landscape, the laws of pollution and toxic dumping do not apply. In *Tropic of Orange* it is as if the destructive pollution caused by overconsumption comes to haunt Los Angeles, thereby suggesting that the sovereignty of the body, like that of the nation, is a shared responsibility.

Tropic of Orange ends with an orchestrated yet unnatural disaster, one that is man-made and yet seems beyond humanity's control. Of the novel's many segments, chapter 20, "Disaster Movie Week – Hiro's Sushi," is among those most loaded with symbolism in its blurring of the spatiotemporal divide between real life and fantasy. According to "HyperContexts," this chapter is labeled as Emi's Wednesday of "Cultural Diversity" (*TO*, 95 and "HyperContexts"). Emi and Gabriel meet for lunch at Hiro's Sushi and debate what cultural diversity is, what is and what is not politically correct, and the merits of having a television inside a sushi restaurant. The narrator comments on Emi's obsession with media and television monitors: "If Emi had her way, she would watch TV at Circuit City. She was used to being in a control room watching her network and the competition simultaneously. At any moment, she could judge which channel had the more exciting screen" (125). Emi's approach to reality is through the virtual, and her job requires her to splice, dice, and edit shows successfully in order to sell products: "Slash and burn. . . . Cut. Cut. Snip. Snip. Snip" (126). Emi explains to Gabriel that it's "just about the money" and that everybody is "on board to buy" (126). In other words, Emi views globalized consumption as the new global order and democracy as secondary to it – or rather as an older version of it. Although Emi's biting sarcasm and glib statements make it difficult to discern when she is being honest and when she is trying to get Gabriel riled up, there is a good deal of truth in what she says. The number of brand names she mentions – "It's about selling things: Reebok, Pepsi, Chevrolet, AllState, Pampers, Pollo Loco, Levis, Fritos, Larry Parker Esq., Tide" (126) – gestures to the way in which she understands her participation in the commodification of bodies. In particular, Emi dismisses programmatic content in favor of the sale of advertising. Disaster Movie Week and reality collide because both are driven by the commodification of nature leading to actual disaster.

The interconnectivity of people to places in Yamashita's novel is significantly technological and media-driven. To describe the relationship between people without referring to the web of life, Yamashita might use the "grid" of life.[11] Yamashita's grid integrates the technological with the biological and pushes the limits of what we define as life. Toward the end of *Tropic of Orange*, Emi's estranged and homeless father, Manzanar Murakami, plays a significant role in challenging traditional schematizations of human existence, and he reconfigures our readings of Yamashita's grid. Manzanar becomes a conductor of freeway symphonies: "Little by little, Manzanar began to sense a new kind of grid, this one defined not by inanimate structures or other living things but by himself and others like him. He found himself at the heart of an expanding symphony of which he was not the only conductor" (*TO*, 238). Manzanar conceives of the new grid of life as having multiple agents conducting the music of movement and life, but this movement is not defined solely by human direction and traditional forms of "living things," as he calls them (*TO*, 238). Yamashita ambiguously positions him and others like him – the "expanding symphony" (*TO*, 238) – as the kinetic heart and soul of a new model of community and organization. The heart of this new group of people (those who challenge national boundaries and official histories) is at the crossroad of mass transit and in the underbelly of Los Angeles. If this is the "vie" part of "C'est L.A. vie" that Yamashita mentions in her foreword, it is a life driven by outcasts, misfits, and the mentally ill who have been forgotten by mainstream society. If Manzanar represents "the freeway crowd" (*TO*, epigraph) in the excerpt from *Parable of the Sower* (Octavia Butler's 1993 futuristic sci-fi novel set in Los Angeles), then the violent and destructive characteristics ascribed to them are replaced by empathy, genius, and love.

Operation Gatekeeper and the net of NAFTA

I follow the motif of environmental degradation from Yamashita's *Tropic of Orange* to *Sleep Dealer*, which include virtual border crossings and material ones, from sea to land, liquid to solid, for noncitizens and green card–holders alike. While *Tropic of Orange* takes place in Los Angeles and the borderlands in it are tangible lands, *Sleep Dealer* is focused on Mexican and Chicano subjectivity and the experience of escaping from the United States. Yamashita's irony and humor make *Tropic of Orange* a quick, even fun read, but *Sleep Dealer*'s darker edge leads viewers to consider the ramifications of unbridled industry and our relationship to the natural world. *Sleep Dealer* is the directing debut of Alex Rivera (2008a), who also coauthored the screenplay with David Riker. It is a futuristic science fiction movie set mostly in the Mexican border town of Tijuana. Rivera admits that his modest budget would not allow him to direct the "biggest" science fiction film ever, but his goal was to create the "'truest' sci-fi ever" by making a film that "seriously imagines where our world might go" (2008b). In the film, the world has already reached a breaking point, and at the US–Mexican border, tensions over human rights and toxic poisoning are coming to a head. In the film, the US–Mexico border appears to be an exaggerated and surreal representation of the US government's security measures and the security measures of powerful, multinational corporations taking control of water sources. The blurring of boundaries between the real and unreal in *Sleep Dealer*'s future is a narratological strategy that causes viewers to pause and reflect on the nonfictional state of US–Mexico relations. The long and tumultuous history between the United States and Mexico has often focused on the lands around the border between the two countries. Part of the US Department of

Homeland Security's effort to secure US borders is the US–Mexico "wall" that is still being built and reinforced to prevent illegal immigration.[12] The rhetoric employed to justify budgetary commitments for the "wall" from the US government is largely based on an economy of overlapping fears – of terrorism; of illegal immigration; of increased trade in weapons and drugs; and an increase in prostitution and human slavery.

The militarization of US borders and the goal of incarcerating illegal aliens crossing the border flies in the face of a US declaration in support of free trade and open borders (NAFTA) and of the existing connections among Canada, the United States, and Mexico. In 1994, the United States began to implement NAFTA.[13] While Joseph Nevins suggests that the US–Mexican border "is today more part of Americans' geographical imagination" than ever before, the rhetoric behind the creation of NAFTA was meant to demonstrate the increasingly borderless nature of North America and the economic benefits of free trade nationally and globally (2010, 13). Concerns have grown about NAFTA's negative impact on illegal immigrants, migrant workers, women, the environment, and US workers, but NAFTA's critics are frequently silenced by accusations that their concerns are invalid or exaggerated.[14] NAFTA was signed within a year of the launch of Operation Gatekeeper. While the United States and Mexico agreed to dismantle economic borders between them, the US Congress was debating building a wall along the physical border and the feasibility of something like Operation Gatekeeper.[15] It is clear that one motivation for both NAFTA and Operation Gatekeeper is the rich array of natural resources in the borderlands. Whole ecosystems surround the "shared" watershed on the US–Mexican border, and experts estimate that 70–75 percent of the Tijuana River basin is located in Mexico.[16]

Literary works exploring the agricultural industry often invite readers to assume an ecocritical perspective. The representation of the earth and humans in these works shifts from one of duality to one of enmeshed materialities. The laboring migrant body becomes not just a receptacle for the products of its surroundings but an integral part of those surroundings, which in turn are understood to engage in a dynamic relationship with the body. It is our revised understanding of the changing relationship between flesh and elements that drives one of the central tenets of this book: the recent attempts to represent the body at the cellular level as both biological and abiological matter indicate a shift in how we consider our humanity and the perceived and increasingly harmful divides between human and nonhuman beings.

Both *Sleep Dealer* and *Tropic of Orange* continually substitute human bodies in places where we would normally imagine there to be animal bodies (animal bodies that produce labor and food, or that perform acts of violence or sex). This repeated ironic juxtaposition draws parallels between the disenfranchisement of the poorest people and that of animals. It is no coincidence that the most memorable images of the dystopian *Sleep Dealer* are those of Memo getting hooked up to a virtual reality machine, through which he controls a robot body via his own life force. The fusion of the biological and technological through laboring bodies of migrants is not necessarily a new idea, but the film sheds new light on the complexities of this fusion. There are a number of instances when migrant bodies mimic animal bodies. While Rivera does not explore this connection beyond offering repeated juxtapositions, in Yamashita's novel the parallels more directly implicate the first world's unbridled consumption as the main roadblock to equal rights for all. The futuristic setting of Rivera's film emphasizes both the disadvantages and the advantages of technology, which leads to increased communication between migrants. That, in turn, counterintuitively leads to isolation and even death; furthermore, the shift from the national to the transnational here benefits the inhabitants of the so-called first world but not the inhabitants of the third.

The plot of *Sleep Dealer* involves three main characters: Memo Cruz, Luz Martínez, and Rudy Ramirez. Memo is from the small Mexican village of Santa Ana del Rio, and his father is mistaken for an aquaterrorist, a person who illegally steals water back from what have become privatized water supplies. Memo's father is killed by a US corporation's drone. The village's water supply, and thus the livelihood of its people, is controlled by a militarized dam complex (a subsidiary of the Del Rio Water Company). Del Rio's activities include filming, hunting, and killing aquaterrorists on a live gladiatorial-style US television show. Memo's passion in life is technology, and he listens in on the lives of others through his homemade transmitter. One evening he overhears a conversation between two people at the San Diego corporate headquarters of Del Rio Security, and his signal is identified by the security company. The company locks onto his coordinates and later flashes images of people vaguely resembling 9/11 terrorists as it broadcasts the attack on Memo's home by the drone pilot for Del Rio Water. The pilot, Rudy, is the American-born son of immigrant

Figure 5.1 Photo of factory employees plugging in to work remotely.

Source: Image courtesy of Alex Rivera, director of *Sleep Dealer*.

parents, and he begins to suspect that he was given faulty information and erroneously killed Memo's father, who was intentionally misrepresented as an insurgent. Because Memo blames himself for the drone attack and the fact that his family can no longer depend on his father's income, Memo travels north to Tijuana in search of work. En route, Memo meets the mysterious and beautiful Luz, a fledgling writer who posts what might be called "mindblogs" for a pay-for-memories network called Trunode.

The Border Patrol and the Bracero Program

In *Sleep Dealer*'s future a person can connect to a network through her "nodes" and input her thoughts in the form of blog posts or diary entries. These same nodes allow people to work at Mexican-based companies that connect their workers through cables to operate robots in the United States. The depictions of Mexican workers in *Sleep Dealer* are eerily reminiscent of industrial dairy cows.

Luz uses her nodes to upload stories and earns her living by making these entries. When a client becomes interested in Memo's story, Luz's motivations for helping Memo are questionable at best. Luz suggests that Memo contact a "coyotek" to implant the nodes in Memo for a cheaper price than he could get through an official business. People who illegally smuggle others across the US–Mexican border are called coyotes (the name indicates a wily creature, both cautious and sinister). *Tropic of Orange* points to the violence inherent in policing bodies as they cross borders, and in *Sleep Dealer* the term "coyotek"

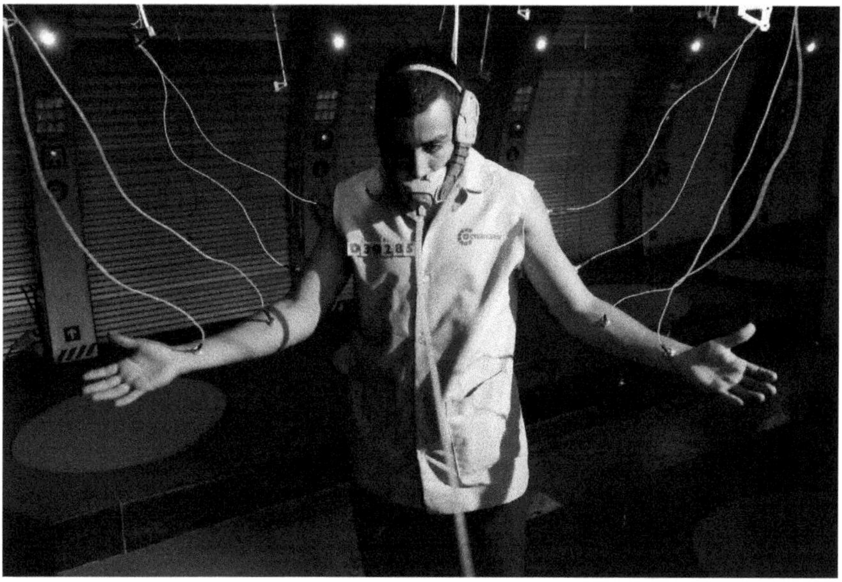

Figure 5.2 Memo Cruz connected through his nodes.

Source: Image courtesy of Alex Rivera, director of *Sleep Dealer*.

suggests that technology is the new and sinister smuggler of human lives. While technology appears to connect humans and advance their lives through increased communication, Rivera's film points out its negative effects. Since 2008, drone warfare has become a reality, and monetized, privatized water supplies are likewise becoming normal. US immigration policies are more related to the tracking and surveillance of bodies as justification for the manipulation of those bodies and natural resources (arguably those resources include the bodies) and less related to the idea that boundaries are meant to delineate and protect populations.

Memo's first attempt to procure nodes goes astray when thieves take his money and beat him up, but the second time Luz does the work and Memo gets them for free. The nodes also function as gateways to enhanced somatic and psychological experiences, allowing a person to plug into a range of sexual, drug-induced fantasies. However, Memo's goal in acquiring nodes is to be able to work in large factories that outsource laboring Mexican bodies to US corporations. When Memo plugs in at work in Mexico, he is operating machinery in San Diego, California. The poor labor conditions, the undocumented and unregistered node implants, and the high risk of electrical shortages (and thus death) all contribute to the term "sleep dealer." Workers are lulled into deep states of sleep when they are plugged in. US corporations are in effect trading with the lives of Mexican workers.

In the post-9/11 future of *Sleep Dealer*, US border security is used to further corporate interests and to control natural resources. For this reason Rudy begins to wonder about the boundaries of the human and the place of ethics in drone attacks. In a scene in San Diego, Rudy is revealed as the man purchasing Luz's stories. After he executes the attack on Memo's father (whom he was told was an aquaterrorist), Rudy asks his own father – a decorated US military veteran with a noticeable accent (unlike Rudy) – if he ever had any doubt about what he did in the war.[17] Rudy's father assures him that he does not regret his actions and that he remains proud of his past military service. Although Rudy is not clearly a part of the US military, the boundaries between the militarization of the dam and government antiterrorist precautions are blurred almost to the point of invisibility – as are the boundaries between the natural and the synthetic.

The visual representations of corporeal communication and of wires running into veins suggest that in *Sleep Dealer*'s future, reliance on technology has overtaken humanity. *Sleep Dealer* weds images of humans, nature, and machines in ways that do not allow the viewer to clearly separate one from the others. The scene that features the killing of Memo's father is an example of how accelerated economic development driven by technology can lead to dehumanization. The previous scene begins with a short montage of images of insurgency demonstrating why companies fight back locals in Mexico. The locals are "sabotaging" corporate security centers and fighting for their rights to clean and free natural resources (that were formerly theirs). Agitated crowds of Mexicans are said to be in constant crisis, and the Mayan Army of Water Liberation is represented by black-masked people shown in grainy images that resemble anti-American terrorists. The Del Rio area is described as the "southern sector water supply" and not part of Mexican territory. Setting aside the incongruities of national borders extending into natural resources of liquid and air, the erasure of any acknowledgment that the watershed is indeed on the Mexican side of the border points to the dangers of allowing privatized security companies to do as they please and to profit from the sale of the earth's resources.

In *Sleep Dealer* multinational corporations have taken control of the southern sector of the globe and continue the long history of embodied violence that border crossers encounter. *Tropic of Orange* also focuses on the various bodies most affected by globalization and colonial rule. As Sze notes, Yamashita's magical realism and postmodern narratological approach push the boundaries of truth and reality in ways that challenge the reader to "understand the contemporary politics around free trade and globalization in an ideological and historical context" (2002, 171). *Sleep Dealer* offers a narrative of disembodied as well as embodied violence and tears down the barrier between ideologies and the colonization of bodies. Through Trunode's virtual reality network, Luz's thoughts can be bought and sold, and their commodification implicitly acknowledges surveillance. To her credit, when Luz begins to understand the kind of violation she's participating in by selling somebody else's dreams and thoughts, she stops reporting on Memo. While the story of Memo's past appears to be easily commodified, his future seems worthless.

This example makes a larger point about the value of the lives of people with the least access to capital. Rapid economic development and the increasing scarcity of natural resources leads to a future in which domination of the poorest by the richest and of the weakest by the strongest becomes status quo. In the world of NAFTA, human rights are trumped by capitalist greed.

In *Sleep Dealer*'s futuristic depiction of a technocratic world, the concomitant struggle and domination over natural (water) and human (labor) resources unveil the imbalance of power in first- and third-world relations. The multiple shots of the border show signs on the US side that read, "WARNING: ENTER MEXICO AT YOUR OWN RISK." Traveling into the United States from Mexico is nearly impossible, while crossing the border in the other direction is an exercise in risk management. A moment of levity occurs in *Sleep Dealer* when Luz takes Memo to the beach. Seeing the Pacific Ocean for the first time, Memo asks about the tall black bars extending out into the water. Luz laughs and replies that the United States has put them up at the end of the border wall to keep out "terrorist surfers." The juxtaposed images of a laid-back California surfer and an anti-American terrorist are absurd, but they expose a raw – and racialized – nerve. Simultaneously, it reveals the futility of trying to extend national boundaries into natural ones, especially liquid ones. The juxtaposition of terrorism and surfing is made all the more poignant by the idea that on the US side of the border surfers are engaging in a leisure sport, while those on the Mexican side appear menacing.

Agriculture and race

In a series of flashbacks of Memo's childhood and father, the viewer learns that Memo's family wanted him to continue the tradition of growing crops on their homestead. At the time, however, Memo was obsessed with technology, electronics, and US television; he considered the ways of his father and village outdated. Memo's father takes him to water the crops and speaks with him about the ways of the land but the viewer sees that in *Sleep Dealer*'s future, natural resources are privatized and corporatized, and that "stealing" them can lead to death. Del Rio Water owns the local water supply, and as Memo and his father walk to buy water by the bag they are tracked by cameras and automated machine guns.

The juxtapositions that Rivera creates are not just those of modern and traditional agriculture but also race and gender inequalities, and they are teased out in troublingly simplified ways. All things modern appear to be produced by the United States and tied to the neocolonial corporatization of natural resources, whereas pastoral ways of life are tied to native culture, less technology, and open and egalitarian access to resources. While the comparisons are reductive and related to traditions of the supposedly noble savage, they reveal Rivera's wish to challenge modern understandings of US–Mexican relations, agricultural practices, and the environmentally dystopic state of our present, not just the future that he depicts as inevitable. In the dreamlike renderings of land in Oaxaca (one of the most biologically diverse areas in Mexico), the combination of indigeneity and natural beauty is highlighted. The name *Oaxaca* is based on a Nahuatl name for a tree native to the area, which boasts some of the most rugged terrain of Mexico. The camera highlights the strength of the unrelenting sun, the beauty of the cornfields, and the struggle of Memo's family to make ends meet. The Del Rio dam complex and its surrounding fortification eerily resembles the present "wall" on the US–Mexican border. Both Baja California (the Mexican state where Tijuana is located) and Oaxaca have long stretches of land bordering the Pacific Ocean: in the north for Baja California and in the south for Oaxaca. These similarities draw attention to the ways in which contemporary Tijuana already resembles the "imaginary" land of Oaxaca in the film. Rapid economic development, a sizable difference in power between Mexico and its neighbor, and a global panic about the scarcity of natural resources are all factors in invisible violations of people south of the US–Mexico border.

Strikingly, both *Tropic of Orange* and *Sleep Dealer* firmly connect race and place and echo the urgency for the type of research done in the fields of environmental justice and the environmental humanities, in which scholars ask how people make meaning and how meaning making can lead to change. Van Jones, a CNN anchor and fan of *Sleep Dealer*, predicts that the movie will "seed a whole new category of film – social justice sci-fi" (quoted in Montgomery 2014). Jones continues and states that "today we are debating drones, jobs and the child refugee crisis at our southern border . . . *Sleep Dealer* puts a human face on all of these issues" (Montgomery 2014). Although much of *Sleep Dealer* is a meditation on technology and drones, it exposes the connections between human and machine. In other words, even though it may seem that the technological fortification of borders would have little if any impact on humans, *Sleep Dealer* proves that the opposite is true.

In Yamashita's novel and Rivera's film, the ways that nature is represented challenges scientific objectivity and exposes the pitfalls of relying on science and technology alone for objective truth. Del Rio Water, a US company, controls Oaxacans' water supply and also appears to have control over media depictions of protests against its violent monopoly. Rivera makes sure that when the viewer sees the way that "American" truth is constructed by the media, he or she will also notice that what appears to be true is false, and that the media sensationalizes reality to benefit corporate interests and national security. In *Tropic of Orange* and *Sleep Dealer*, issues of environmental justice are explicitly related to questions of racial equality. Natural resources in the form of water, food, and human organs are exploited and fiercely guarded – readers and viewers of these texts are intrigued by their surreal and fantastical nature, which encourage an exploration of how to reconcile the surreal and imaginary with the real of the present. The ridiculousness of militarized water sources and buses being dragged across the US–Mexican border by five-hundred-year-old beings with wings has to be reconciled with the realization that the fictional is more real than not. Most readers and viewers are aware of the growing debates about legitimizing the privatization of water and air and of the developing international laws centered on these same issues. Beneath the obvious problems depicted in these works – poisoned oranges and dirty nodes – are the invisible risks that are even more sinister because of their invisibility and unquantifiable nature. As Beck points out, "the risks of civilization today typically escape perception" (1996, 21). The parts of these equations that escape perception are the deeper forms of colonial violence such as cocaine-laced oranges. What Rivera and Yamashita lay bare is the grave danger of being distracted from invisible harms by visible ones.

The obvious similarities in these two works are their nod to the fantastical, their focus on US–Mexican relations and the countries' borders, and the interesting characters that draw us into the stories. Once readers are drawn in, it is easy to get lost in the narrative and not notice the authors' commitment to identifying the connections between colonial domination and environmental degradation and the place of the body in the environment in the postcolonial era. Recall the quote from *Tropic of Orange*, when Bobby is smuggling his "niece," Xiayue, into the United States: "Get rid of the Chinagirl look. … Now get her a T-shirt and some jeans and some tennis shoes. Jeans say Levi's. Shoes say Nike. T-shirt says Malibu. That's it" (*TO*, 203). Xiayue's body is dissected and divided into parts according to brand and product – certainly pointing to the ills of capitalism and also a moment that sharply focuses the reader's attention on the way in which the body is dismembered.

The last chapter of *Tropic of Orange* ends with Bobby's struggle to keep two invisible lines of the hemisphere together. While the previous chapter ends with the statement that Manzanar "could not run out of time" (*TO*, 265), Bobby does seem to be running out of it. In chapter 49, "American Express – Mi Casa/Su Casa," Bobby arrives late to the Pacific Rim Auditorium to find Rafaela and Sol watching the great fight between El Gran Mojado (Arcangel) and SUPERNAFTA. Bobby witnesses the mortal blow to Arcangel's heart and then finds Sol and Rafaela. After Arcangel "dies," Rafaela tells Bobby to cut the orange but keep the halves of it together. In a surreal and symbolic ending, Bobby lets go of the oppositional forces of the orange's two halves: North and South, the United States and Mexico. They no longer appear to be tethered to an exact latitudinal range. The narrator asks the questions on readers' minds: "What are these goddamn lines anyway? What do they connect? What do they divide? What's he holding on to?" (268). Those watching him would see a man with "arms open wide like he's flying" (268), but he is supposedly struggling to keep two things together. Yet the narrator's description suggests that Bobby is liberated and flying into an "embrace." Bobby "lets go. Go figure. Embrace. That's it" (268). And as the novel ends with Bobby's arms in a wide embrace, the reader understands that North and South are no longer clearly divided. Bobby's embrace seems peaceful but is accompanied by large-scale death and violence, indicating that change will not come easily, and that the boundaries between the literal and metaphorical North and South are fraught with histories of domination of one power over another.

Voice-overs

Tropic of Orange has three epigraphs, from Michael Ventura (a California-based journalist and screenwriter), Octavia Butler (a writer of science fiction), and Guillermo Gómez-Peña (a Chicano performance artist, poet, and activist). A sarcastic note to the reader from the author follows the epigraphs: "Gentle reader, what follows may not be about the future, but is perhaps about the recent past; a past that, even as you imagine it, happens. Pundits admit it's impossible to predict, to chase such absurdities into the future, but c'est L.A. vie. No single imagination is wild or crass or cheesy enough to compete with the collective mindlessness that propels our fascination forward. We were all there; we all saw it on TV, screen, and monitor, larger than life" (*TO*, preface). The direct address by the narrator, breaking the imaginary fictional boundary, is an ironic disclaimer about the fiction that follows. Yamashita's authorial voice invites play between time and space, future and past, fiction and reality. Implicit in her preface is an understanding that people are not only simultaneously in the past and future (that is, reliving the past), but also co-creators of the future. The voyeuristic nature of what "propels our fascination forward" indicates our obsession with – and responsibility for shaping – the media's portrayal of "reality," and thus it also invites us to coauthor the future while breaking what seems like a feedback loop to the past. The epigraphs are meant to foreshadow what follows in the novel.

The three epigraphs work together to question origin stories, forms of communication, and borders between countries. The first one reminds the reader that "Las Californias" was a name given to a mythical island populated only by beautiful Amazonian warriors. Spanish explorers thought that the real California was an island, and Michael Ventura indicates that California's beauty is about "letting go of where you came from" and letting go of "old lessons" (quoted in *TO*, epigraph). Why would Yamashita begin the novel with the mission of letting go? More than a foreshadowing of the various characters who will change and die, the first epigraph points to the palimpsest that is California's history (and Mexico's as well), and to the notion that history is a co-creator of the future. The epigraph from Octavia Butler underlines the central role that freeways play in life in Los Angeles. Ostensibly, this epigraph is about circuits of transit, how although it is "illegal" to walk on California's freeways, everybody does it. "Everybody" refers to society's castoffs, who are "armed with sheathed knives . . . [and] visible holstered handguns" (*TO*, epigraph). Passing cops "paid no attention," writes Butler, because people "get killed on the freeways all the time" (*TO*, epigraph). In selectively excerpting the text from Butler's novel, Yamashita shapes the reader's understanding of freeways: places where "sinister" and disposable bodies inhabit space and are ignored by the police and left to their own devices. The freeways are depicted as the "most direct" but also the most dangerous route between two points in Los Angeles.

While Yamashita foreshadows the importance of the control of trade routes across national boundaries, she also places the dystopian excerpt from Butler between two other epigraphs on the same page. Taken together, they tell a different story than each does on its own. The third epigraph is a fragment from Gómez-Peña's poem "Freefalling toward a Borderless Future." The poem is an ode to a "borderless future" that divides the modern citizen's body into nationalistic limbs and parts: a "Canadian head," "U.S. torso," "Mexican genitalia," "South American legs," and "Antarctic nails" (quoted in *TO*, epigraph). The fragment ends with the speaker "jumping borders at ease / jumping borders with pleasure" (*TO*, epigraph). The three epigraphs collectively constitute a pastiche of Los Angeles's mythical roots and routes. California's reputation as the place where dreams come true (at least, in Hollywood) proves to be a series of contradictions, and the "borderless future" is firmly bordered by body parts. They depict not a whole body or a unified people, but groups of continents and countries that are demarcated through body parts. The mythical and the real are magically blended and cannot be untethered, and Yamashita's epigraphs further muddle the distinctions between real reportage and pure art.

Yamashita's chosen epigraphs indicate that she will be giving the reader fragments of stories and histories, juxtaposing them in a particular way and leaving it to the reader to piece them together. On their own, the epigraphs are short excerpts, but together they make a unified statement against colonial domination, against the slicing up of bodies, and in favor of combining the past and future. In fact, they advocate adding the present as well, so that the intricate layers of truth and fiction can interact with one another to create the real. One thing that Yamashita does very well is to hold fragments from other creative texts up for further examination, fragments that show the faults of systems that have retrofitted colonialism as capitalism. The recalibration of colonialism and its disguise as capitalism is not a clear critique of global capitalism as the source of the world's problems. Rather, it points to the individual's responsibility not only for building a network of hope and self-sufficiency, but also for helping create the chaos that requires such a network. Yamashita seems to critique with an openness that leaves it up to readers to work out where they are implicated in the wider scheme of things and how individuals can enact change.

Sleep Dealer and *Tropic of Orange* both focus on how media-driven external forces and the environment become enmeshed with our bodies. The voice-over in the official *Sleep Dealer* trailer (Rivera 2008a) connects US demands for cheap and undocumented labor from Mexico and the deaths of Mexican workers. With interspersed clips of Memo "connecting" through his nodes and virtually manning machines across the border, the all-American voice announces, "A young man risks everything to plug into the new American dream. All the work, without the workers." The "dream" in *Sleep Dealer* is one of labor without workers or consequences, but Rivera shows bodies collapsing as a direct result of their virtual labor. The viewer sees Memo's life force slowly drained from him as the wires leach energy from his veins. Rivera underlines the psychosomatic connection between virtual reality and physicality in a way that does not let the viewer ignore it. Things that seem unreal and extraneous nonetheless strongly affect one's material self. The virtual becomes real when the physical body shows signs of such enmeshment.

In the first ten minutes of the film, the viewer watches as Memo eavesdrops on conversations between people in his village and their distant relatives. Memo later explains that in the beginning he could pick up only local conversations, but then he reverse engineered the satellites of Del Rio Security, based in San Diego, to expand the reach of his eavesdropping. Memo's activities seem innocent enough. He longs to experience life outside the confines of his village, and he gets great pleasure from listening to other peoples' lives and watching US television shows. The ones that he enjoys most are in direct conflict with his heritage and family values. His escapist fantasies involve different versions of moving away from his village to more exciting and urban destinations. He switches from one radio station to another and hears snippets of life from Tijuana. Bright lights, big cities, and good pay seduce Memo. One unnamed voice states, "But I'm already working as a busboy in New York. Well, it looks like New York. It might also be Los Angeles" (Rivera 2008a). There are many layers of irony here: Memo himself will later be working – virtually – in different cities that begin to blend together; he too will at first be excited about his job and later suffer from it; and just like the stories of the people he eavesdrops on, his own stories will become the property of others. Unbeknownst to him, he will follow those people down a path of destruction that at first entertains him but then leads to great suffering. Memo is punished for his voyeurism by the death of his father, and Luz is later punished for hers by the loss of Memo's trust and a general feeling of malaise. These repeated patterns, which ask us to question the cost of our gaze and the media's glare, come to a head at the end of the film. When Rudy tries to make amends for his actions, he does so by publicly shaming Del Rio Water and making a spectacle of what had been kept invisible. Rudy's determination to take a leap and translate intangible forms of violence into tangible ones that can be read by the wider public is also a move to make amends for his own role in drone attacks and war.

American studies and true science fiction

In the scene that features the murder of Memo's father, the white, garishly American announcer wearing a suit pits Rudy against Memo's father and uses the banner of the American flag to cloak the extreme violence needed to continue mining natural resources in contested territory. The announcer points to the camera as he conspiratorially remarks, "This show contains graphic violence against evildoers. You won't want to miss it!" (Rivera 2008a). Images of otherwise serene territory are transformed by infrared footage, replete with the explosion of trucks and the soundtrack of rioting. The announcer points out that advanced flying cameras flank the plane Rudy is remotely piloting. The excitement over the level of surveillance seems equal with that of the impact of the drone, and the viewer is granted insight into how power manifests itself. The director's desire to make the "'truest' sci-fi film" (2008b) might resonate with scholars looking at American studies from an ecocritical perspective. *Sleep Dealer* brings current and past issues to the forefront of ongoing debates about water rights, trade agreements, and human rights in the region around the US–Mexican border. In the ebb and flow of globalization and technological advances lie the human and nonhuman bodies of evidence – markers of changing tides. Often the entities most negatively affected by change are those with the least agency and visibility. It is this delicate balance of systems that American studies has only recently begun to explore. The environmental justice movement began as an attempt to redress wrongs – the tacit complicity of the US government and its residents in inappropriate land use, toxic dumping, dangerous labor conditions, and the denial of a voice to the poor and working classes most affected (who are often ethnically marked) – but as the movement continues to grow, its concerns are being recognized as universal and indispensable to dialogues within American studies.

The discourse of globalization can create political and personal paralysis even for those who hope to make a difference. The narrative of *Tropic of Orange* creates an intricate portrait of present-day Los Angeles, with all of its flaws and beauty, and draws the reader into the story of each character. *Sleep Dealer* picks up the thread of the exploitation of human labor and natural resources and presents a tale about multinational corporations that attempt to own the bodies and land of Mexico. One widely held view of ecocriticism is that it "seeks to evaluate texts and ideas in terms of their coherence and usefulness as responses to environmental crisis" (Kerridge and Sammells 1998, 5). Yet both *Sleep Dealer* and *Tropic of Orange* might be seen as responding and entering into new dialogues with their audiences about the very incoherency of the world. In her work on *Tropic of Orange*, Ruth Hsu convincingly suggests that part of Yamashita's narrative strategy is to "decenter" readers' notions of Los Angeles and to disorient their sense of space and time (2006, 77). Memo's memories of his family's home in Oaxaca and its destruction, the death of his father, and his teen years in the arid beauty of Oaxaca are all recounted in flashbacks.

Rather than disseminating romanticized idealizations of humans' connection to earth, Yamashita and Rivera are deploying images and constructs of our progressive distance from nature. Where Yamashita leaves off (before 9/11), Rivera picks up, and through his film he offers a powerful commentary on US antiterrorist policies that cloak existing corporate interests. They also push their audiences to think about the ways in which humans increasingly rely on technology. *Sleep Dealer* and *Tropic of Orange* answer calls like that of Ursula Heise for "environmental literature and ecocriticism . . . to engage more fully with the insights of recent theories of transnationalism and cosmopolitanism" (2008, 383). Cultural productions of the environmental justice movement increasingly demonstrate the relevance and importance of the field of ecocriticism outside of academia. Taken together, *Tropic of Orange* and *Sleep Dealer* add urgency and weight to Adamson and Slovic's proposed "third wave" of ecocriticism, which "transcends ethnic and national boundaries" while respecting "ethnic and national particularities" (2009, 6), and to Heise's call for a transnational turn in ecocriticism. In tackling issues of globalization and international commerce, *Sleep Dealer* and *Tropic of Orange* foreground the biopolitical violence that accompanies the corporate-driven division of natural resources on the US–Mexican border.

Notes

1 The previous chapters have demonstrated that throughout the twentieth century, Western civilization has understood humans to be connected to the nonhuman largely through the production and consumption of food. *The Grapes of Wrath* (Steinbeck [1939] 1976), *Sea of Cortez* (Steinbeck and Ricketts [1941)] 2009), *Stealing Buddha's Dinner* (Nguyen 2007), *My Year of Meats* (Ozeki 1998), and *Heroes and Saints* (Moraga 1994) are principally concerned with the natural landscape only insofar as it has to do with the politics of consumption and the control and delineation of nature.

2 I thank Carl Gutiérrez-Jones for suggesting that I watch *Sleep Dealer*.

3 Parts of this chapter appeared in a previous publication, Athanassakis (2009).

4 *Maquilapolis* (Funari and de la Torre 2006) is a movie that exposes the infamous labor practices of the maquiladoras in Tijuana. Based on principles of community-driven activism and environmental justice, this film addresses many of the issues raised in both *Sleep Dealer* and *Tropic of Orange*.

5 One of the main aims of the Department of Homeland Security is to "protect our homeland" by restructuring governmental agencies from a "confusing patchwork" into a uniform entity (Bush 2002).
6 For more on environmental justice and ecocriticism, see Adamson, Evans, and Stein (2002). For the connection between ecocriticism and race, see Martínez-Alier (2002, 172).
7 For more on the intersection between postcolonial studies and ecocriticism, see Head (1998).
8 Just as Rudy Ramírez in *Sleep Dealer* realizes that he is responsible for the death of somebody whose life resembles the story of Rudy's immigrant parents, so too Gabriel realizes that he is part of the elite that benefits from Rafaela's subjugation.
9 Ulrich Beck suggests that in a global risk society nation-states can no longer pretend to have dominion over risk (2002, 41).
10 "El Gran Mojado" is translated as "The Big Wetback" (see page 257), but it can also mean "The Great Wetback."
11 Although Yamashita commented in an interview that she first used the grid at the beginning of the novel for her own organizational purposes, she admitted that it can be read in different ways (Glixman 2007). Yamashita elaborates: "As I said, the hypercontext at the beginning of the book was a spreadsheet that I initially used to map out the book. . . . I hope that the book can be read on several levels. Every reader takes away a different read, a different book" (Glixman 2007).
12 The "wall" between the United States and Mexico is not a true wall but a series of barriers constructed at various times and made of a variety of materials. Joseph Nevins writes: "At the beginning of the 1990s, what existed there [in the San Diego borderlands] in terms of a boundary fence in the area had gaping holes" (2010, 6; see also 6–14 and 211–18). See also Massey, Durand, and Malone (2002).
13 The campaign for NAFTA began during the administration of President George H.W. Bush and continued under President Bill Clinton. The agreement was signed by Clinton on September 14, 1993, and implemented on January 1, 1994 (2016; United States Department of Justice 1998).
14 In reference to the environmental and human costs of NAFTA, economists Gary Hufbauer and Jeffrey Schott write, "critics grossly exaggerated their magnitude" (2005, 4; see especially pages 1–78).
15 For more on NAFTA's opponents, see Center for Immigration Studies (2000, 3 and 17, note 1).
16 Lawrence Herzog estimates 70 percent (1990, 201), and the United States National Oceanic and Atmospheric Administration (2007) uses the figure of 75 percent.
17 Although a brief image of Rudy's father at war is ambiguous, the desert setting suggests that he participated in the US occupation of Iraq or Afghanistan.

References

Adamson, Joni, Mei Mei Evans, and Rachel Stein, eds. 2002. *Introduction to the Environmental Justice Reader: Politics, Poetics, and Pedagogy*, 3–14. Tucson: University of Arizona Press.

Adamson, Joni, and Scott Slovic. 2009. "The Shoulders We Stand On: An Introduction to Ethnicity and Ecocriticism." *MELUS* 34 (2): 5–24.

Athanassakis, Yanoula. 2009. "LA and TJ: Immigration, Globalization, and Environmental Justice in *Tropic of Orange* and *Sleep Dealer*." *Journal of American Studies in Turkey* 30 (1): 89–110.

Beck, Ulrich. 1996. *Risk Society: Towards a New* Modernity. Translated by Mark Ritter. Thousand Oaks, CA: Sage Publications.

———. 2002. "The Terrorist Threat: World Risk Society Revisited." *Theory, Culture and Society* 19 (4): 39–55.

Buell, Lawrence. 2005. *The Future of Environmental Criticism: Environmental Crisis and Literary Imagination*. Malden, MA: Wiley-Blackwell.

Bush, George W. 2002. "Proposal to Create the Department of Homeland Security." Department of Homeland Security. http://www.dhs.gov/xabout/history/publication_0015.shtm.

Butler, Octavia. 1993. *Parable of the Sower.* New York: Warner Books.

Calavita, Kitty. 1994. "U.S. Immigration and Policy Responses: The Limits of Legislation." In *Controlling Immigration: A Global Perspective*, edited by Wayne A. Cornelius, Philip L. Martin, and James Frank Hollifield, 55–82. Stanford, CA: Stanford University Press.

Carson, Rachel. 1962. *Silent Spring.* New York: Houghton Mifflin.

Center for Immigration Studies. 2000. "Five Years After NAFTA: Rhetoric and Reality of Mexican Immigration in the 21st Century." http://www.cis.org/sites/cis.org/files/articles/2000/naftareport.pdf.

Comfort, Susan. 2002. "Struggle in Ogoniland: Ken Saro-Wiwa and the Cultural Politics of Environmental Justice." In *The Environmental Justice Reader: Politics, Poetics, and Pedagogy*, edited by Joni Adamson, Mei Mei Evans, and Rachel Stein, 229–46. Tucson: University of Arizona Press.

Cronon, William. 1995. "The Trouble with Wilderness; or, Getting Back to the Wrong Nature." In *Uncommon Ground: Rethinking the Human Place in Nature*, edited by William Cronon, 69–90. New York: Norton.

Deming, Alison H., and Lauret E. Savoy, eds. 2002. *The Colors of Nature: Culture, Identity, and the Natural World.* Minneapolis: Milkweed Editions.

Funari, Vicky, and Sergio de la Torre, dirs. 2006. *Maquilapolis.* San Francisco, CA: California Newsreel. DVD.

Gaard, Greta. 2001. "Women, Water, Energy: An Ecofeminist Approach." *Organization and the Environment* 14 (2): 157–72.

Glixman, Elizabeth P. 2007. "An Interview with Karen Tei Yamashita." http://www.eclectica.org/v11n4/glixman_yamashita.html.

Glotfelty, Cheryll. 1996. *Introduction to the Ecocriticism Reader: Landmarks in Literary Ecology*, edited by Cheryll Glotfelty and Harold Fromm, xv–xxxvii. Athens: University of Georgia Press.

Head, Dominic. 1998. "The (Im)possibility of Ecocriticism." In *Writing the Environment: Ecocriticism and Literature*, edited by Richard Kerridge and Neil Sammells, 27–39. New York: Zed Books.

———. 2008. "Ecocriticism and the Transnational Turn in American Studies." *American Literary History* 20 (1): 381–404.

Herzog, Lawrence A. 1990. *Where North Meets South: Cities, Space and Politics on the US-Mexico Border.* Austin: University of Texas Press.

Hsu, Ruth Y. 2006. "The Cartography of Justice and Truthful Refractions in Karen Tei Yamashita's *Tropic of Orange*." In *Transnational Asian American Literature: Sites and Transits*, edited by Shirley Geok-lin Lim, John Blair Gamber, Stephen Hong Sohn, and Gina Valentino, 75–99. Philadelphia: Temple University Press.

Hufbauer, Gary Clyde, and Jeffrey J. Schott. 2005. *NAFTA Revisited: Achievements and Challenges.* Washington, DC: Institute for International Economics.

Kerridge, Richard, and Neil Sammells, eds. 1998. *Writing the Environment: Ecocritcism and Literature.* New York: Zed Books.

Lee, Sue-Im. 2007. "'We Are Not the World': Global Village, Universalism, and Karen Tei Yamashita's *Tropic of Orange*." *Modern Fiction Studies* 52 (3): 501–27.

Martínez-Alier, Joan. 2002. *The Environmentalism of the Poor: A Study of Ecological Conflicts and Valuation*. Cheltenham: Edward Elgar.

Massey, Douglas S., Jorge Durand, and Nolan J. Malone. 2002. "System Assembly: A History of Mexico-U.S. Migration." In *Beyond Smoke and Mirrors: Mexican Immigration in an Era of Economic Integration*, 24–51. New York: Russell Sage Foundation.

Montgomery, David. 2014. "Alex Rivera's Lost Cult Hit 'Sleep Dealer' about Immigration and Drones Is Back." *Washington Post*, July 7. http://tinyurl.com/gro3w4p.

Moraga, Cherríe L. 1994. *Heroes and Saints*. In *Heroes and Saints and Other Plays*, edited by Cherríe L. Moraga, 85–149. Albuquerque, NM: West End.

Nevins, Joseph. 2010. *Operation Gatekeeper and Beyond: The War on "Illegals" and the Remaking of the U.S.-Mexico Boundary*. 2nd ed. New York: Routledge.

Nguyen, Bich Minh. 2007. *Stealing Buddha's Dinner: A Memoir*. New York: Viking.

Ozeki, Ruth. 1998. *My Year of Meats*. New York: Penguin.

Rivera, Alex, dir. 2008a. *Sleep Dealer*. Los Angeles: Maya Entertainment. DVD.

———. 2008b. "*Sleep Dealer*: Sci-Fi with Director Alex Rivera." Interview. January 20. http://emanuellevy.com/interviews/sleep-dealer-sci-fi-with-director-alex-rivera-2/.

Rooney, Katie. 2007. "Naomi Klein on Disaster Capitalism." *Time*, September 27. http://content.time.com/time/arts/article/0,8599,1666221,00.html.

Shiva, Vandana. 2005. *Earth Democracy: Justice, Sustainability and Peace*. Cambridge, MA: South End.

Steinbeck, John. (1939) 1976. *The Grapes of Wrath*. Reprint, New York: Penguin.

Steinbeck, John, and Edward F. Ricketts. (1941) 2009. *Sea of Cortez: A Leisurely Journal of Travel and Research*. Reprint, New York: Penguin.

Sze, Julie. 2000. "'Not by Politics Alone': Gender and Environmental Justice in Karen Tei Yamashita's *Tropic of Orange*." *Bucknell Review* 44 (1): 29–42.

———. 2002. "From Environmental Justice Literature to the Literature of Environmental Justice." In *The Environmental Justice Reader: Politics, Poetics, and Pedagogy*, edited by Joni Adamson, Mei Mei Evans, and Rachel Stein, 163–80. Tucson: University of Arizona Press.

United States Department of Agriculture, Foreign Agricultural Service. 2016. "North American Free Trade Agreement (NAFTA)." http://www.fas.usda.gov/topics/nafta.

United States Department of Justice, Office of the Inspector General. 1998. "Background to the Office of the Inspector General Investigation." http://www.justice.gov/oig/special/9807/gkp01.htm.

United States National Oceanic and Atmospheric Administration. 2007. "NOAA, State Officials Dedicate $1.2 Million in New and Renovated Facilities for Tijuana River National Estuarine Reserve." August 13. http://www.publicaffairs.noaa.gov/releases2007/aug07/noaa07-r430.html.

Wallace, Molly. 2001. "Tropics of Globalization: Reading the New North America." *symplok* 9 (1–2): 145–60.

Worster, Donald. (1977) 1985. *Nature's Economy: A History of Ecological Ideas*. Cambridge: Cambridge University Press.

Yamashita, Karen Tei. 1997. *Tropic of Orange*. Minneapolis: Coffee House Press.

CODA

Environmental interplay

> Some call me Nature. Others call me Mother Nature. I've been here for over four-and-a-half billion years, twenty-two thousand five hundred times longer than you. I don't really need people but people need me. Yes, your future depends on me. When I thrive you thrive. When I falter you falter, or worse. But I've been here for eons. I have fed species greater than you and I have starved species greater than you. My oceans, my soil, my flowing streams, my forests: they all can take you or leave you. How you choose to live each day, whether you regard or disregard me, doesn't really matter to me. One way or another your actions will determine your fate, not mine. I am Nature, I will go on. I am prepared to evolve. Are you?
>
> Conservation International 2014

In October 2014 Conservation International released a series of seven YouTube videos that anthropomorphize Mother Nature, Water, Soil, the Ocean, the Coral Reefs, the Rainforests, and the Redwoods. Narrated by Hollywood stars including Julia Roberts, Robert Redford, Penélope Cruz, and Ian Somerhalder, the short videos are a pointed commentary on humans' disregard for nature.[1] The overarching message is crystal clear: nature will go on, but humans likely will not. In "Mother Nature Is Speaking," Julia Roberts (as the voice of Mother Nature) lets the audience know that they are irrelevant to the planet's future. The video's menacing tone is likely meant to produce a sense of anxiety and frustration in the viewer, who realizes that the limits of the earth's resources may have already been surpassed. The feeling that "Mother Nature" is angry with you is crushing, and the sound of the uncannily familiar voice is deafening.

The star wattage of Roberts alone is enough to garner public attention, but this particular video's scaffolding depends on a foundation of unsettling the viewer. As Jennifer Jacquet explains, a pivotal component of effective shaming is building layers of "concealed irony" (2015, 138). In her book on the uses of shame, Jacquet predicts more cases of concealed irony as effective resistance tactics because "it's so playful and because it asks more of the crowd, since, to fully appreciate the act, you have to understand the backstory" (2015, 139). A large percentage of viewers write about Julia's voice, and they are, in fact, "in" on the larger backdrop of the video.[2] Viewers go beyond what Conservation International likely expected as a response.

The bait-and-switch methodology of the Julia Roberts video relies on an economy of backstories and irony. Conservation International (CI) carefully selected one of the world's most recognizable "girl-next-door" actresses to deliver the message that it is humanity's resilience, not the planet's, which will soon expire. The combination of the images, music, and voices is disquieting; the video is less playful than it is threatening. The online responses to the video indicate that the danger of such apocalyptic threats is that people may conclude that their gestures to recycle cans or conserve water are futile. M. Sanjayan, a senior scientist for CI and codirector of *Nature Is Speaking*, acknowledged to *The Guardian*'s Greg Harman that "not everyone's going to like this. It's not happy talk" (quoted in Harman 2014). Rather than being upset that climate change talk is not "happy talk," the reactions I noticed from viewers were peppered with distrust of Hollywood stars who themselves enjoy the privileges of wealth and whose films leave sizable carbon footprints. Numerous comments indicated that megastars are in fact *un*ironically telling the other half (or 99 percent) how to live.

As footage of glacial avalanches and tiny schools of fish accompany Julia Roberts's grave tone, we are given a sense that we are out of our depth. The optics of CI's videos collectively communicate the idea that humans indeed have little awareness of the magnitude or finitude of the impact we have made, and can make, on the world around us. Recent projects like the *Nature Is Speaking* series imagine how nature might engage with and respond to a postindustrial and technocratic reality, and what forms that response might take (including indifference). When "natural" catastrophes occur, people often describe it as Mother Earth being angry or striking back at humanity for its wayward behaviors. Even the most well-meaning social media campaigns continue to gender and anthropomorphize materiality in troubling ways. As with the example of CI's project, which for all intents and purposes is successful, the public is fickle and sensitive to being told how to "fix" things for which they do not feel responsible. CI's campaign slogan, "Nature is our best defense against climate change," positions nature as a tool against anthropogenic ills, yet it ultimately pits nature against humans. Sanjayan, cognizant of the complicated landscape – and the slippery slope – of speaking to audiences about their agential relationship to climate change, admits that "with any campaign, even one as carefully planned as this one, you have no idea how it's going to work" (quoted in Harman 2014).

Texts about the environment are traditionally less direct and confrontational than the videos from Conservation International. Among the many issues the environmental humanities are trying to make sense of are questions of how we define the success of environmental and ecocritical texts, what speaks to the public, and what galvanizes people. Artists, writers, and directors are exploring even more sophisticated ways to engage individuals and reach them through emotional registers ranging from joy to sadness, love to hate, hope to despair. They are also navigating a range of mediums and tactics to increase the sensory depth and bandwidth both of their works and of their audiences. As our notions of material agency expand, so too do our attempts to activate and reach that agency.

Susanne Antonetta's simple statement, "separation and separation and separation" (2001, 11), remains an anthem for the ways in which our agency is continually stratified and muted. Antonetta's *Body Toxic*, like a number of texts in my book, demonstrates how the vitality of the material body overturns outmoded renderings of the human body and its surroundings. In anticipation of the visual and written texts yet to come in the book, I stated that reading about these works, along with other ecocritical texts, entails a profound reconsideration of predatory environmental practices that are repackaged as necessary markers of progress. It means an estrangement from our realities and usual practices of knowledge production that force us to question how we go forward from here. In this last section, I would add that these texts also invite readers to think beyond ideas of linear history and time. Temporally, they behave in unpredictable ways, inhabiting what we conceive of as the past, present, and future all at once; they play with scale, moving quickly from the invisible and minute to the planetary and galactic; and they offer insights into how we are interconnected in ways that we cannot yet conceive.

Chapter 1, "Bodies Interrupted," considered Antonetta's disbelief that "we've gone and created immortality and the problem is how to mortalize it again. . . . We've made immortality for our waste, which grows larger and more important and more alive, and bulks itself out to inhabit the spaces we dwindle ourselves away from" (2001, 208–9). And yet the very place from which she is "dwindled" away is the "anti-place" of America (2001, 3). Her outrage is directed at powerful conglomerates that cordon off space and create places that are "no place," and have little legal responsibility for the "accidents" and "natural disasters" that occur. Antonetta's memoir and other works in my book juxtapose the immortality of "our waste" with the mortality of our corpus, and they feature subjects whose bodies are focalized examples of the tragic endgame of corporate power.[3] Ciba-Geigy's Chemical Corporation site in Dover Township (Toms River, New Jersey) was declared a Superfund site in 1983.[4] The EPA's website on Ciba-Geigy and Toms River states that it "does not pose an immediate threat to human health or the environment" (EPA 2016). Yes, "1.2 million gallons of groundwater are treated each day" as the EPA continues its efforts of "digging up [47,000] buried drums and disposing of them off site" (EPA 2016). The website lists "Human Exposure Status" and "Contaminated Ground Water Status" as "Under Control" (EPA 2016).[5] This is an impossibility and a path-dependent course that relies on the reabsorption or "off-siting" of risk as evidence of EPA progress/safety. In efforts to quell "irrational" bodies and rebellions, it offers severance from the rational. First Ciba-Geigy and then the Superfund site that metaphorically replaces it together serve as the ultimate anti-place that haunts Antonetta. It is the fictional and poetic representation of an uncannily real portrait of how toxic bodies are not legally cognizable.

Narratives of our responsibility for ecological harm become targets of anger and anxiety as much as they are epicenters of change. The first and last sections of my book contain discussions of disparaging online comments, first against Antonetta's *Body Toxic* (in chapter 1) and then against Conservation

International's videos. It is not just that, as Lawrence Buell has stated, "toxic discourse challenges traditional understandings of what counts as an environmental movement or ethos" (1998, 639). Stories of interrupted bodies garner attention because they signify failure and incite phobias of transmission. They are stories of contagion only because humans immediately think of the risk of contagion and contamination to themselves. Interrupted bodies do not demand that we quantify the risk to ourselves; in fact, they do not care whether or not we do so. Bodies that register differently from others, that communicate in odd ways, or that are not easily categorized by the rest of society hold in their rebellious materiality the potential to disrupt and disturb our normal tools of apprehension and calculation. As I conclude this book on environmental texts I think back to the works that have most moved and engaged me and I realize that they are the ones that have looked at things askance, and helped me imagine what it would be like to do the same.

The interplay between material and immaterial, the clean and the toxic, the safe and the unsafe invites us to transform our patterns of thought around what is fixed and what is mutable.[6] There are compelling reasons why this particular kind of body discourse would aim to produce anxiety and paranoia – disruption requires a wrinkle in time and space. The overturning of a safe teleology necessitates an elasticity and openness that pushes people to reimagine subjectivity and belonging.[7] Writing in 1998, Lawrence Buell's approach is one that depends on fright as an instigator of change: "even if the theory of environmental justice proves too idealistic or partisan for most legislators to endorse, the fear of environmental poisoning that energizes it will likely have at least as good a chance of remaining a compelling public issue" (1998, 643–4). Pastoral traditions and dreams of being one with nature become nightmares of deception and freakish moments of the uncanny. But the approach of fear mongering may have passed its expiration date.

The works discussed in my book take diverging approaches to real events and use different emotional registers and tones. Antonetta's memoir and the other texts in *Environmental Justice in Contemporary US Narratives* are causally linked by the very different ways in which they seek to understand, expose, and illuminate what happens when predictable anthropogenic catastrophe is disguised as something else. Moreover, they explore how the reallocation and obfuscation of systems of risk production work symbiotically to allow different modalities of violence to continue unfettered.

In a time when data is a currency of its own and attention is the most valued commodity online, and when the virtual reflexively seems to be shaping the real, the humanities and sciences are more seriously working together to come up with ways to make a difference beyond their expected scope. First coined by biologist Eugene F. Stoermer in the 1980s, the term "Anthropocene" is a way to designate the profound and immutable changes humans have made to the Earth's systems.[8] The implications for humans and the chances of their long-term survival are dire. Stoermer and Nobel Prize–winning chemist Paul J. Crutzen copublished a short piece entitled "The 'Anthropocene'" and solidified its entry into the modern-day lexicon as an epoch when "mankind" has become a "major geological force" (2000, 18). In 2012, James Syvitski, director of the International Geosphere-Biosphere Programme, struck a more positive tone when he wrote that humans contain great "strength" in their ability to develop solutions to complex problems, and thus, he proposes, the Anthropocene's "final chapter" is unfinished because "the narrative will depend on our collective self-awareness and the capacity to correct our course, for the relentless pressure on our planet portends unprecedented destabilization" (Syvitski 2012). The Anthropocene as a new epoch and term carries a heavy symbolic mantle. Whilst considering *The Shock of the Anthropocene*, Cristophe Bonneuil and Jean-Baptiste Fressoz differentiate between viewing our present moment as fixed versus fluid and urge readers "to see the Anthropocene as an event rather than a thing . . . without becoming mere chroniclers of a natural history" (2016, xii). Bonneuil and Fressoz's call to conceptualize the Anthropocene as an event is a way to breathe life into what could easily be seen as a nonevent and, troublingly, a fait accompli. To speak of materiality and the environment in 2016 is to necessarily address the discourse of the Anthropocene. In Dale Jamieson and Bonnie Nadzam's creative work *Love in the Anthropocene* they suggest that the quandary of the place of our emotional lives, especially love, in the time of the Anthropocene is not "a narrow scientific question," but rather "a challenge," because "the story of the Anthropocene begins with geology, but it is ultimately a story of the human heart" (2015, 27). The looming "unprecedented destabilization" that Syvitski predicts is met with lighter reactions: love, mischievous play, and even optimism.

With all the forecasting of catastrophe comes the promise of a new vantage point. In Teresa Shewry's research on narratives of hope in oceanic literature (*Hope at Sea: Possible Ecologies in Oceanic Literature*), she contends that hope allows for political engagement with intractable issues and is "a way of brushing up against and complicating narratives that situate the future as already given" (2015, 183). Indeed, with so much bleak material outlining a decrepit future it seems that joy, laughter, hope, and irreverence tap into the parts of humans' emotional registers needed in order to move past natural and unnatural catastrophes and see, or sense, things from a different perspective.[9]

The many catastrophes in the first and last chapters of this book point to anthropogenic causes beginning on US soil with cataclysmic and immeasurable repercussions. Catastrophe (from the Greek, κατα-στρέφειν) is to literally turn down (κατά) and turn over – overturn – with some degree of unexpected suddenness. In Western classical texts it signified the act of razing to the ground that which is up: a complete leveling and destruction. The discourse of ancient epics and lyric texts has long captivated me. Why must destruction and rage precede reconciliation and regeneration? The key element of so many works is that catastrophe is tethered to a temporal component. It is a surprise, an attack, and an unexpected turn of events. But in the thousands of years since many of Western civilization's cultural touchstones were written, the word has taken on a different meaning; and in climate speak it is almost a neologism by comparison. *Catastrophe* is increasingly understood to be an attritional occurrence, and one that is a bricolage of events. It is thus an opening for productive inquiry because its surfacing signifies a time for re-excavation. The past requires documentation to remind us that we inhabit the present and enter the future as capable merchants of change. Imagining alternate histories and futures in ways that deeply move people is a tall but necessary order for contemporary writers, one that inevitably also changes our present. With catastrophe thus comes a tilling of the soil, so to speak, and a way to dislodge and unearth obviated stories: the ultimate role of this world's most gifted writers and artists.

The works discussed in this book hold their readers and viewers responsible for engaging in a critique of mainstream environmental and economic policies, while also pointing out the inherent ambivalence of a planet that will go on regardless. William Empson referred to the pastoral "process" of constructing myth around matter (and making that myth adaptable to meet our needs) as one of "putting the complex into the simple" ([1935] 1960, 23). Ecocritics and environmental humanists often crave the very uniformity that we know has led to troubling practices, and we repeatedly rehearse those practices in our efforts to break away from them. In this book I hope to have demonstrated that the simplest stories that could be ignored and forgotten – those about sick, sad, weird, and crazy bodies – significantly complicate our knee-jerk reaction to a multifaceted world. Then the stories end and we are left with their absence. Our imaginative potentiality is borne in the grooves of that absence, and I am steadfast in my knowledge that it is great and limitless.

Notes

1 Since the initial release of the seven videos, Conservation International has continued to create and post videos including "Home," "Mountain," and "Ice" (see Conservation International 2016).

2 As of April 2016 there were over 1,660 comments.

3 The 1980 Comprehensive Environmental Response, Compensation, and Liability Act (CERCLA) created a way for the EPA to generate a list of Superfund sites. Signed by President Carter in 1980, the "Superfund" legislation, CERLA, held as its dictate to work with the EPA on creating a list of hazardous areas, or Superfund sites, also known as the National Priorities List (NPL). The idea behind the act was that the dumpers of the most highly toxic wastes would be forced to pay for cleanup or that the taxation on the petroleum and chemical industries would create a "superfund" that would fund cleanup.

4 US tax dollars were considered a last resort in the case that money couldn't otherwise be raised. The Ciba-Geigy Superfund site is one of two sites in Ocean County alone, and one of 65 overall in New Jersey, by far the leader of toxic dumping. The EPA language for corporate or individual entities identified as offenders is "potentially responsible parties" (PRPs). Even the identification of participants in lethal practices takes on the language of uncertainty and deniability.

5 Ciba-Geigy operated its plant from 1952 to 1990 – seven years post-designation as a Superfund site.

6 Lawrence Buell (1999), Carolyn Merchant, and other voices in ecocritical discourse would agree that, as Merchant has stated, we are experiencing an ontological break with reality that demands a radical shift in perspective: "we must reexamine the formation of a world view and a science that, by reconceptualizing reality as a machine rather than a living organism, sanctioned the domination of both nature and women" (1980, xxi). Even the vocabulary available to us seems spatially bound and dictated by the scientists that Merchant goes on to say are in need of reevaluation: "Francis Bacon, William Harvey, René Descartes, Thomas Hobbes, and Isaac Newton" (1980, xxi).

7 Nikolas Rose discusses emerging forms of citizenship: "Different citizenship practices can be seen in the increasing importance of corporeality to practices of identity" (2007, 133). Rose indicates that the creative possibilities of redefining one's citizenship and subjectivity are crucial to understanding our present and future.

8 Prior to Stoermer's use of Anthropocene, "Holocene" has been the designation for our current geological epoch, spanning the last 11,700 years. The derivation of Holocene is from the Greek ὅλος, meaning whole or entire, and καινός, meaning new, fresh, or unused; it is thus understood as the epoch of the wholly or entirely recent.

9 A number of recent undertakings come to mind as projects that are pushing the envelope of traditionally closed systems of communication. *Dear Climate* (2014) is a multimedia production that includes podcasts, exhibits, and creative commons posters and invites people to collaborate in a variety of ways. The Oceanic Preservation Society's project to display endangered animals on the Empire State Building with moving images (August 3, 2015) was a concerted effort to promote *Racing Extinction*, a documentary directed by Louie Psihoyos (director of *The Cove*) that launched in 220 countries during the 2015 Paris Climate Change Conference. These are just two examples from a long list of similar projects.

References

Antonetta, Susanne. 2001. *Body Toxic: An Environmental Memoir.* New York: Counterpoint.

Bonneuil, Cristophe, and Jean-Baptiste Fressoz. 2016. *The Shock of the Anthropocene: The Earth, History and Us.* Translated by David Fernbach. New York: Verso.

Buell, Lawrence. 1998. "Toxic Discourse." *Critical Inquiry* 24 (3): 639–65.

———. 1999. "The Ecocritical Insurgency." *New Literary History* 30 (3): 699–712.

Conservation International. 2014. "Nature Is Speaking – Julia Roberts Is Mother Nature." https://www.youtube.com/watch?v=WmVLcj-XKnM.

———. 2016. "Nature Is Speaking Film Series." http://www.conservation.org/nature-is-speaking/Pages/default.aspx.

Crutzen, Paul J., and Eugene F. Stoermer. 2000. "The "Anthropocene." *Global Change Newsletter* 41: 17–18. http://tinyurl.com/mlcvfzr.

Dear *Climate.* 2014. Marina Zurkow, Una Chaudhuri, Oliver Kellhammer, Fritz Ertl, and Sarah Rothberg. http://www.dearclimate.net/#/homepage.

Empson, William. (1935) 1960. *Some Versions of Pastoral.* Reprint, Norfolk, CT: New Directions.

EPA. 2016. "EPA Superfund Program: CIBA-GEIGY CORP., TOMS RIVER, NJ." http://tinyurl.com/h994fkp.

Harman, Greg. 2014. "'Nature Is Speaking': Will Consumers Listen?" *The Guardian*, October 6. http://tinyurl.com/l7ba6lq.

Jacquet, Jennifer. 2015. *Is Shame Necessary? New Uses for an Old Tool.* New York: Pantheon.

Jamieson, Dale, and Bonnie Nadzam. 2015. *Love in the Anthropocene.* New York: OR Books.

Merchant, Carolyn. 1980. *The Death of Nature: Women, Ecology, and the Scientific Revolution.* New York: HarperCollins.

Psihoyos, Louie, dir. 2015. "Racing Extinction." http://racingextinction.com.

Rose, Nikolas. 2007. *The Politics of Life Itself: Biomedicine, Power, and Subjectivity in the Twenty-First Century.* Princeton, NJ: Princeton University Press.

Shewry, Teresa. 2015. *Hope at Sea: Possible Ecologies in Oceanic Literature.* Minneapolis: University of Minnesota Press.

Syvitski, James. 2012. "Anthropocene: An Epoch of Our Making." *International Geogsphere-Biosphere Programme Global Change Magazine* 78. http://tinyurl.com/zb5qyeo.

Index

Note: *italicized* page numbers indicate a figure on the corresponding page.

For Product Safety Concerns and Information please contact our EU representative GPSR@taylorandfrancis.com
Taylor & Francis Verlag GmbH, Kaufingerstraße 24, 80331 München, Germany

www.ingramcontent.com/pod-product-compliance
Ingram Content Group UK Ltd.
Pitfield, Milton Keynes, MK11 3LW, UK
UKHW020949180425
457613UK00019B/599
9780367027001